CHILDREN AS EQUALS

Exploring the Rights of the Child

Edited by
Kathleen Alaimo
Brian Klug

D0920355

University Press of America,® Inc.
Lanham · New York · Oxford

Copyright © 2002 by
University Press of America,® Inc.
4720 Boston Way
Lanham, Maryland 20706
UPA Acquisitions Department (301) 459-3366

12 Hid's Copse Rd.
Cumnor Hill, Oxford OX2 9JJ

Library of Congress Cataloging-in-Publication Data

Children as equals : exploring the rights of the child /
edited by Kathleen Alaimo, Brian Klug.
p.   cm
Includes bibliographical references and index.
1. Children's rights. I. Alaimo, Kathleen. II. Klug, Brian.

HQ789 .C4277 2002
305.23—dc21   2002021482 CIP

ISBN 0-7618-2300-X (clothbound : alk. ppr.)
ISBN 0-7618-2301-8 (paperback : alk. ppr.)

In Memory of
JoAnne Fleming Warner
(1936-1999)

For the children in our lives
Johanna
Beatrice
Tania
Adam
Joff

Contents

Foreword

The adoption of the United Nations Convention on the Rights of the Child (UNCRC) in 1989 strongly affirmed the universality of human rights. Countries from every region of the world expressed a commitment to act within their borders and through international cooperation, to make children's rights a reality for all children without distinction of any kind. It marked a new stage in human history on the scale of the abolition of slavery and the recognition of women's rights. Children's rights were at long last recognized as fundamental human rights, alongside the human rights of other members of the human family.

Children's rights have gained a new and unique profile since the adoption of the UNCRC. In addition, the UNCRC has changed the vision of children forever. They can no longer be perceived as simply vulnerable, not-yet ready to participate in decision-making processes and expected to become mature and responsible by the magic effect of attaining the age of majority. Rather, they are envisaged increasingly as subjects of rights, entitled to protection at all times, respected in their individuality and dignity.

Children can no longer be disregarded in policy making, in budgetary decisions, or even in statistical work. Such activities are not indifferent to children; they advance or compromise their development. And the best interests of the child need to be a primary consideration when such policies and decisions are shaped and implemented. The situation of children needs to be perceived as a meaningful indicator of social progress, including consideration of those children who remain invisible and struggle to survive behind a curtain of silence and discrimination, who are neglected or forgotten on the basis of their gender, disability, social or ethnic origin or wealth, or because they live in remote and impoverished areas. Each child is important and entitled to develop his or her talents and abilities to their fullest potential, to be healthy, to gain skills and to play, to be protected from violence, abuse and exploitation.

Children's rights generate obligations and responsibilities we all need to respect and fulfill. The family is the natural environment for the development and well-being of the child, and it is also the first opportunity for the child to experience democracy. But all members of society have a responsibility to ensure the necessary protection, assistance, and support for the child to grow and assume a responsible life in the community.

Governments have a primary responsibility in this regard. Children's rights must become central to the national political agenda and to the process of development. In many countries throughout the world this is becoming a reality. An important process of reform has been generated, including at the constitutional level, through the adoption of codes on the rights of the child and the enactment of specific legislation, including on juvenile justice, inter-country adoption, sexual exploitation, child labor, violence and abuse. Child rights institutions have been established to ensure an integrated approach to children's policies, as well as an effective coordination of efforts and a relevant monitoring system. Independent offices have been created to voice children's interests and defend children's rights.

Information and advocacy campaigns have been launched to promote a culture of respect for children's rights and help end harmful social practices and traditions. More and better data on children is now available and increasingly used to influence public policies and governmental allocation of resources. The rights of the child have been introduced in school curricula, as well as in training programs of professionals working for and with children. Civil society organizations have adopted the principles and norms of the UNCRC as a reference for their work, are actively involved in its implementation and have developed important national and international coalitions.

Moreover, children's rights have become a major thrust for international development cooperation. And, in a unique manner, they have influenced the international peace and security agenda, including the work of the United Nations Security Council.

So much has been achieved since the adoption of the UNCRC. And yet so many children remain untouched by the progress made. At the beginning of a new century we continue to be confronted by serious challenges which clearly compromise children's rights. The proliferation of armed conflicts, the spread of HIV/AIDS, together with the decline in overseas development aid, increasing poverty and widening disparities in the world, all continue to threaten the positive trend the previous decade had shaped.

We are at a challenging crossroad. Looking ahead, we realize that a sound investment in children and the realization of their rights can safeguard peace, promote development and achieve social justice. And the successes of recent years give us grounds for optimism. Progress has been considerable in those countries where policies were guided by the principles of the best interests of the child, equity and non-discrimination, and where resources were allocated for the realization of children's rights. We must not miss this opportunity!

Marta Santos Pais
Director
UNICEF Innocenti Research Centre
Florence, Italy
January 2002

Acknowledgments

Numerous individuals, organizations, and institutions have contributed to the realization of this book. Andrew Linzey (Blackfriars Hall, Oxford) provided the initial inspiration with his "just a thought" suggestion. Our colleague, the late JoAnne Fleming Warner promoted the idea of a conference on children's rights to commemorate the sesquicentennial of Saint Xavier University; that conference became the impetus for the book. We joined with our colleagues, Avis Clendenen, Julie McNellis, and Jack Montgomery, to form a team (actually a planning committee) which organized and launched a successful international conference on children's rights; later they provided steadfast support for this book project. Jack especially helped us to maintain our sanity during the final crazy days. Richard Yanikoski, president of Saint Xavier University, and George Matthews, former academic vice-president, encouraged us to give continued life to the conference through a publication. Scott Jordan facilitated an approach to our publisher, University Press of America.

UNICEF offered resources and assistance. In particular, Tony Bloomberg generously provided contacts, advice, and encouragement. Karen Kancius of the United States Committee for UNICEF helped us in various ways.

The Center for Educational Practice and the Arts and Sciences Dean's Fund of Saint Xavier University provided financial support for technical production of the manuscript. The John D. and Catherine T. MacArthur Foundation and the Ronald McDonald House Charities, major funders of the conference, marked some of those funds for a book project.

Jean Newcomer's technical expertise was critical to the successful completion of this book, which might well still be languishing in our computer files. In addition, she assisted with preparing the Index and demonstrated admirable patience with our frenetic work schedule.

We would like to acknowledge the many friends and close relatives with whom we have explored the subject of children's rights. Brian drew inspiration from Francesca's writings on human rights, Tony's work for Amnesty International, and Harold's lifelong commitment to civil rights. Kathy leaned heavily on Dominic, who spent many evenings discussing the book with her, and many more days caring for their children while she was otherwise occupied. Special thanks to Johanna who spent a great deal of time "minding" her younger sister, and to Beatrice who spent a great deal of time "minding" her older sister. Kathy's sister Diane died before the book's completion, though their many days of discussion about the topic will be remembered.

Finally we acknowledge each other — partners in an intellectual exploration we did not anticipate but which has proved a challenge and an inspiration.

KA & BK
Chicago
January 2002

Introduction

Kathleen Alaimo and Brian Klug

In March 1997, Saint Xavier University, Chicago, held a multidisciplinary, international conference, "Children in the World: Exploring the Rights of the Child," to mark its 150th anniversary. All of the essays in this book, with the exception of Alaimo's and Klug's, are based on presentations given at this conference.[1] Like the conference itself, the aim of the book is to "explore" the idea of children's rights.

Every essay (except Tanenhaus's) refers explicitly to the United Nations Convention on the Rights of the Child (UNCRC), adopted by the General Assembly in 1989, which is thus a unifying theme of the book.[2] The title, *Children as Equals*, refers, in the first place, to the premises on which the UNCRC and similar instruments are based. The Preamble to the UNCRC, invoking the Charter of the United Nations (1945), proclaims "the inherent dignity" and "the equal and inalienable rights of all members of the human family."[3] Since children are no less members of "the human family" than adult women and men, this assertion implies that the child is equally possessed of inherent dignity and equally entitled to rights. But what do we mean by "child" and by "rights"? To which rights are children entitled? Do children's rights vary according to their age and competency? Are rights necessarily in the best interests of the child? How, in practice, can children's rights be secured? What about the rights of parents? These are among the questions explored by the essays. In the second place, the title suggests that, as it were, all children are created equal; that no child should suffer discrimination on grounds of race, color, sex, ethnicity, religion, and so on. This principle is contained in article 2 of the UNCRC, whose language is almost identical to article 2 of the Universal Declaration of Human Rights (1948). The fact that the language is so similar testifies to the fact that, as Cohen (Chapter 3) and Lenzer

(Chapter 12) both emphasize, children's rights are human rights. In short, children matter, and they matter in their own right. Moreover, no child matters more than any other child, nor less than any adult. Calling children "equals" is intended to convey this set of ideas, which provides common ground for all the essays. A varied language regarding children's rights exists within this common framework. The contributors to this volume explore the layers of meaning embedded in the expression "children's rights."[4]

The book does not aim to present a unified view; on the contrary, it explores a variety of approaches to a range of issues, beginning with the very concept of the child. Alaimo (Chapter 1), reviewing Western history over several centuries, connects the idea of children's rights to changing ideas about childhood. She traces the story up to the UNCRC, and argues that "[t]he contemporary movement for children's rights is both an incorporation of and reaction to several historical visions of childhood." Klug (Chapter 2) uses the story of Wendy and Peter Pan to tease out the complexities in the concept of the child implicit in the UNCRC. He emphasizes that children's rights "are not simply human rights for the young; they are specifically rights for a child...to *be* a child." Both essays explore the connection between how we visualize children and what we take their rights to be.

Cohen (Chapter 3) introduces the UNCRC — its origins, provisions, implementation, and impact — and describes developments since 1989, including new child rights treaties. She sees the UNCRC as representing a "shift in child status from 'object' to 'person,'" and concomitantly "from a 'child-caring' perspective to a 'child-rights' perspective." Flekkøy (Chapter 4) discusses the implications of the UNCRC for developmental psychology, and vice versa, offering a refreshing perspective on the issue of "competence" among children of various ages. She also focuses on "the keystone concepts of 'the best interest of the child' and 'the evolving capacities of the child.'" Both concepts are central to Ladd's essay (Chapter 5), which offers a philosophical analysis of what we mean by "children's rights," and Bellon's (Chapter 6), which lays a basis for a moral theory of rights for children. Ladd uses both concepts to help clarify three questions: What kinds of rights should be accorded to children? What should be the balance between them? What is the appropriate role of child, parents, and state in decision-making that affects the child's interests? Bellon argues, "The two principles together — best interests and evolving capacities — require that we treat children as whole beings, whose well-being is shaped in large part by our decisions and actions toward them, and by the decisions and actions children make for themselves."

The essays by Tanenhaus (Chapter 7), Smith (Chapter 8), Pitts (Chapter 9), and Levesque (Chapter 10) are all concerned, in different ways, with children's rights in the United States. Tanenhaus revisits a landmark case in Illinois, *People v. Turner, 1870*, which "disrupts conventional narratives that trace the evolution and expansion of state power over children from the establishment of houses of refuge in the 1820s to the creation of juvenile courts at the turn of the twentieth century." Tanenhaus notes that this case extended (albeit temporarily) due process rights to children, and as such represents an important dissent in the emergence of state paternalism. Writing as attorneys with family law experience, both Smith and Pitts argue that the voice of the child should be heard in cases involving custody, abuse and neglect. Both of them draw on their first-hand experience as practicing attorneys, and present powerful case studies to support their arguments. Smith addresses the vexed question of children's rights versus parents' rights. She argues against the "marketplace model" for family relationships, and advocates a "legal system founded on a jurisprudence of the child-centered family." Pitts points out that in theory children are persons with rights under the federal Constitution, but in practice they are denied their due process rights of access to court and representation through independent counsel. He distinguishes between two kinds of legal representation — *expressed* interest and *best* interest — for the child, and argues that, "paradoxically, the principle of the best interests of the child can work against the child's best interests," especially when the child is denied the right to express a pertinent view. Levesque's essay (Chapter 10) moves back from the judiciary to the legislature, and situates the United States within a global context. Noting that the United States has yet to ratify the UNCRC, he argues against the view that ratification would not have a significant impact on the well-being of children in the U.S. Describing the Convention as a "living document," he calls for a public debate about the future of children's rights. He argues that the UNCRC holds "the potential to transform child policy-making in the United States."

The final two essays examine the role of colleges and universities in exploring the rights of the child. Kitchen (Chapter 11) describes an interdisciplinary course she has designed and taught, World Justice and Care for Children, which offers a "global study of human rights for children." Her experience is that students respond warmly when children's rights are moved from "the margins of university life" to "the center of their education." Lenzer's essay (Chapter 12) is in two parts. In the first part, she explains how she and her colleagues came to found the new multidisciplinary field of Children's Studies. She argues that Children's Studies and children's rights go hand in hand, since children "deserve to be understood and analyzed in the whole of their existence by the research, academic and policy community." The second half of her essay is a thoughtful reflection on the role of the modern state vis-à-vis nongovernmental organizations. She cautions that "the children's rights movement cannot afford to continue its activities without regard to the larger social and economic developments that are shaping the world for future generations. Nor can it afford to proceed in isolation from the general human rights agenda." On that thought-provoking note, the book concludes its exploration of the rights of the child.

This brief résumé of the book is intended to provide a handy "road map." However, it does not begin to do justice to the richness of the discussion in these essays. Nor does it indicate sufficiently the extent to which they dovetail. In the final analysis, readers must explore the book for themselves; hopefully this will lead them to further explore the rights of the child.

Notes

1. Though based on presentations given at the conference, the essays have been thoroughly revised and substantially expanded.

2. To date, the UNCRC has been ratified by all nations except the United States and Somalia.

3. See the text of the UNCRC reprinted as an appendix to this volume. A useful selection of general human rights documents is reprinted in P. R. Ghandhi, *Blackstone's International Human Rights Documents* (London: Blackstone Press, 2000). Two important resources for documents related to children's rights are Beverly C. Edmonds and William R. Fernekes, *Children's Rights: A Reference Handbook* (Santa Barbara, CA: ABC-CLIO, 1996) and Philip E. Veerman, *The Rights of the Child and the Changing Image of Childhood* (Dordrecht, Boston, London: Martinus Nijhoff Publishers, 1992).

4. Protection rights, provision rights, entitlement rights, liberation rights and participation rights are just some of the terms used in contemporary discussions of children's rights.

Chapter 1

Historical Roots of Children's Rights in Europe and the United States[1]

Kathleen Alaimo

In 1977, Barbara Chrisholm observed, "Not long ago it was absurd to talk about the rights of the child, but today it is a serious social issue."[2] Indeed, today the expression "children's rights" is a lightning rod for heated discussions among experts and the general public. Most people regard children's rights as a relatively recent phenomenon, emerging out of the human rights movement following the Second World War. Many of those involved in advocacy for the children's rights movement point to the 1959 United Nations Declaration of the Rights of the Child, and the more powerful 1989 United Nations Convention on the Rights of the Child (UNCRC), as well as groundbreaking court cases of the 1960s and 1970s[3], as key moments in the history of children's rights. For many proponents, children's rights is a quite modern idea whose time has come.

The general public views children's rights as a very recent phenomenon and many Americans are quite wary of the idea, linked as it is in their minds with such high profile cases as Gregory Kingsley "divorcing" his natural/biological parents. In that context, *Newsweek* observed that much of the unfounded fear about children's rights is "the stuff of Dan Quayle speeches, raising the specter of litigation over insufficient allowances and too much spinach for dinner."[4] More open-minded persons sense that children's rights have something to do with protecting and providing for children. They often associate the publicity surrounding exploited child labor (especially in the developing world) with this version of children's rights. Or they link phrases such as "the best interests of the child," often heard in child custody cases, with the idea of children's rights.

My aim in this essay is to trace the historical roots of children's rights in the West over several centuries. At the same time, I shall try to clarify the ways in which the contemporary understanding of children's rights is distinctive. Both points need to be emphasized, as the important work of Joseph Hawes suggests. On the one hand, in the preface to his history of the children's rights movement in the United States, he correctly notes, "Although most current members of the children's rights movement believe that they and their cause are relatively new, they are actually part of a long history of efforts to use public power and pressure to improve the lives of American children...." On the other hand, in the final chapter he observes, "In many respects, the children's rights movement is a creature of the last thirty years."[5] Although the two statements appear confusing, there is no contradiction here; the qualifier "in many respects" makes all the difference. The implication of what Hawes says is clear: a history of children's rights must take full account of the changing nature of the meaning embedded in the phrase "children's rights" and in the practices associated with that phrase.

My focus in this essay will be on the idea of children's rights, a sort of intellectual history. I intend to connect the idea of children's rights to changing ideas about childhood in the West, tying the discussion to the 1989 UNCRC. I will use familiar historical periodization and take examples from the literature on legal and institutional history in the United States and Europe. My argument is that children's rights has a long history that is tied to the history of childhood and children.[6] As (adult) ideas about childhood and children have changed over time, so too has the concept and practice of children's rights. Since the face of children's rights has changed throughout history, we must be alert to differences in its appearance over time.

Children's Rights Defined

The UNCRC affirms not only the child's right to protection from harm and abuse, but also the right to childhood, to develop into an autonomous adult, and to have a voice in matters that affect and concern the individual child. Contemporary literature on children's rights identifies several categories of rights: protection rights, provision rights, participation rights.[7] Another distinction found in the contemporary literature is that between protection rights and liberty rights, a distinction that underscores some of the tensions inherent in children's rights. If adults take responsibility for the protection of children, doesn't that potentially limit their freedom? If children, based on their evolving capacities, have the right to make some of their own decisions, how can adults protect them from possible harm?

An historical perspective suggests that protection rights have a long history, while provision rights (entitlements) emerge most clearly in the nineteenth century (especially the second half of the nineteenth century). It should be noted that most historical accounts fold provision rights into protection rights, perhaps with good reason. Participation rights or liberty rights appear as a by-product of the civil rights and human rights movements of the later twentieth century.[8] Yet, historians interested in youth have traced the emergence of urban youth culture in the *early* twentieth century, suggesting that young people at that time were successfully carving out autonomous space.[9] This is not to say they were agitating for "rights" but that their voice was a significant part of the culture of the time and laid a foundation upon which later generations of young people could build. The unusual case of English schoolboys on strike in 1911 to demand the abolition of caning, more play time, payment for school work, and improved heating suggests precocious political activity.[10]

The fact that different labels — protection, provision, participation — attach to children's rights at different periods contains a clue. It suggests that evolving understandings of childhood shaped different conceptions of rights for children throughout history. In early modern times (1500-1750), the image of children as willful and tending toward sinfulness supported a climate of strict discipline and punishment that afforded only the barest forms of protection against gross abuse. As the image of childhood innocence and dependency deepened in the nineteenth century, adults made extensive efforts to protect and care for children, going so far as to use public and private organizations to intervene in the closed world of the family. In the later twentieth century, awareness of the evolving capacity of children (in contrast to a fixed state of dependency and assumed incompetence) has led to a more liberal view of their autonomy and rights-bearing potential. Despite these differences from one period to another, the concept of children's rights, in all its forms, asserts that "children have some legitimate claims even against their own families."[11]

I would like to suggest that the UNCRC offers a vision of childhood and children's rights that is rooted in several historical, and sometimes contradictory, antecedents. The contemporary movement for children's rights is both an incorporation of and reaction to several historical visions of childhood. These include 1) a pre-industrial model in which the worlds of children and adults were more closely integrated, and all lived under the yoke of patriarchal authority; 2) the eighteenth-century Enlightenment model which emphasized the evolving rational capacity of children as well as their individuality; 3) the model embodied in the efforts of the French Revolution (1789-1799) to transform the familial subjects of the king into individual citizens of the state; 4) the early nineteenth century vision of Romanticism which cast childhood as joyfully different, even better, than adulthood; and 5) the later nineteenth-century model of the Paternalist State establishing that childhood stood in need of protection and services. The contemporary children's rights movement takes something from each of these historical visions, but also contributes a new ingredient: that of the right of the child to a voice in his or her own affairs. So that while the UNCRC should be seen as part of a larger post-1945 international movement in support of human rights, taking its cue from the 1948 Universal Declaration on Human Rights, the idea of the "rights of the child" in the Convention represents a distillation of historically constructed visions of childhood.

In the following sections I shall trace the way in which these visions of childhood evolved and how they shaped different conceptions of rights for children. Although every period is significant, in some the history is more complex or less clear than in others. Consequently I do not devote an equal amount of space to them all. I treat the pre-industrial early modern period at some length in order to lay a solid basis for the subsequent discussion, and because this history is perhaps less well known. Finally for reasons of continuity of theme, the brief section on Romanticism in the early nineteenth century appears out of chronological order — immediately after the discussion of the Enlightenment and prior to the discussion of the French Revolution.

The Pre-Industrial Early Modern Conception of Childhood and Children's Rights

In his book, *When Fathers Ruled: Family Life in Reformation Europe*, Steven Ozment observed, "In the sixteenth century, children were raised and educated above all to be social beings; in this sense they had more duties towards their parents and society than they had rights independent of them."[12] Social cohesion seems to have been paramount. Yet a tradition, rooted in Judaism and Christianity, already existed in Europe that urged parents to recognize and fulfill their duties towards their offspring. Vivian Fox has argued that English children, including poor children, did indeed have rights in the early modern period based both on their individual status and on their vulnerability. Fox describes a 1609 case in Somerset, England, in which the justices of the peace asserted the right of very young children to "nourishment," assessing the biological mother 3 pence a week and the "reputed father" 9 pence a week to pay for another woman to nurse and rear the child.[13] The Protestant and Catholic Reformations brought renewed attention to children, recognizing in particular the important place of childhood and childhood education in the making of a Christian. During this era of religious turmoil, family child rearing as well as institutions outside the family, such as schools, attracted the attention of social commentators.

In general, early modern children were intimately tied to the institution of the family, where from about the age of seven they began a slow initiation into the world of work, a world inhabited by both adults and children. The economic contribution and therefore the economic value of children were considerable. This should be seen in stark contrast to the modern era (especially since 1880) where the economic value of children has declined and they have became economic liabilities.[14] We should not overstate the labor value of children in the early modern period: after all, many were idle and constituted an expense especially in their younger years. However, they were understood as a potential labor force for the family. And in those areas where rural or cottage industry began to develop, especially in the seventeenth century, this "proto-industrialization" increased the labor of children and therefore their economic value. Reports exist of children as young as four and five working in the textile districts of England, and at least some child laborers were not working with their families.[15]

Agricultural child labor and proto-industrial child labor accustomed people to the idea that children should work, and that this work would bring them into contact with adults. This is the basis upon which the employment of children in factories in the early nineteenth century occurred. In this context, the nineteenth-century movement against child labor and in favor of child schooling is a significant shift in thinking that helped to bring about a key transformation in the conception of childhood and in the formulation of children's rights.

The demographics of childhood in the early modern period are perhaps relevant to this discussion. High infant and child mortality prevailed, along with short life expectancy among adults. One in four children died before their first birthday; survival to the age of ten varied but was fraught with danger too. Generally, the deaths of children constituted the majority of deaths in any community. In late seventeenth-century Florence, two-thirds of all deaths were of children under the age of five.[16] Did the pervasiveness of childhood death contribute to a casual attitude towards children that itself increased mortality? Historians have debated this question with fervor. Many argue that the causes of child mortality (death at birth, death due to abandonment, death associated with wet-nursing) were factors most often related to poverty and do not necessarily indicate a low regard for children. In fact, in 1556 the French State issued an edict making infanticide a capital crime; thereafter aid to abandoned children increased significantly in both the public and private sectors. Some have interpreted this expansion of charity as evidence of the appeal of the idea of childhood innocence in the face of harsh circumstance.

High adult mortality had its effects as well. Parental death, especially the death of a father, opened issues of child custody and inheritance of property. Throughout Europe, and later in the colonies of North America, communities developed specific provisions to protect the property rights of orphans. And for orphans without property, laws governed their placement with other families. The arrangements developed under English Poor Law were "not merely exercises in discretionary charity" but rather established the right of poor children to a settlement.[17] In the Chesapeake colonies of Virginia and Maryland, with high adult mortality and slim kin networks, orphan courts handled the custody of children to insure their care and took responsibility for the protection of children's property. These arrangements were generally formalized by court order. Lois Green Carr found that by the end of the seventeenth century, in one county in Maryland, the court was handling the situations of three-fourths to four-fifths of orphans.[18]

Though schooling was certainly quite limited in this period, several surprises emerge. For example, in 1530, Martin Luther argued that children belong to God and to the community, not just to their parents, and considering the maintenance of social order as a public trust, he made one of the earliest arguments for compulsory schooling. In 1583, the German community of Nordhausen passed the following ordinance:

> Although no decree ought to be necessary to compel parents to do their duty to their own children, we are aware of a great failing on their part because so many of them do not know what it means to instruct children. Parents and guardians shall therefore send their children to

school so that in their early childhood they may learn to pray, know God and acquire discipline, decency, and sound skills.[19]

This ordinance is significant because it contains many of the elements that have gone into the conceptualization of children's rights: the well-being of the child (religious salvation, self-governance, skill acquisition); the best interest of the child and the idea that parents do not always have the child's needs in mind; education as an essential experience early in childhood; and state interest.

The Puritan colony in Massachusetts had a similar statute in place in 1642. It regulated and supervised parental behavior on the grounds that many parents and masters were neglectful in training and educating their children. The statute stated that parents were responsible for insuring that their children could read, exercise skills necessary to be self-supporting, and understand Christian religious precepts. Failure to fulfill these responsibilities could lead to punishment, including fines or loss of physical custody of children. The Massachusetts Bay Colony considered this responsibility important enough to appoint local officials to "redress this evil."[20] A Danish law of 1630 also assigned public guardians responsibility for children whose parents neglected to send them to school or teach them a trade.[21]

Though one can find some sense of a child's right to support, property, and even education in the early modern period, the picture is not simple. In most cases, the "right to support" was tied to mandatory placement as an apprentice or servant with another family or tied to child labor for one's own family. Apprenticeship contracts arranged by one's parents, as well as court-ordered placements (binding out), typically held boys until the age of twenty-one and girls until the age of eighteen. English Poor Laws, also used in the British colonies, mandated the binding out of poor, idle, or vagrant children. And when labor demands were high, such as in the Virginia colony in the early seventeenth century, London's street children could be swept up and transported to Virginia's struggling colony with or without their consent, with the promise that "under severe masters they may be brought to goodness."[22] As Mary Ann Mason has suggested, questions regarding the legal placement of children revolved around their labor value.[23]

Though there is evidence to suggest that parental responsibility towards children was a recognized concept with community consequences for failure, still parental and specifically paternal authority was extremely broad. Discipline was a parental duty, and corporal punishment was almost universally accepted as appropriate. The legal provisions in the *Body of Liberties* promulgated in the

Massachusetts Bay Colony in 1641 provided for the capital punishment of children over sixteen who assaulted their parents. In continental Europe the ideology of monarchical absolutism had its counterpart in paternal absolutism. On the eve of the French Revolution, complaints about the arbitrary use of *lettres de cachet,* mechanisms to have subordinate family members arrested without cause, weighed into the revolutionary mix.

It is important to note that excessive use of force was not condoned in the disciplining of children, including apprentices. Contracts for indentured apprentices stipulated that they were not to be mistreated. Court records provide evidence that excessive punishment was censored. And even the Massachusetts *Body of Liberties* set some conditions. Parents could not act arbitrarily but rather had to bring their rebellious offspring to the public arena of the courthouse.[24] Another condition of these so-called "stubborn child" provisions is that they applied to older children, specifically those sixteen years or older. By implication, such severe punishment seems to have been considered inappropriate for younger children. This is confirmed, perhaps, by the phrase in the statue that reads "of sufficient years and *understanding,* viz. sixteen years of age." I emphasize the word "understanding" because it signals a rather early example of the notion of evolving capacities.

So, what was the idea of childhood and children's rights in the early modern period? Given the high proportion of children in the population, their very high death rate, the young age of leaving home, limited formal schooling, early entry into economic productivity, and a revived interest in the religious salvation of children, we can, I think, conclude as follows: Those children who survived were generally closely integrated into the world of adults and the world of labor; and yet, the idea of children's special needs appears in nascent form along with the notion that these needs established a public interest in children. In addition, one must note that the early modern interest in the protection of children was rooted in a worried concern, if not fear, that uncared for children might become a liability to the community. Thus, in 1737, the selectmen of Watertown told poor parents to place their children with families "where they may be taken good care of."[25] Were they acting out of concern for children's rights? Interest in the legal protection of children and even in their right to basic maintenance and instruction was motivated by the hope that this would result in productive and disciplined members of the community. Finally, it is important to understand that early modern European and American society was a compacted, hierarchical world in which few persons possessed rights; even most adult males had little public autonomy. The family was perhaps the one arena in which men, as male heads of households, exercised extensive rights over others. In this hierarchical formation of the family, children and wives simply could not possess rights; if they had, the very meaning of paternal rights would have been undermined. To the extent that paternal rights carried obligations, those subordinated to it might claim some protection — perhaps even protection rights.

The Enlightenment Ideal

Numerous Enlightenment thinkers focused on childhood education and the ways in which children learn. So, it is not surprising that many historians view the "long" eighteenth century (from the last decade of the late seventeenth through the first decade of the nineteenth century) as a time when a pronounced sensitivity to childhood emerged, with a clear articulation of childhood as a distinct stage of life having its own ethos and in need of its own institutions.

To some extent, this development was linked with the Enlightenment critique of traditional Christianity including the idea of original sin; when the Enlightenment adopted a view of humanity as inherently benevolent it moved towards a recasting of the nature of childhood. According to Hugh Cunningham this resulted in "the shift from a prime focus on the spiritual health of the child to a concern for the development of the individual child."[26] The Enlightenment's attention to the development of the individual child is an important milestone leading to the twentieth-century concept of the rights of the child. A brief introduction to the work of two seminal Enlightenment thinkers who contributed in different ways to this development should clarify the significance of the Enlightenment in the history of childhood and children's rights.

John Locke (1632-1704), considered the founding philosopher of English liberalism, wrote about children in *An Essay Concerning Human Understanding* (1690) and *Some Thoughts Concerning Education* (1693). In these writings, he laid some of the groundwork for a change in the conceptualization of children and children's rights. Among Locke's well-known ideas is his view that the mind is a "blank slate" without innate ideas; from this Locke theorized that all knowledge comes from experience. Based on this understanding of the sources of human knowledge, Locke asserted the power of education in the shaping of the child: "nine parts of ten are what they are — good or evil, useful or not, by their education."[27] The importance of childhood education was so undisputed in Locke's mind that he declared "errors in education should be less indulged than any." Locke appears to have recognized the individuality of each child, noting that children possess "various tempers, different inclinations, and particular defaults" and advised that parents/educators must watch children at play in order to discover their true nature and then adjust their education. He urged parents and educators to treat children as rational creatures and rejected corporal punishment as inappropriate to the raising of "wise, good, and ingenuous men." Locke wrote of the "tender age and constitutions" of children and the importance of cultivating a "child's spirit, easy, active, and free."[28]

Locke's thinking marks an important shift in the conceptualization of childhood in the West. Yet there are limits to his apparent child-centeredness. Locke seems most interested in "habit formation" that would internalize restraint and create the productive self-governing adult. Thus Locke wrote: "All the plays and diversions of children should be directed towards good and useful habits."[29] In other words, Locke's primary concern was the future adult not the child.

Jean-Jacques Rousseau (1712-1778) took a different tack in his educational treatise disguised as a novel, *Emile* (1762). In the preface, he complained: "The wisest writers devote themselves to what a man ought to know, without asking what a child is capable of learning. They are always looking for the man in the child, without considering what he is before he becomes a man."[30] Reacting to Locke's assertion that the child is a rational creature, Rousseau cautioned "Reasoning should not begin too soon." He asserted "Nature intends that children shall be children before they are men." Rousseau warned, "If we insist on reversing this order we shall have fruit early indeed, but unripe and tasteless, and liable to early decay; we shall have young savants and old children." And, he observed, "Childhood has its own methods of seeing, thinking, and feeling." In a quintessential example of Enlightenment humanism, he articulated a radically novel view of childhood:

> Men, be humane, that is your first duty: be so for all conditions, all ages, all that is germane to man. What does wisdom avail you except as it concerns humanity? Cherish childhood, look with favor on its games, its pleasures, its friendly instincts...when laughter is always bursting forth and the soul is ever at peace. Why do you so want to rob these young innocents of the pleasures of such brief and fleeting hours and of such precious gifts, which they are too young to misuse? Humanity has its place in the general order; childhood, too, in the span of human life; we must look upon man in mankind and the child in childhood.[31]

Rousseau also advocated state-sponsored public education of children — specifically for boys — on the grounds that this alone could form a solid bedrock for democratic government. He specifically addressed the issue of parental rights (father's rights) by noting that a provision for public education would not undermine the authority of the father but would transform it into the authority of the citizen. As Rousseau noted, "Families dissolve, but the State remains."[32]

Rousseau was genuinely concerned with the process of growing up. He implied that children had a right to a happy childhood, characterized by freedom and closeness to nature. One eighteenth-century contemporary referred to *Emile* as the "charter of youthful deliverance." Unfortunately, Rousseau seemed to accord this right to boys, not girls.

Nonetheless, the influence of Rousseau was immediate and widespread both in his recasting of childhood and his elevation of motherhood. More than a century later, during the French working-class revolution of 1871, known as the Paris Commune, women workers cited Rousseau as they elaborated their vision of an ideal society where "we must seek to perfect above all others the child." Until utopia could be achieved, these practical women called for reforms that would support child health and development, including day nurseries with playrooms that "contain everything to keep children amused."[33]

The Vision of Romanticism

Poets, artists, writers of the Romantic era (which spanned the late eighteenth and early nineteenth centuries) took up and popularized Rousseau's ideal of an innocent, natural, carefree, happy childhood. Romantic writers rejected the Lockean emphasis on utilitarian education and instead called for freeing the child's imagination. Romanticism proclaimed childhood as the best part of life, and attributed qualities of purity and innocence to the child, which enabled children to recognize truth and beauty. Ironically, this idealization of childhood coincided with the emergence of the first industrial societies, which seemed to encourage the exploitation of children. Moreover, Romanticism's idealization of childhood did not initially produce a widespread alteration of child-rearing practices, which continued to aim at habit formation. Yet the Romantic's conception of childhood, derived from Rousseau, would gradually shape the nineteenth century response to children and contribute to a notion of children's rights. The notable Yale child psychologist, Arnold Gesell sounds much like a Romantic writer in his 1912 publication *The Normal Child and Primary Education*: "Child life and child motives are elusive, creative, elastic, and intuitive.... But the child is circumvented at every turn by well-meaning adults out of harmony with his intent; even his play is crippled by formal limitations and adult conceptions of organization and courtesy."[34]

The Era of the French Revolution

In 1992, Lynn Hunt, a noted historian of the French Revolution, published a collection of primary sources titled *The French Revolution and Human Rights*, with specific sections devoted to the rights of male citizens, the poor, the propertied, religious minorities, questionable professions, women, free blacks, and slaves. The absence of documents on children's rights might lead a reader to conclude that the French Revolution, which so profoundly altered the political consciousness and practices of the West, did not concern itself with the rights of children but only with the "rights of man." In fact, the Revolution attacked arbitrary authority of many forms including the arbitrary authority of the family patriarch. Revolutionary legislative proposals sought to dismantle the patriarchal family and establish a new place for children in the family. Notable examples of these efforts are such specific provisions as the elimination of primogeniture and the institution of equal inheritance, the elimination of distinctions between legitimate and illegitimate children, abrogation of the *lettres de cachet,* a liberal divorce law, and provisions for child support as well as maternal custody claims. The revolutionaries in France also studied seriously the question of public education for all children in France, but failed to implement the plan as the Revolution struggled for survival in the mid-1790s. A serious blow to exclusive paternal authority resulted from the revolution's conception of the nation as a population of individuals, each with a direct relationship to the state, including children as future citizens. According to Sylvia Schafer, paternal authority contracted during the early years of the Revolution.[35]

However, most of the Revolutionary era family legislation did not survive, and the nineteenth century opened with the patriarchal vision of the Napoleonic Code firmly in place, not only in France but throughout much of Europe. Despite the ideas of the Enlightenment, the actions of the French Revolution, and the visions of Romanticism, the legal situation of children remained relatively unchanged in the early nineteenth century. In Europe, the Napoleonic Code specified the legal subordination of children to their fathers until the age of twenty-one. In France, fathers retained the right of correction — the right to request a child's detention — well into the twentieth century. While fathers were obligated to support their legitimate children, they also had uncontested control over their children's wages and property. Children's rights seem to have been limited to protection against extreme abuse or parental unfitness. For example, parents who had prostituted their own children could lose their parental rights, while children who had been acquitted of crimes might be removed from parental custody.[36]

State Paternalism and the Child's Right to Protection and Provision, c. 1830-1920

During the nineteenth century, government authorities and trained professionals eventually replaced philanthropists in conceptualizing and protecting childhood, thus inaugurating the age of "child-saving." The motives for publicly-sponsored child-saving combined old and new: concerns about children's morality, public order, productivity, population quality and quantity, joined a new concern to save children so they might enjoy childhood. Particularly in the half-century from 1870 to 1920, the rights of children in relation to parents, employers, and others expanded in the form of rights to protection and services that presupposed a vision of childhood as a distinctive and vulnerable time of life. This process occurred relatively rapidly under the patronage of the state.

In the four decades prior to 1870, the main development regarding children's rights occurred in reference to industrial child labor. The child labor reform movement was the first important child-oriented reform movement of the nineteenth century. Humanitarian concerns motivated this movement in which reformers cast child laborers as defenseless victims of industrialization and launched an eventually successful campaign to regulate and ultimately eliminate industrial child labor.[37] Influenced at least in part by Romanticism's cult of childhood, the reformers viewed industrial child labor as unnatural.[38]

Factory work was physically exhausting for children who as young as seven worked sixteen hours a day in damp, poorly ventilated workplaces where corporal punishment was common. Foremen used harsh methods to keep exhausted children awake as this report from a young factory worker indicates:

> [T]he overlooker walks round the room with a stick in his hand, and he touches that child on the shoulder, and says 'Come here.' In the corner of the room is an iron cistern filled with water, he takes the boys and takes him up by the legs and dips him over head in the cistern and sends him to work for the remainder of the day.[39]

Even employers conceded that sleepy child laborers would be "aroused by any means necessary, including the lash."[40] In addition to physical punishment, other health hazards existed. Child laborers inhaled cotton dust, metal filings, acidic dyes while machines chopped their limbs.

Moral hazards also concerned contemporaries. The factory (unlike the family farm or craft shop) contained large numbers of strangers who might molest and corrupt children. (Many contemporaries conveniently overlooked the fact that this had been the fate of many apprentices and servants in domestic environments). With nineteenth-century factory conditions as a backdrop, one commentator lamented that the factory child laborer had "taken off the robe of innocence, and cast it far from him." And the poet Coleridge referred to child laborers in English cotton factories as "our poor little white slaves."[41] Clark Nardinelli has concluded, "The literature on the employment of children may well be the most emotional of all the writings on the industrial revolution in England."[42]

The plight of the working child not only aroused popular sympathy but also stirred the intervention of the state. This response was both a cause and an effect of the new status of childhood as an age of innocence and development. The most significant aspect of the child labor reform movement is that it opened a public discussion about the social meaning of childhood, specifically opening the door to the radical notion that perhaps children should not work at all, that perhaps they had a right not to work, a right to a different childhood — one of development — physical, moral, intellectual, social. Practically, however, the child labor reform movement of the 1830s and 1840s achieved very little; it was not until the 1870s and later that child labor declined significantly, and this was due to the development of an alternative model of social existence for children, namely, schooling. When the protection right (laws against industrial child labor) was joined to a provision right (entitlement to education), the campaign to eliminate child labor took off.

Between 1870 and 1920 the ideology of childhood, developing since the eighteenth century, offered a compelling rationale for a wide-range of child-focused social reforms designed to secure protection and care rights for children. Three features distinguish this period. First, the state with its army of professionals became the guarantor of these rights. Second, children were increasingly separated from adults as childhood came to be seen as a distinctive stage of life with age-specific requirements. Third, parental authority and autonomy in child-rearing were increasingly challenged by the state in its ever more persistent exercise of *parens patriae.*[43] As Elbridge Gerry, one of the founders of the New York Society for the Prevention of Cruelty to Children, declared in 1882, "at the present day in this country, children have *some* rights, which even parents are bound to respect."[44]

There has been a great debate among historians about how to interpret the intent and the consequences of these state-sponsored child-saving measures. Social control was part of the agenda, and the policing of families resulted.[45] At the same time, significant, and often beneficial, changes occurred in children's lives. First, schooling replaced work as the social expectation for all children. From 1870 on, laws made school attendance compulsory for children, but also made schools free, public, and professional. Second, child health improved steadily. Public health measures such as school medical services expanded and 1888 witnessed the founding of the American Pediatric Society. Third, parental neglect and abuse were subjected to intense scrutiny and challenge not only by private philanthropies, such as the Society for the Prevention of Cruelty to Children with branches across the United States by the 1870s, but increasingly by government authorities. Questioning the assumption of unlimited parental rights, professional child-savers challenged parents who neglected, abused, and endangered their children. Reformers thus invented the modern concept of child abuse. In 1889 both France and Great Britain passed laws against child endangerment including that caused by parents. Commenting on the French law, a contemporary authority asserted that "above the father's interest, above the interest of society, there is also and above all the interest of the child."[46] In Britain this legislation was called the Children's Charter.[47] In Norway, the Child Protection Act of 1896 brought children in a variety of circumstances under state tutelage, including delinquents, truants, and those neglected by their parents.[48] International meetings on the protection of children became regular events in the 1880s, 1890s, and early 1900s, with scientific experts increasingly dominating the agendas. Fourth, children in trouble with the law were removed from the grip of the adult penal system and ensconced in the octopus-like safety network of a newly fashioned juvenile justice system. Illinois founded the first juvenile court in 1899, a practice followed in Britain in 1908 and in France in 1912. Juvenile court operated on different principles than its adult counterpart: reform and treatment not punishment; preventive action; indeterminate sentences that depended on a child's response to treatment; probation or supervised freedom. The new juvenile courts entered the life of the family too. A 1911 Illinois law gave juvenile court a mandate to administer financial aid to parents for the care of their dependent children.

In segregating and protecting children, these public policies and institutions aided in the creation of a dependent childhood, characterized by children's loss of autonomous action and highly regulated by adult guardians. Moreover, by the early twentieth century child-saving as a state policy targeted not only deprived children but all the children of a nation and even extended the age-definition of child to include those up to the age of twenty-one. To what extent were child-saving policies rooted in a concept of children's rights? The protection of children, limited in the early modern period to protection against extreme physical abuse and protection of property, became a dramatically enlarged field by the end of the nineteenth century. Alleged parental neglect, incompetent parenting, and the realities of poverty emerged as legitimate criteria for state intervention in the life of the child. The child's right to protection led inexorably to the child's right to provisions of various sorts, with the state responsible for providing these services. Freedom from work and access to public schooling were merely the tip of the iceberg. Health care, acceptable housing, playgrounds and uplifting recreation emerged as elements of children's rights. Schafer has noted that the definition of protection in the influential French dictionary by Littré (1877) provided both a negative and positive meaning. Protection was both an act of guarding someone against danger or harm and an act of cultivation or assistance.[49]

Child-saving policies owed much of their justification to Romanticism's conceptualization of childhood. The definition of a happy childhood involved a variety of contrasts to adult life: adulthood stood for responsibilities, work, and the indoors, while childhood was associated with playfulness, school, and the outdoors. In this context, the rights of the child consisted mainly in the rights to a certain experience of childhood. Moreover, to attain these rights, children had to be made dependent on adults so those adults could protect them — quite the opposite of autonomous adulthood. Prohibitions on child labor, perhaps the greatest accomplishment of state paternalism, made children economically dependent on adults over a longer period. In the

United States, as part of the national campaign to restrict child labor, an adult reformer drafted in 1913 a "Declaration of Dependence by the Children of America in Mines and Factories and Workshops Assembled." Speaking for children, it stated, "[W]e declare ourselves to be helpless and dependent...that we may be protected in the enjoyment of the rights of childhood."[50] Turning the political language of the American Revolution on its head, this document signals the peculiar understanding of rights that shaped the children's rights movement of the late nineteenth and early twentieth centuries.

The Contemporary Age

In the aftermath of the First World War, the protection-provision view of children's rights expanded into the international arena. In 1924, the League of Nations adopted a declaration of children's rights known as the Declaration of Geneva, building on the 1919 Covenant of the League of Nations which had made numerous provisions for the protection of children. Women's groups, social scientists, and public health experts dominated the reform efforts associated with children's rights to welfare provisions. In the United States, President Hoover's White House Conference on Child Health and Protection convened in 1930; volumes of recommendations were distilled into a "Children's Charter" which recognized "the rights of the child as the first rights of citizenship."[51] Through the first half of the twentieth century, children's rights still embodied the idea of a child's right to protection against harm as well as access to certain basic entitlements such as schooling and health care. In addition, the role of government as guarantor of those entitlements marked the period. The state as "superparent" altered the traditional relationship between parents and children. According to Mason,

> Never again would a father command absolute custody and control of his children, including their wages and services, in exchange for maintenance and education. The state now severely limited the child's ability to deliver wages or services while assuming the obligation to educate children. The state also set minimum standards for child raising that a parent had to meet in order to retain custody of a child.[52]

It is tempting to see in this process the diminution of parents' rights, an increase in parental duties, and the establishment of children's right to a certain quality of life. Non-parental adults and the state as parent asserted children's rights on behalf of children claiming to know the best interest of the child.

After the Second World War, as human rights became a focus of international attention, a seemingly new approach to children's rights emerged. The markers are well known: the 1959 United Nations General Assembly's Declaration of the Rights of the Child; the announcement of 1979 as the International Year of the Child; and the 1989 United Nations Convention on the Rights of the Child.[53] The 1959 Declaration asserts that each child has the right to a "happy childhood" and its principles bear the stamp of the protection-provision view of children's rights based on an assumption of childhood dependency and vulnerability. However, the Declaration also emphasizes the individuality and autonomy of the child. The 1989 Convention is even more explicit in this regard, asserting rights for children that would guarantee their individuality and autonomy, such as the child's right to free expression and association. This articulation of children's rights might be interpreted as a reaction against the overwhelming shift towards dependency and powerlessness characterized in the ideas of Romantic childhood and the practice of state-sponsored child-saving protectionism. Also, the new understanding of children's rights, which extends to participation based on evolving capacity in matters of self-interest, can be seen as a reaction against the excessive segregation of the child from the adult that seemed to be so essential to the vision of innocent childhood.

In the United States this new trend found expression in a number of notable court cases in the 1960s and 1970s. In *Tinker v. Des Moines Independent School District* (1969), the Supreme Court declared that "young people do not shed their rights at the school house door." In *Goss v. Lopez* (1975) the Court found that students cannot be suspended without a hearing and an opportunity to tell their side of the story.[54] In 1978, a group of lawyers founded the Youth Law Center in San Francisco to provide legal services to minors. In Belgium and the Netherlands, Children's Law Shops provide legal information and assistance to children. The Children Act of 1989 gave British children a legal voice in decision-making related to their welfare.[55] As children claim legal and civil rights they interact more with adults, shedding some of the distinctiveness attributed to them in the past. This development is not without problems: How should the right of the child to be a child (read "dependent, protected, separated") be balanced against the right of the child to be a person (read "an individual with rights to some autonomy and participation")?

Conclusion

As with the concept of childhood, the idea of children's rights has a long history shaped by changing economic, social, cultural, and political circumstances. The idea of children's rights articulated by the UNCRC is different than that held by Reformation moralists, Enlightenment theorists, and late nineteenth-century social scientists, but it is not without precedent. Traces of this concept of rights, that children have legitimate claims to make "against" external agents, can be found throughout the centuries surveyed here.

The UNCRC represents the accumulation of expanding notions of children's rights to protection and provision based on the following factors: their vulnerability due to age, their developmental status, the extent of parental resources, and even parental abilities. The UNCRC asserts the principle of the best interests of the child (article 3) much like nineteenth-century reformers did. For example, in an 1881 Kansas child custody case, *In re Bort,* the court denied both parents custody, committing the two children to their grandmother's care and custody, writing: "We understand the law to be, when the custody of children is the question, that the best interest of the children is the paramount fact. Rights of father and mother sink into insignificance before that."[56] On the matter of children's access to information, the UNCRC suggests that children should have access to information and ideas of all kinds, but that dissemination should be consistent with the moral well-being of the child and requires the state to protect the child from harmful materials (articles 13 and 17); this position may be a far cry from the "moral panic" concerns of the early twentieth century but it retains some elements of the "protect the innocent" ideal. In the nineteenth and twentieth centuries the promotion of the child's right to protection and provision set the stage for conflicts between the state (as superparent) and parental authority; the UNCRC instructs states to "take all appropriate legislative, administrative, and other measures for the implementation of rights recognized" (article 4) but also calls for states to "respect the responsibilities, rights, and duties of parents or... other persons legally responsible for the child" (article 5). The UNCRC seems to direct states to a more collaborative and supportive relationship with families than nineteenth century child-savers.

So what's new in the UNCRC? In her history of child custody in America, Mason notes that traditionally children had "no voice of their own."[57] The UNCRC brings to the table a new recognition of the child's right to a voice. If Reformation moralists viewed the child as sinful, and

Enlightenment theorists viewed the child as rational, and social scientists of the late nineteenth century viewed the child as malleable, we view the child as independent and assertive. The UNCRC reflects this by acknowledging that children have the right to express an opinion in matters that concern them (article 12) and by asserting the importance of the idea of evolving capacities (article 5), as opposed to a fixed state of dependency. According to Marta Pais, article 12 transforms the child into a "principal," an agent in his or her own life.[58] Yet even this clearly new emphasis in the conceptualization of children's rights has some historical precedent. In 1872 a mother filed a suit in Pennsylvania to reclaim her daughter from the grandmother's custody. In determining the question of whether the mother or grandmother should have custody of the little girl, the court wrote:

> Beside, the wishes of the child herself, now about seven years of age, are not wholly to be overlooked. With an intelligence little less remarkable in one so young, she communicates her inclinations and begs that they not be disregarded. In short, she clings to the respondent, her grandmother."[59]

The court awarded custody to the girl's grandmother. Perhaps the apparent novelty of children's rights today may be less dramatic than either advocates or opponents believe. But more importantly, children's rights have attained a degree of codification and consensus that is impressive in scope. The UNCRC makes a distinctive contribution to the history of children's rights by enumerating standards for treatment of children throughout the world based on the principle that as members of the human family children possess "inalienable rights."

Notes

1. I presented an earlier version of this essay at the 2nd Annual Meeting of the Society for the History of Children and Youth, 27-28 July 2001, Marquette University. Special thanks to Brian Klug for his thoughtful questions and suggestions.

2. Cited in Philip E. Veerman, *The Rights of the Child and the Changing Image of Childhood* (Dordrecht, Boston, London: Martinus Nijhoff Publishers, 1992), p. xv.

3. Two important cases in the United States were *In re Gault* (1967) 387 US 1 concerning due process of juvenile offenders and *Tinker v. Des Moines Independent School District* (1969) 393 US 503 concerning free speech rights of students.

4. Ben Cohn, "From Chattel to Full Citizens," *Newsweek,* September 21, 1992, p. 88.

5. Joseph M. Hawes, *The Children's Rights Movement: A History of Advocacy and Protection* (Boston: Twayne Publishers, 1991), pp. ix, 96.

6. Veerman, p. 10 makes this same point but does not develop the historical trajectory.

7. See for example, Beverly C. Edmonds and William R. Fernekes, *Children's Rights: A Reference Handbook* (Santa Barbara, CA: ABC-CLIO, 1996), pp. 2, 5-8.

8. See David Archard, *Children: Rights and Childhood* (London: Routledge, 1993), pp. 45-69 for a discussion of the child liberationist movement of the 1960s and 1970s.

9. In Paris, working-class youth had by the early 1900s "articulated their own subculture through the abundant and varied diversions of the 'city of light': dance halls, cafes, cinemas, sports, and newspapers." W. Scott Haine, "The Development of Leisure and the Transformation of Working-Class Adolescence, Paris, 1830-1940," *Journal of Family History* 17:4 (1992), p. 452.

10. David M. Pomfret, "'Something Horrible to Witness': Young People and Political Activism in English and French Cities, 1890-1949," paper presented at the 2nd Annual Meeting of the Society for the History of Children and Youth, 27-28 July 2001, Marquette University.

11. Hawes, *The Children's Rights Movement,* p. 87.

12. Cited in Hugh Cunningham, *Children and Childhood in Western Society since 1500* (London: Longman, 1995), p. 56.

13. Vivian C. Fox, "Poor Children's Rights in Early Modern England," *The Journal of Psychohistory* 23:3 (Winter 1996), pp. 286, 290.

14. See for example, Viviana A. Zelizer, *Pricing the Priceless Child: The Changing Social Value of Children* (New York: Basic Books, 1985).

15. Cunningham, *Children and Childhood,* pp. 85-87.

16. Ibid., pp. 90-91.

17. Fox, "Poor Children's Rights," pp. 292-293.

18. Cited in Paula S. Fass and Mary Ann Mason, *Childhood in America* (New York: New York University Press, 2000), p. 352.

19. Cited in Cunningham, *Children and Childhood,* p. 118-119.

20. Colonial statute reprinted in Fass and Mason, *Childhood in America,* pp. 537-538.

21. Målfrid Grude Flekkøy, "The Scandinavian experience of children's rights," in Bob Franklin, ed., *The Handbook of Children's Rights: Comparative Policy and Practice* (London and New York: Routledge, 1995), p. 176.

22. Correspondence of the Virginia Company, 1619-1620 and the Declaration of the Privy Council of England, 1620 reprinted in Fass and Mason, *Childhood in America,* pp. 241-243.

23. Mary Ann Mason, *From Father's Property to Children's Rights: The History of Child Custody in the United States* (New York: Columbia University Press, 1994), p. 3.

24. Hawes, *The Children's Rights Movement,* and Mason, *From Father's Property,* discuss the Massachusetts *Body of Liberties.*

25. Cited in Hawes, p. 7.

26. Cunningham, *Children and Childhood,* p. 62.

27. Cited in Cunningham, *Children and Childhood,* p. 63.

28. See excerpt from *Some Thoughts Concerning Education* reprinted in Isaac Kramnick, ed., *The Portable Enlightenment Reader* (New York: Penguin Books, 1995), pp. 222-28.

29. Cited in Cunningham, *Children and Childhood,* p. 66.

30. Cited in Cunningham, *Children and Childhood,* p. 65.

31. See excerpt from *Emile* reprinted in Kramnick, ed., *The Portable Enlightenment,* pp. 229-233.

32. From *Discourse on Political Economy,* excerpt reprinted in Kramnick, p. 234.

33. From documents reprinted in Lisa DiCaprio and Merry Wiesner, eds., *Lives and Voices: Sources in European Women's History* (Boston: Houghton Mifflin, 2001), pp. 308-310.

34. Cited in Robert H. Bremner, ed., *Children and Youth in America: A Documentary History,* volume 2, (Cambridge, MA: Harvard University Press, 1971), p. 1123.

35. Sylvia Schafer, *Children in Moral Danger and the Problem of Government in Third Republic France* (Princeton, NJ: Princeton University Press, 1997), p. 27-28.

36. Ibid., pp. 29-33, 44.

37. Early efforts to regulate child labor occurred in England in 1833, Prussia in 1838, France in 1841, and Massachusetts in 1842.

38. This movement concerned specifically urban, industrial labor since after all the idea and practice of child labor were not considered unusual at the time.

39. The Sadler Committee gathered testimony from child laborers as part of a British government inquiry into child labor. The Report of the Sadler Committee is frequently cited and excerpts are available in many print and electronic sources. This quote is cited in William J. Duiker and Jackson Spielvogel, *World History* (St. Paul: West Publishing Co., 1994), p. 780.

40. Reported in 1835 by the wife of a French factory owner and cited in Lee Shai Weissbach, *Child Labor Reform in Nineteenth-Century France* (Baton Rouge: Louisiana State University Press, 1989), p. 11.

41. Cited in Cunningham, *Children and Childhood,* p. 139.

42. *Child Labor and the Industrial Revolution* (Bloomington: Indiana University Press, 1990), p. 34.

43. Literally 'parent of his country,' the phrase refers to the state acting as guardian of minors and other legally incompetent persons.

44. Cited in Hawes, *The Children's Rights Movement,* pp. 20-21.

45. A groundbreaking example of this interpretation can be found in Jacques Donzelot, *The Policing of Families,* tr. Robert Hurley (New York: Pantheon Books, 1979).

46. Cited in Schafer, *Children in Moral Danger*, p. 82.

47. Harry Hendrick, *Child Welfare in England, 1872-1989* (London: Routledge, 1994), p. 54.

48. Flekkøy, "The Scandinavian experience," in Franklin, ed., *The Handbook of Children's Rights*, p. 177.

49. Schafer, *Children in Moral Danger*, p. 47.

50. Cited in Cunningham, *Children and Childhood*, pp. 160-161.

51. Edmonds and Fernekes, *Children's Rights*, pp. 182-185.

52. Mason, *From Father's Property*, p. 118.

53. Edmonds and Fernekes, *Children's Rights* and Veerman, *The Rights of the Child* provide full text of many significant children's rights documents.

54. *Tinker v. Des Moines Independent Community School District* (1969) 393 US 503; *Goss v. Lopez* (1975) 419 US 565.

55. See Christina Lyon and Nigel Parton, "Children's rights and the Children Act 1989," in Franklin, ed., *Handbook of Children's Rights*.

56. Cited in Bremner, ed., *Children and Youth*, pp. 132-33.

57. From *Father's Property*, p. xv.

58. Cited by Michael Freeman, "Children's rights in the land of rites," in Franklin, ed., *Handbook of Children's Rights*, p. 73.

58. Bremner, ed., *Children and Youth*, pp. 128-130.

Chapter 2

Wendy and Peter Pan: Exploring the Concept of the Child[1]

Brian Klug

The Concept of the Child

When we speak of the rights of the child, of whom are we speaking? The answer, of course, is any child and all children. But what do we mean by "child"? In one sense of the word, anyone who is somebody's daughter or son — a first generation descendant — is a child; and as Wendy says to "the lost boys" when she begins her bedtime story, "Almost everything is a descendant."[2] But this is not the sense of the word that is apropos. When we speak of the rights of the child, we mean "child" as distinct from "adult," not "parent" (although we might speak of children's rights vis-à-vis their parents). So, the question is, How do we distinguish a child from an adult? One answer is, by age, a child being a minor, a person under full legal age. On the face of it, this is the answer contained in the United Nations Convention on the Rights of the Child (UNCRC). Article 1 stipulates that for the purposes of the Convention, "a child means every human being below the age of eighteen years unless, under the law applicable to the child, majority is attained earlier." But how much earlier? Though it might be hard to specify, there must be a lower limit. Suppose, *ad absurdum*, a nation were to lower the age of majority to, say, five. This would make the provisions of the UNCRC inapplicable to human beings over the age of four. There is nothing in article 1 to prevent this, but it would go against the whole spirit and intention of the Convention. This shows that formal legal status — being a minor — is not at the heart of the

UNCRC's definition of the child. There is a substantive concept that lies in the background of article 1. This is the concept of the child that I wish to explore. A child, we are saying, is not an adult. Then what is an adult? Not a child. We can play this game till pigs can fly or Peter Pan grows up, but it will not get us any nearer to distinguishing the one from the other. Let us begin with the obvious: the fact emphasized by René Descartes, the seventeenth-century French philosopher, who points out that "we were all children before being adults." He emphasizes this fact because it has, he thinks, profound human significance. As adults, he says, "our judgments" are not as "pure or solid as they would have been had we the full use of our reason from the moment of our birth and had we never been led by anything but our reason."[3] We do not need to follow him further than this, nor even so far. If we set aside his exclusive focus on reason and judgment, and if we take his observations quite generally, they seem to hint at something like the following concept of childhood: a period in life that precedes adulthood, in the course of which we develop certain faculties, the full possession of which constitutes an adult's estate. Or, more succinctly, a child is someone growing up.[4] This is the concept of the child encapsulated in the UNCRC, with its focus on the child's "development," its emphasis on "the evolving capacities of the child," and the principle that the rights of the child should correspond to those evolving capacities.[5] It is a broad concept, covering everything from infancy to adolescence.[6] "A child," concludes historian Anna Davin, "is someone at a certain stage in the life cycle."[7] If this "stage" is understood to subsume several successive stages, and if it is understood that the next stop is adulthood, then we seem to have a working answer to our question.

Or do we? I remember, as a child, wincing when grown-ups used the word "stage" to talk about children's feelings, interests, and experiences. This was because it sounded patronizing; as if "stage" came with "mere" clinging to it; as if the things that mattered to me and my friends were trivial; as if we were going through a phase out of which we would grow, and childhood were just a preliminary to the real thing: being grown-up. Of course, I have grown out of that stage now. I no longer mind if childhood is called a stage. (It does not bother me in the least.) However, there is something in my juvenile reaction to the word that I think is true and which I wish to carry forward into this essay. If childhood is a step in the direction of adulthood, it is not merely a means towards the end of growing up; it is also a state in its own right. When we speak of children having rights, we think of childhood as an end in itself.[8]

At the same time, a child is not a completely different form of life from that of an adult human being. Consider, in contrast, the caterpillar. A caterpillar is a stage in the life cycle of a butterfly or moth. But tell that to the caterpillar, which thinks it is a worm with legs and not a member of the lepidopteran family. If it senses the life it harbors within, if it feels those six insect feet kicking in its belly, or the brush of wings against the inside of its skin, it probably thinks an alien creature has invaded its body. Munching its way across green leafy pastures, what does it know about life on the wing? To all intents and purposes, when the butterfly hatches, the caterpillar dies. It does not grow up. Children, in contrast, grow up. (All except one, of course, but we shall get to him soon.) They do not incubate the adult within; they develop in the direction of adulthood over time.

So, let us by all means think of the child as someone at a certain stage in life. But we must be clear that there are two sides to this concept. On the one hand, a child is someone evolving into an adult. On the other hand, there is more to being a child than potentially being a man or woman: there is the actual thing itself, today, now, for its own sake, and not for the sake of a future grown-up state. These two elements are in tension, and it is easy to forget one when insisting upon the other. Yet, if we are to hold on to our concept of the child, they should fit together, like two sides of a coin, or a thing and its shadow. How can we unite them in our minds?

In this essay, I take my cue from Wendy. When she discovered Peter foolishly trying to stick his shadow on with soap, she resorted sensibly to needle and thread.[9] I shall imitate her example, after a fashion, by trying to sew the two sides of our concept together; only the thread I shall use is imaginary. Specifically, I shall try to imagine, side by side, the two central figures in J. M. Barrie's story. Other characters will come into the picture, but the focus will be on Wendy and Peter. This is partly because Barrie himself emphasizes their relationship, and partly because, on my reading, they reflect the two sides of our concept of the child.[10] Consequently, I shall ignore vast tracts of the narrative and drama. I say "narrative and drama" because the story I refer to is told in two places: the novel *Peter and Wendy* and the play *Peter Pan.*[11] I shall draw on both sources freely, ignoring differences between them, taking what I want and neglecting to point out what does not suit my purpose. Some might call this cheating, but it isn't. I am playing by the rules, the ones I have made up for the occasion. (Peter would approve.) For the aim of the game is not really to arrive at an adequate reading of the story. The aim is to use the story to bring our concept of the child to the imagination: to imagine the idea of growing up. (Peter would scowl.) Keeping this image — the image of the child — in mind, I shall conclude by arguing that when we speak about children's rights, we are not speaking simply about human rights for young people. It makes a world of difference that it is the *child* of whom we speak.

The World of the Child

Peter Pan

If we conceive of the child as someone at a certain stage in life, a young person who is growing up, then nothing and no one seems as antithetical as Peter Pan, "The Boy Who Would Not Grow Up."[12] This singular fact is his defining difference: "All children, except one, grow up."[13] So, does Peter Pan represent another concept of the child, a viable alternative to the one I am exploring in this essay? If so, and if he were to write his own Convention on the Rights of the Child, or if one were to be written for the likes of him (except that he has no peer), it would have to be a substantially different document, based on the principle of the *non*-evolving capacities of the child. I imagine him (or his lawyers) erasing the word "development" every time it occurs in the UNCRC. Article 29, for example, states that the education of the child shall be directed to the "development of the child's personality…" *That* would have to go, for a start. In fact, the whole of this article, as well as the previous one, would be anathema to Peter Pan, especially the bit about making "primary education compulsory" (article 28 (a)).[14] In place of the present articles 28 and 29, with their several sub-clauses and sub-sub-clauses about the right to education, there would be a terse statement along these lines: "States Parties recognize the right of the child not to go to school." I suppose the supreme right in Peter Pan's Convention would be this: "Every child has the right not to grow up." All other rights would spell out the ramifications of this basic right. In the light of this, it is worth asking the question, Could Peter Pan conceivably exist?

The question can be put this way: Is Peter Pan a real boy? In the story, he is certainly called a boy by the narrator, by other characters, and by himself. "Boy" is the first word Wendy uses when she is woken by his sobs in her nursery and sees him for the first time. She addresses him thus: "Boy, why are you crying?" Crying is certainly something boys do; so is denying they cry, which Peter does a minute later. Wendy thinks he is crying because (as he has just told her) he does not have a mother. "'I wasn't crying about mothers,' he said rather indignantly. 'I was crying because I can't get my shadow to stick on. Besides, I wasn't crying.'" The logic of this retort does rather tend to reinforce the impression that Peter is a veritable child. He loves to play, like a child, and can "never resist a game." He is "greedy" for stories, especially if they are about him.[15] He is cocky and conceited, cunning and naïve, selfish, generous, heartless, kind. He is mischievous. He has a strong sense of fair play and wants to kill pirates. (He also wants to *be* one.) So far, so real.

He could still be a real boy when he tells Wendy that he does not want to grow up. "'I don't want ever to be a man,' he said with passion. 'I want always to be a little boy and to have fun.'"[16] Any boy might say this with passion. But, given the sort of boy Peter is, does it mean the same when *he* says it? Let us consider the implications of the difference — the defining difference — between Peter and other children. All children, except Peter, grow up. To begin with, this does not mean that *in fact* all other children grow up. The facts of life are sadly different. The point, I take it, is that *in principle* they grow up; they grow up, all other things being equal. (Hence the special poignancy of the death of a child: the sense that they have lost a future into which they were still growing.[17]) So, when other children say, "I don't want to grow up," they are, as it were, defying nature (like an apple on a tree saying, "I don't want to fall down"). But when Peter says it, what does it mean? For he is in the opposite case. Not growing up is not just a contingent fact about him, something that happens to be true; it is written into his very nature. He *sounds* like a real child when he says, "I don't want ever to be a man. I want always to be a little boy and to have fun." It *sounds* like a protest against fate. But it cannot be one, not *really*, since it precisely *is* his fate to be the boy who never grows up. So, how exactly should we hear his plaint?

While we are pondering this, let us turn to the question of Peter's parentage. If he is a real child, whose child is he? He tells Wendy that he does not have a mother, and that he has not "the slightest desire to have one." This does not mean that he *never* had one. Indeed, he goes on to tell Wendy that he ran away from home when he "heard father and mother talking of what I was to be when I became a man." However, it is difficult to accept this story at face value, partly because he says, almost in the same breath, "I ran away the day I was born." Either he was unbelievably precocious as a newborn infant, or he is confused, or this is a piece of honest make-believe. (For Peter, "make-believe and true were exactly the same thing"; as far as I am aware, he never lies.) And then there is the story he tells about the day he flew home, only to find "the window was barred, for mother had forgotten all about me, and there was another little boy sleeping in my bed." The narrator remarks, "I am not sure that this was true, but Peter thought it was true…" So, even if *Peter* thinks his account of his origins is true, *we* might not be so sure. In the final analysis, we cannot be certain that he was born at all. For the narrator says, "Now, if Peter had ever quite had a mother, he no longer missed her."[18] If Peter were a real boy, this "if" and "quite" would be unthinkable. Real children come from the womb; there are no ifs and quites about it.[19]

Furthermore, real children have a determinate age that changes with the years. They have birthdays. But not Peter.[20] Not only does he never grow up, he never grows older. When Wendy asks him how old he is, he replies, "I don't know, but quite young."[21] "Quite young" is quite broad. But based on his behavior and appearance, we can surely set some outer limits. He is not, on the one hand, a toddler. And although his pranks are adolescent, there are clear indications that he is pre-pubescent. (His horror of beards suggests that he thinks puberty is beyond the pale.[22]) He strikes me as somewhere in the region of eight or nine or ten years old. And yet, he still has "all his first teeth."[23] He still has them, moreover, at the end of the tale, after the years have come and gone and "rolled on again," and Wendy is married with a daughter named Jane, and the nursery window blows open of a sudden, and Peter drops on the floor. "He was exactly the same as ever, and Wendy saw at once that he still had all his first teeth."[24] He, however, does not yet realize that she has changed and become a grown-up woman. She tries to prepare him for the shock: "Peter! Peter, do you know how long it is since you were here before?" "It was yesterday." Now, it is one thing to say, as Wendy tells her daughter just before Peter drops in, that he has "no sense of time," and that "all the past was just yesterday" for him. He would not be the first child, nor the last, to live in the moment. It is another thing to say that *time*, as it were, has no sense of *him*. This makes him timeless. Which makes him different not just from other children but from all humankind. As Jane observes, "Everybody grows up and dies except Peter, doesn't they?"[25] All children, except one, grow up. All people, except one, are mortal. Peter is that one. Then who or what is Peter?

This question rings a bell. In their "final bout" aboard the pirate ship the *Jolly Roger*, Captain Jas. Hook and Peter Pan are locked in combat. The children are watching, spellbound. To the brigand, Peter "is less like a boy than a mote of dust dancing in the sun." The elusive Pan pirouettes and lunges, and the Captain's cutlass goes clattering to the deck. Hook appears undone! But instead of pressing home the advantage, Peter picks up the weapon by its blade, and "presents the hilt" to his foe. "'Tis some fiend fighting me!" exclaims the perplexed Captain. "Pan, who and what art thou?" Peter's reply hangs in the air, poised like the sword of Damocles. "The children listen eagerly for the answer, none quite so eagerly as Wendy." Then Peter's spirit strikes. "I'm youth, I'm joy, I'm a little bird that has broken out of the egg."[26]

Handing the Captain back his sword, Peter is keeping the fight — the game — alive. He is perpetuating the moment. This is what drives him; or rather, he *is* that drive. He is youth: not *a* youth, not an individual child, but youth itself. Refusing to grow up, he is not an actual boy protesting against fate; he is the spirit of that protest. If from start to finish he is "a strange boy," it is not because he is unlike other real children, but because unlike other children he is not real. Wounded by Hook and stranded on Marooners' Rock in the mermaids' lagoon, the waters rising inexorably, Peter revels in the unfamiliar feeling of fear: he feels it as "a drum beating in his breast *as if* he were a real boy at last" (emphasis added). He exclaims, "To die will be an awfully big adventure." But his exhilaration is pathetic, for he is *not* a real boy. When Tinker Bell is fading away after drinking from the poisoned chalice, Peter "rises and throws out his arms he knows not to whom, perhaps to the boys and girls *of whom he is not one*" (emphasis added).[27] He is not one of them because he cannot age and he cannot die — because he does not live. And yet uniquely, he can reach them. "There were no children there, and it was night-time; but he addressed all who might be dreaming of the Neverland, and who were therefore nearer to him than you think; boys and girls in their nighties, and naked papooses in their baskets hung from trees."[28] He is "nearer than you think" to children in the world, nearer than anyone could possibly be, because he is no distance at all from them; he is *part* of them, but not *one* of them. (Which is why, despite the fact that he is joy, he is "tragic."[29]) This, as I read it, is "the riddle of his being" of which he can never "quite get the hang."[30] Nor can we, because he does not quite hang together: he keeps having adventures without time ever lapsing. If he *seems* viable as a person, it is because his exploits and experiences appear to make up a segment of a human life.[31] But actually, they don't, for Peter Pan only ever occupies the present moment; he does not exist on either side of it. The story creates the illusion of a real boy by making that moment last longer than an instant — which perforce it must, for otherwise there would *be* no story. However, when the fairy dust has settled, the story does not fly: Peter Pan could not be a real person. And yet, what he personifies *is* real, or a real part of what it means to be a child. If we try to imagine childhood as purely a state in its own right, wholly an end in itself, something that exists for its own sake only and not at all in relation to the future adult that the child becomes — we imagine Peter Pan. And if Peter Pan is ultimately unimaginable — if he could not conceivably exist — then this image of childhood is incoherent too. Or incomplete: it is only half the story. Turning to Wendy, we meet Peter's other half. More accurately, we meet a girl who represents the other element in our concept of the child: the emerging adult.[32]

Wendy

In the young Wendy, the emphasis on the future adult is so pronounced that she is in danger of ceasing to be a child altogether. She is "every inch a woman, though there were not very many inches."[33] She is so closely identified with her mother, who she pretends to be at the beginning of the story, and whose style of life she leads at the end, that she is practically a miniature Mrs. Darling.[34] In the Neverland, the boys go down on their knees outside the house they have built for her, begging her to be herself: "O Wendy lady, be our mother." For a moment she demurs (or pretends to), protesting that she is "only a little girl" and has "no real experience." But Peter explains that what they need "is just a nice motherly person." "Oh dear," she sighs, "you see I feel that is exactly what I am." As if to prove the point, she promptly chides them, "Come inside at once, you naughty children; I am sure your feet are damp."[35] They call her "Mummy," and she plays the part by frequently saying, "Oh dear."[36] She is a "housewife." In their home under the ground, she makes the rules, cooks the meals, does the washing, darns the clothes, tells them stories, and tucks them up in bed at night. She loves to give them their medicine, "and undoubtedly gave them too much." She is such a nice motherly person, and her hands are so full with "those rampagious boys of hers," that there are "whole weeks" when she is "never above ground." In fact, the prospect of looking after them was the main attraction by which Peter had lured her to fly away with him to the Neverland in the first place. "'Wendy,' he said, the sly one, 'you could tuck us in at night.' 'Oo.' 'None of us has ever been tucked in at night.' 'Oo,' and her arms went out to him. 'And you could darn our clothes, and make pockets for us. None of us has any pockets.' How could she resist?" Even when the children have their great adventure with the pirate ship, her point of view is strictly grown-up. "No words of mine can tell you how Wendy despised those pirates. To the boys there was at least some glamour in the pirate calling, but all that she saw was that the ship had not been scrubbed for years." It is exactly what Mrs. Darling would have noticed; both of them liked everything to be shipshape and "just so."[37]

So, Wendy is "Mother Wendy."[38] But there is also Wendy the would-be girlfriend or mate. For, while her feelings for Peter are partly maternal, they are also romantic. In the frame of this story, such feelings are not in the repertoire of a child; they are distinctly adult. Tinker Bell and Tiger Lily, who are attracted to Peter in the same way, are both portrayed as young women rather than as little girls. (Tinker Bell, of course, is a fairy, but love conquers the species divide.[39]) Wendy understands that they are her rivals in love. She feels pangs of sexual jealousy when Peter mentions their names. (Tinker Bell feels the same way, only more so: she "hated" Wendy "with the fierce hatred of a very woman."[40]) All of this, naturally, goes over Peter's head. Finally, Wendy forces the issue. It is the dramatic climax of their relationship:

> WENDY (knowing she ought not to probe but driven to it by something within) What are your exact feelings for me, Peter?
> PETER (in the class-room) Those of a devoted son, Wendy.
> WENDY (turning away) I thought so.[41]

Wendy knows she ought not to inquire into his feelings about her. But why shouldn't she? Perhaps she feels it is intrusive, or unbecoming, or unwise. But fundamentally, it is inappropriate. For there is nothing within Peter that answers to the "something within" Wendy that is driving her. Peter is "in the class-room"; that is to say, he is being a good little boy, behaving himself, giving "Miss" what he thinks is the right answer, the one she wants to hear. But his answer could not be more wrong. There could not be a deeper gulf between them than the one that opens up at this moment. It is the gap between her grown-up emotion and his youthful naiveté. It is a woman falling for a boy as if he were a man. The *faux pas* is too great. She turns away.

Ironically, it is precisely Peter's boyish insouciance that saves Wendy. In the story, he rescues her from the pirates. In this reading of the story, he saves her from a fate worse than Hook: growing up too soon. He saves her, that is, from being possessed by the future adult, the "something within" that is driving her. "She was one of the kind that likes to grow up. In the end she grew up of her own free will a day quicker than other girls."[42] So, if Peter is The Boy Who Would Not Grow Up, Wendy is The Girl Who Could Not Wait. Both, in their opposite ways, are unlike other children: he is the exception to the rule that all children grow up, she is its exceptional illustration, its clearest exponent. In Wendy, the future adult presses so hard that you wonder:

Why only a day? Why doesn't she grow up a week ahead of other girls, a month, a year, five years; or even an entire childhood? Who or what keeps the woman in Wendy at bay? It is Peter, oblivious to her amorous advances. For, as I shall try to elucidate, if Wendy would have got her man, she would have lost her portion in the Neverland — to where we now must turn.

The Neverland[43]

How do you approach the Neverland? It is a baffling question, whether you mean the place or the topic. Peter Pan's directions for going there are "Second to the right and then straight on till morning."[44] But what sort of directions are these? Surely, they lead no place. But in that case, they point the way, since "no place" is just what "Neverland" means — which is a good way of approaching the topic. For this no place is an island, like another land that never was: More's Utopia, whose name means the same.[45] The story of Peter Pan and Wendy, in other words, belongs to utopian literature. The Neverland is an island paradise for children.[46]

Being for children, this no place is like no other no place on earth. The categories are different. I do not mean the creatures, though there are numerous unearthly or fabulous beings, including mermaids, fairies, and Never birds. I mean the fabric of reality: space and time do not behave themselves here, or do not behave the way they do in an adult (no) place. Time is not unreal, it's just unruly: "[I]t is quite impossible to say how time does wear on in the Neverland, where it is calculated by moons and suns, and there are ever so many more of them than on the mainland." The seasons do not take their proper turns: "It is summer time on the trees and on the lagoon but winter on the river, which is not remarkable on Peter's island where all the four seasons may pass while you are filling a jug at the well." And space expands like a toy balloon, so that all ten children can tramp into Wendy's house at the same time, even though it has been built to fit her snugly: "In they went; I don't know how there was room for them, but you can squeeze very tight in the Neverland." The whole island seems squeezed very tight, given its geography of mountains, forest, river, and lagoon. This is because its scale is proportioned to the fun it sustains: it is "very compact, not large and sprawly with tedious distances between one adventure and another, but nicely crammed."[47] In short, the island is a whole world, a *child's* world where even time and space play up.

It is a *world*, not a *place*, not a location on the globe, not even an imaginary one. It is no use trying to find it on a map, because only mainland shows up on maps. You can only get there by flying, which means being a child, for when you grow up you forget how to fly. It took the children "many moons" to get there, "and, what is more, they had been going pretty straight all the time…" But which moons are being counted here? The one that revolves round the earth once a month, or the plethora that appear in the Neverland sky? (After all, the children are already high on fairy dust.) Furthermore, the Neverland is so perilously close that "in the two minutes before you go to sleep it becomes very nearly real"; hence the need for night-lights. A mere "film" separates it from the mainland — which Peter (and Tinker Bell) break through at the beginning, startling Mrs. Darling as she dozes in the nursery. Summing up, we can say with some assurance that there is no way to make sense of these facts. Then what is the nature of the gap that separates island from mainland?[48]

Is it fantasy? Is the island mere make-believe? It is, if you approach it with the point of view of someone in "the grown-up world," someone like Mr. Darling in the city, "where he sits on a stool all day, as fixed as a postage stamp."[49] If that is your approach, the island will forever recede, and be a land you never find: a Neverland.[50] To put it another way, in an adult accounting of "the real world," the world of a child exists purely as make-believe; it has no standing other than as fantasy. But when Wendy, John, and Michael approach the Neverland for the first time, and are fired upon by Long Tom, the pirates' big gun, whose thunderous boom fills them with terror, the children "learn the difference between an island of make-believe and the same island come true."[51] So, it is *not* make-believe; it is real. But what does this mean? What would Mr. Darling say it means? He would scoff at the very notion. He would say (I presume), "The idea of a make-believe island that comes true is itself make-believe," and file it under Stuff and Nonsense. In a way, he would be right. For what does it mean to say that the island has "come true"? It does not mean that what was once make-believe has now become real by the normal criterion of reality, the one used on the mainland; it means the *criterion* has changed. The *perspective* has shifted from adult's to child's.

Thus, on the island, the children still distinguish between make-believe and true — but on their own terms.[52] Sometimes, their distinction corresponds to the one made on the mainland. For example, the children know, in a perfectly straightforward sense, the difference between real and pretend dinners.[53] But at other times, the distinction seems to cut across the usual one. So much so, that it is hard to say that there is a *criterion* of reality on the Neverland: a hard and fast basis for telling the difference between true and pretend. When the boys construct Wendy's house, they really do gather branches, and lay a mossy green roof on top of its red walls. There are windows with yellow blinds, and a door that actually opens. The sole of Tootles' shoe makes "an excellent knocker," while John's hat, with its top pushed out, furnishes a chimney. The moment it is perched upon the roof, the chimney starts to smoke. Is the smoke as real as the rest? Perhaps so, on the principle that function follows form, as if this were a law of children's nature. Or is the smoke just pretend, like the roses "peeping in" at the window, which, on Peter's stern command, "they made-believe to grow"?[54] It is hard to say, and wrong to try. For the point is this: the smoking chimney *makes sense* in this world. There is, in short, a *world* of difference between Mr. Darling's office and Peter's island. Going from the one to the other, from the mainland to the island, is a sea-change.[55]

For the children, it is a homecoming. "Wendy and John and Michael stood on tiptoe in the air to get their first sight of the island. Strange to say, they all recognized it at once, and until fear fell upon them they hailed it, not as something long dreamt of and seen at last, but as a familiar friend to whom they were returning home for the holidays." They can even pick out, from their crow's-nest in the sky, features of the island beneath them — features that in a sense belong to them. "'I say, John, I see *your* flamingo with the broken leg.' 'Look Michael, there's *your* cave.' 'John, what's that in the brushwood?' 'It's a wolf with her whelps. Wendy, I do believe that's *your* little whelp'" (emphasis added). They have never visited the island before, but it is theirs. So much so, that "the island was looking out for them. It is only thus that anyone may sight those magic shores."[56] In other words, the Neverland comes naturally to the children. They feel like they are coming home (or that home is coming to them) because they *are* at home here. Here everything is on *their* terms, not on terms set by adults.

Now, to speak of "their" terms is to speak of the terms set by Peter. For the Neverland is not just his place of abode, it is his domain, his dominion. The island is animated by his spirit and subject to his will. "Feeling that Peter was on his way back, the Neverland had again woke into life." This is how it pays homage to Peter. The wild beasts go on the prowl, greeting him "in the way they think he would like them to greet him." The mermaids "for the same reason" commence combing their hair. The pirates "for the same reason" slink ashore in their longboat. "The whole island, in short, which has been having such a slack time in Peter's absence, is now in a ferment because the tidings has leaked out that he is on his way back; and everybody and everything know that they will catch it from him if they don't give satisfaction." Peter lords it here; even the sun is "another of his servants." His chief antagonist understands this boy's sway. "'So, Pan,' said Hook at last, 'this is all your doing.' 'Aye, James Hook,' came the stern answer, 'it is all my doing.'"[57]

In other words, the entire Neverland serves the purpose of this youth — who is the spirit of youth. It is *his* island, where children can be children; this is its very *raison d'être*. And it is Wendy's reason for being there, whether she knows it or not. It is true that Peter lures her to his island by appealing to her maternal longings. But he has already won her "intense admiration" because he is acquainted with fairies. Moreover, he uses mermaids as bait as well. "'And Wendy, there are mermaids.' 'Mermaids! With tails?' 'Such long tails.' 'Oh,' cried Wendy, 'to see a mermaid!'" Fundamentally, Peter addresses her as a child, and his island is a child's safe haven. Among the marauding beasts, predatory pirates, and other Neverlandish hazards, Wendy is perfectly safe. She is safe, as a child, from the encroachments of the adult within. Here on the island she can indulge her sense of responsibility to her heart's content. She can darn umpteen pairs of socks, dish out bucketsful of bitter-tasting medicine, tuck up lost boys in bed all night, mutter "Oh dear" every other minute; and still be a child. For she *really* does these things; but she does them in a child's world. So, there is no danger that she will grow up overnight. On Peter Pan's island, growing up is "against the rules."[58] I think this means against its concept: growing up is *inconceivable* on the Neverland, the land of never growing up.

Even after the children return to the mainland, Wendy receives visits from Peter.[59] She accompanies him back to the Neverland the following year "to do his spring-cleaning"; and again two years later, for the same purpose.[60] The deeper point being this: taking her to his island, he brings her back to the present, against the tenacious pull of the future adult. Thus, when the woman in Wendy woos Peter, her very childhood is at stake. For Pan, the universal spirit of youth, is the soul of the Neverland. If Peter ceased to be Pan, the Neverland would vanish. And if Wendy were to win Peter's hand, he would cease to be Pan: he would be a man. No Pan, no Neverland. No Neverland, no childhood. So, when Wendy courts Peter and risks losing Pan, she risks all.[61] Not that she knows it. And not that there is the slightest chance of the gallant Peter being her beau; for he is nature's own gentleman.

In sum, Peter, the spirit of youth, is not a real boy. Wendy is a flesh-and-blood human being; but take Peter away from Wendy, and she reverts prematurely to being a little woman. Put them together, and a real child comes into being. A real child, according to the concept under discussion in this essay, is someone at a certain stage in life, a young person growing up. A real child is evolving into an adult — but concomitantly has the experience of not being one. This experience — of not being grown-up — is precisely what the Neverland provides for. Put it this way: In the story's accounting of "the real world," childhood is not just a preliminary to the real thing: the things that matter to a child are just as real as the bills the Darlings have to pay or their dinner party at number 27.[62] In effect, the Neverland is a representation of make-believe on the mainland, representing it as real; this is "the difference between an island of make-believe and the same island come true." Within its "magic shores," the world of the child is real — as real in its own right as the grown-up world. Thus, through the alchemy of the Neverland, our concept of the child is transmuted into an abiding image that floats before our mind's eye: Wendy and Peter Pan side by side in flight.

The Rights of the Child

If we can manage to keep this image in mind, perhaps we shall not lose sight of whom we are speaking when we speak of the rights of the child.[63] Wendy, as a little girl, needs to be given the chance to take responsibility for matters that will concern her as a grown woman. But she is *not* a grown woman; and to treat her as such would be, as it were, to adulterate her youth. One way of talking about this is to say that a vein of play must run through all her work; otherwise she will become a drudge, even if a contented one (for she wants to do the work). She is entitled to that vein; and equally to the process that leads it to wane over time. Peter grants her the first right, though he would deny her the second.[64] But she is entitled to both because both belong to a child's estate. She is, in short, entitled to her childhood.

The right to childhood is not mentioned in the UNCRC, but it is proclaimed by the convention as a whole; it is the sum of its parts.[65] If we forget the sum, we are liable to mistake or misapply the specific rights the Convention enumerates. The Preamble, citing the Charter of the United Nations, recognizes "the inherent dignity and...the equal and inalienable rights of all members of the human family." It is an apt metaphor: if *children* do not belong to the human *family*, then no one does. But if they belong to it *as* children, and if this is what the UNCRC intends, we must remember of whom the Convention speaks. A child is not just a young human being. A child, according to the concept that informs the Convention, is someone at a certain stage in a human life. The rights of a child, therefore, are not simply human rights for the young; they are specifically rights for a child: for a child to be a child.

Without Peter, Wendy is not a child: she is a grown-up woman in the body of a little girl. And whereas Peter without Wendy could not conceivably exist, variations on the theme of Wendy are unhappily commonplace. Children, in all sorts of ways, in all kinds of circumstances, have adulthood thrust upon them before they have had the chance to be children. It would certainly be ironic if, in the name of their rights, children were denied the very thing to which they are most entitled. Thus, we must continually try to keep the child in view as we explore the rights of children laid down in such instruments as the UNCRC.

After the children return home, Wendy looks out the window and sees Peter playing a prank: he is "hovering in the air, knocking off tall hats with his feet." *Wendy* sees him, but the grown-up victims of his playfulness do not; they are "too old." "You can't see Peter if you are old." Uniquely, it seems, Wendy, the grown woman, now mother of Jane, can. Perhaps that's because, despite her maturity, Wendy wishes she could fly back to the Neverland with him: "'If only I could go with you,' Wendy sighed." Once upon a time, something within her drove her towards growing up. Now the inner voice is different: "Something inside her was crying, 'Woman, woman, let go of me.'"[66]

What about us — us rational, reasonable, sensible, moderate, mature, adult human beings: Can we see him too? Can we glimpse the mote that dazzled Captain Hook, and recognize it as the spirit of our youth? Can we know of whom we speak when we speak of the rights of the child? Perhaps — if we are still prompted by that same inner voice the woman Wendy hears: Peter Pan's.

Notes

1. I am grateful to Kathleen Alaimo for prompting me to write this essay, and for her numerous helpful observations, suggestions, and references. I have also benefited from discussing certain points or themes with Jane Rubenstein, Lenore Metrick-Chen, Nan-Nan Lee, Jack Montgomery, and Joan Cohan.

2. J. M. Barrie, *Peter Pan,* in his *Peter Pan and Other Plays,* ed. Peter Hollindale (Oxford: Oxford University Press, 1995), p. 131 [act 4, scene 1]. The play *Peter Pan* was first performed (in London) in 1904. It underwent several revisions, and was not published until 1928. On February 22, 1908, a

new scene was added near the end of the play. This scene, which was not performed again in Barrie's lifetime (he died in 1937), was first published in 1957 as *When Wendy Grew Up: An Afterthought*. It corresponds closely to the final chapter — also called "When Wendy Grew Up" — of the novel. The novel was published in 1911 under the title *Peter and Wendy* (see note 9). In the 1921 edition, the title was expanded to *Peter Pan and Wendy*. In more recent editions, the title has been contracted to *Peter Pan*. In this essay, I draw upon all three sources: the play as published, the added scene as published, and the novel. For the purposes of the discussion, I treat the added scene as part of the play (though I cite it separately). I quote from Barrie's ample stage directions without distinguishing them from the script, treating them as integral to the work. For the lost boys, see note 35.

3. René Descartes, *Discourse on Method*, in his *Discourse on Method and Meditations on First Philosophy*, tr. Donald A. Cress (Indianapolis: Hackett, 1993), p. 8. The *Discourse* was published in 1637. The "method" that Descartes sets out in the *Discourse*, summarized in the rules laid down in Part Two, is not only a way of *employing* reason but of *cultivating* it: "Moreover, I felt that in practicing this method my mind was gradually getting into the habit of conceiving its object more rigorously and more distinctly..." (pp. 12-13). I am not sure, however, what he would make of the idea that reason is a capacity that *evolves*.

Part Four of the *Discourse* contains Descartes' famous first principle, "I think, therefore I am" (p. 19). The (implicit) foundation of Peter Pan's metaphysics is slightly different: "I pretend, therefore it is."

4. Hence the expression "grown up" as a synonym for "adult." The word "adult" seems to contain within itself the germ of this concept. The word derives from the Latin *adultus*, the past participle of *adolescere*, to grow up. *Adolescens* is the present participle. It is as if "adults" have accomplished what "adolescents" are still in the process of doing.

5. The "development" of the child is mentioned twice in the Preamble. It comes up again in article 7, and recurs in several later articles, where it is sometimes analyzed; e.g., article 27 specifies "physical, mental, spiritual, moral and social development." The notion of "the evolving capacities of the child" is introduced in article 5. Note also the importance attached to *preparing* the child for later life; according to article 29, one of the aims of education is to prepare the child "for responsible life in a free society."

6. Perhaps it is even broader than that. The Preamble to the United Nations Declaration of the Rights of the Child (1959) notes that the child needs special safeguards and care "before as well as after birth" (in P. R. Ghandhi, *Blackstone's International Human Rights Documents* [London: Blackstone Press, 2000], p. 51). This phrase is cited in the Preamble to the UNCRC. At the other end of the spectrum, adolescence shades into adulthood; it does not end at midnight when a person turns eighteen. The discussion in this essay does not apply straightforwardly, if at all, to the concept at its margins — at either end of the spectrum. It concerns the broad middle range. As for "second childhood," that is, of course, a different idea altogether: it is derivative from

the concept under discussion in this essay, rather than being part of it. The UNCRC is not a charter for the senile.

7. Anna Davin, "What is a Child?" in *Childhood in Question: Children, Parents and the State,* ed. Anthony Fletcher and Stephen Hussey (Manchester: Manchester University Press, 1999), p. 33.

8. The phrase "end in itself" is borrowed from Kant. "The ground of such a principle is this: rational nature exists as an end in itself" (Immanuel Kant, *Grounding for the Metaphysics of Morals,* tr. James W. Ellington [Indianapolis: Hackett, 1981], p. 36.) However, I am not suggesting for one moment that Kant himself sees childhood as an end in itself.

9. J. M. Barrie, *Peter and Wendy,* in his *Peter Pan in Kensington Gardens and Peter and Wendy,* ed. Peter Hollindale (Oxford: Oxford University Press, 1999), pp. 89-90.

10. Barrie's emphasis is reflected in the title of his novel, *Peter and Wendy.* Their closeness is underscored from the start. Wendy's mind is "scrawled all over" with Peter, even before she has met him, whereas he is only "here and there" in the minds of her brothers, John and Michael. When her mother asks her about Peter, she says confidently "he is just my size." The narrator tells us, "She meant that he was her size in both mind and body; she didn't know how she knew it, she just knew it" (*Peter and Wendy,* pp. 74, 75).

11. See note 2.

12. This is the subtitle of the play "Peter Pan."

13. *Peter and Wendy,* p. 69. This is the opening sentence of the novel. When I quoted this sentence to Niall Keenan, a St. Benet's mate, he observed wryly that he knew several people who had never grown up. I take his point.

14. "'I don't want to go to school and learn solemn things,' he told her passionately" (*Peter and Wendy,* p. 217).

15. *Peter Pan,* p. 98 (act 1, scene 1); *Peter and Wendy,* pp. 90, 148, 96, 226. See also *Peter Pan,* p. 153 (act 5, scene 2).

16. *Peter and Wendy,* p. 92. I do not mean that Peter represents what it *means* to be a boy, as if, for example, every boy wants to kill a pirate. Nor, for that matter, do I mean to imply that no girl ever harbors this hope. The story reflects the Edwardian era in which it was written, including ideas about children and gender that were current at the time. But this is beside the point. The point here is simply that these elements in Peter's personality are consistent with his being a real boy, albeit a boy of a certain sort. Likewise, I do not mean that every child wants to remain a child, nor that this is something that a given child wants always. All I mean is that such a wish is characteristic of children, and the sort of wish a real child might express. It is also characteristic of children to want to play at being grown-up. Peter is a typical child in this respect too.

17. James Barrie was six years old when his thirteen-year-old brother David died. According to Hollindale, "David's death was undoubtedly the origin of Peter Pan" (Introduction to *Peter Pan,* p. xxiii). The death of a child also lies in the background of Wendy, whose name Barrie coined, adapting it

from the sobriquet given him by Margaret Henley, who died at the age of five. "She had tried to say James was her friend, but it came out 'fwend' and then 'fwendy' in her infant pronunciation. James made the change from fwendy to Wendy, and he had the name he wanted for his heroine" (Susan Bivin Aller, *J. M. Barrie: The Magic Behind Peter Pan* [Minneapolis: Lerner Publications, 1994], pp. 81-82). Knowing this, adds poignancy to the final event in the narrative: Peter Pan flies off to the Neverland with a little girl named Margaret, daughter of Jane, daughter of Wendy, so she can be his mother (*Peter and Wendy*, p. 226) Margaret was also Barrie's mother's name.

18. *Peter and Wendy*, p. 90; *Peter Pan*, p. 99 (act 1, scene 1); *Peter and Wendy*, pp. 128, 167,170.

19. I am speaking of a world prior to the advent of cloning, test tubes, and incubators.

20. Here I am cheating slightly, but ever so. That Peter does not have birthdays is implied by the fact that he does not age at all. But I am also thinking of Peter Pan in an earlier incarnation. In *Peter Pan in Kensington Gardens* (1906), we are told, "Peter is ever so old, but he is really always the same age, so that does not matter in the least. His age is one week, and though he was born so long ago *he has never had a birthday*, nor is there the slightest chance of his ever having one" (emphasis added) (*Peter Pan in Kensington Gardens* in *Peter Pan in Kensington Gardens and Peter and Wendy*, p. 12.). This children's book consists of six chapters previously published as part of *The Little White Bird* (1902), which was thus the first published text containing a character called Peter Pan. The story is quite different, and there is no Wendy, but there are strong family resemblances between the earlier and later versions of Peter. The earlier Peter, however, seems to be a younger child than the later one. The earlier one is recalled when "our" Peter (the one who knows Wendy) says that when he left home, he "ran away to Kensington Gardens and lived a long time among the fairies" (*Peter and Wendy*, p. 92). Moreover, several elements in the earlier story are imported into the later, including the tale about Peter returning home and finding another boy in his stead, with the window to his room barred.

According to the map at the Marlborough Gate entrance of Kensington Gardens, London, the famous Peter Pan statue sculpted by Sir George Frampton is "taken largely" from *The Little White Bird*. However, we could just as easily be looking at "our" Peter as we gaze at the juvenile piper standing astride a tree trunk swarming with life, both animal and fairy, while a Wendy-like figure clambers over the top, apparently attempting to join him. A small metal plaque on the ground in front of this tableau says, "Children: Please do not climb on this beautiful statue — you will harm it." As I stood there and read the inscription, I wondered, "What would Peter do if he were in my shoes now?"

21. *Peter Pan,* p. 99 (act 1, scene 1).

22. "I don't want to be a man. O Wendy's mother, if I was to wake up and feel there was a beard!" (*Peter and Wendy*, p. 217.)

23. *Peter and Wendy*, p. 77. He also retains his "first laugh" (p. 94).

24. *Peter and Wendy,* pp. 220, 223.

25. *When Wendy Grew Up,* in *Peter Pan and Other Plays,* pp. 161, 159 (act 1, scene 1). Peter not only telescopes the past into a single day, "yesterday," he is also exceedingly forgetful. For example, within a year, much to Wendy's dismay, he completely forgets their adventures in the Neverland. "'Who is Captain Hook?' he asked with interest when she spoke of the arch enemy" (*Peter and Wendy,* p. 219). Peter's forgetfulness goes hand in hand with his not growing up: he has neither future nor past.

26. *Peter Pan,* p. 145 (act 5, scene 1). "I'm a little bird that has broken out of the egg." This harks back to the earlier Peter Pan story (see note 20), in which babies are said to be birds before they are born as human beings. Peter himself was initially a bird. After he flies the coop (his parent's home) at the age of one week, he ends up on the island that comes to be known by his name (which is where all the birds that turn into boys and girls are hatched). The wise old Solomon Caw tells Peter that henceforth he is "a Betwixt-and-Between," meaning that he is part human, part bird. (*Peter Pan in Kensington Gardens,* pp. 10, 13, 14, 17). He retains his kinship with birds in the later story. When he re-enters the Darling house to bar the window against Wendy's return, he "flutters about the room joyously like a bird..." Just before the curtain falls at the end of the play, "the Never birds and the fairies gather closer" (*Peter and Wendy,* pp. 149, 154 [act 5, scene 2].) See also *Peter and Wendy,* p. 139: "Or suppose we tell of the birds that were Peter's friends..."

27. *Peter and Wendy,* pp. 77, 214; *Peter Pan,* pp. 125 (act 3, scene 1), 136-37 (act 4, scene 1). See also p. 118, where he warns Wendy against the mermaids: "They are such cruel creatures, Wendy, that they try to pull boys and girls *like you* into the water and drown them" (emphasis added). The next stage direction says that Wendy is "too guarded by this time to ask what he means precisely by 'like you,' though she is very desirous of knowing." By "like you," I take him to mean "of whom you are one" rather than "of your sort." In other words, he is saying, "They try to drown all boys and girls; so, you are at risk, and I am not."

28. *Peter and Wendy,* p. 185.

29. He is "the tragic boy" (*Peter and Wendy,* p. 224). Some will say that Peter's tragedy is that he is without a loving home. Others might say it is the fact that the world changes — that Wendy grows up and becomes a woman, and so on. I think these things are sad or painful, perhaps, but what is tragic is his exclusion from humankind. He stares in at the window "at the one joy from which he must be for ever barred" (p. 214): a human life.

30. *Peter Pan,* p. 153 (act 5, scene 2).

31. He does not, however, appear to have a human body made of flesh and blood. He can float on air; he "is no weight at all"; and, at least until Wendy does the cooking, all his meals are "pretend." Captain Hook gives the order, "Cleave him to the brisket," but suspects he does not have one. (*Peter and Wendy,* p. 103; *Peter Pan,* pp. 124 [act 3, scene 1], 127 [act 4, scene 1], 144 [act 5, scene 1].) He has a detachable shadow. He cannot be touched — except

by fairies (pp. 98 [act 1, scene 1], 117 [act 2, scene 1]). In short, to the extent that he is an individual being at all, Peter Pan is more spirit than matter, more elfin than human, less boy than will-o'-the wisp.

32. Wendy, in contrast to Peter, is a real human being. It would miss the point to object that since both are merely characters in a work of fiction she is no more real than he is. She is real, as are the other children in the story, in the sense that she is a *conceivable* person. (She is a real *possibility*.) Wendy is a real person in the "world" of the story, just as Juliet is in Shakespeare's play or Anna Karenina in Tolstoy's novel. Peter is not. Not that he isn't a real element in the story; of course he is. But he is not a real *person*. (How can I say this, when his personality is so vivid and his predicament so touching?)

33. *Peter and Wendy*, p. 91.

34. Their houses are closely identified too. In the stage directions for the opening scene of act 1, the family home is called "the Darling house." When Wendy wakes up in the house that Peter and the boys have made for her in the Neverland, she strokes it and calls it a "darling house." Moreover, the real house "wanders about London looking for anybody in need of it, like the little house in the Never Land" (*Peter Pan*, pp. 87 [act 1, scene 1], 116 [act 2, scene 1]).

35. *Peter and Wendy*, pp. 131-32. The boys comprise Peter, the lost boys, and Wendy's brothers John and Michael. The lost boys "are the children who fall out of their prams when the nurse is looking the other way. If they are not claimed in seven days they are sent far away to the Never Land" (*Peter Pan*, p. 101 [act 1, scene 1]). Their number varies from time to time. When the Darling children visit the Neverland, there are six. So, counting John and Michael, Wendy has eight children in her care. Peter, arguably, makes nine, but she prefers to think of him as the father of the household (*Peter and Wendy*, pp. 160-61).

36. *Peter and Wendy*, pp. 158, 159, 161, 164, 165.

37. *Peter and Wendy*, pp. 157, 132-135, 170, 135, 97, 192, 71, 183. No doubt, the idea of womanhood represented by Wendy and her mother is very narrow; it is relative to a particular period, culture, and class, and it is part of a larger script about gender that pervades the story. But all this is beside the point for the purposes of my argument in this essay. The point is that Mrs. Darling embodies a version of what it means to be an adult, and that in Wendy the emphasis falls on the future adult. A whole essay could be written about Wendy and Peter based on their different gender roles. This would be to view the story through the lens of a different topic. I write what I see through mine. (See also note 16.)

38. *Peter and Wendy*, p. 151.

39. That Tinker Bell is physically mature is made clear by the description of her attire when she accompanies Peter Pan on his quest to retrieve his shadow: she is "exquisitely gowned in a skeleton leaf, cut low and square, through which her figure could be seen to the best advantage" (*Peter and Wendy*, p. 88). She wears a negligee, not a child's robe or nightgown (p. 169). She is, incidentally, "slightly inclined to *embonpoint*" or plumpness, unlike the fairy with the hourglass figure in Walt Disney's animated film (p. 88).

40. *Peter and Wendy*, pp. 162, 111.

41. *Peter Pan*, p. 130 (act 4, scene 1). See also p. 135.

42. *Peter and Wendy*, p. 220.

43. In his Explanatory Notes, Hollindale says it is the Neverland in the novel, the Never Land in the play as published, and the Never Never Land in the play as performed (*Peter and Wendy*, p. 232; *Peter Pan*, p. 311). It is also the Never Never Land in the published text of *When Wendy Grew Up*. Hollindale mentions that in the first draft of the play it was the Never, Never, Never Land. But never mind whether there is a "never" more or less, for it is the same non-existent place nevertheless.

44. *Peter Pan*, p. 98 (act 1, scene 1). In the novel, the narrator, noting that these directions are useless, offers a disarming explanation for why Peter gives them: "Peter, you see, just said anything that came into his head" (*Peter and Wendy*, p. 102).

45. Thomas More, *Utopia*, 1516. The name "Utopia" combines the two Greek words *ou* and *topos*, "no" and "place." In pointing out this parallel, I am not offering an explanation for why Barrie called the island the Neverland (or the Never Land or the Never Never Land: see note 43). In his Explanatory Notes, Hollindale says, "there was an actual district in Australia called the Never, Never, Land" (*Peter and Wendy*, p. 232). Perhaps this suggested the name to Barrie. In any event, my speculations linking the Neverland and Utopia are strictly interpretive and not in the least historical. I certainly see no reason whatsoever to mention, even in passing, that More's work is prefaced by a letter addressed to a certain "Peter" (Peter Giles).

46. By "paradise," I do not mean to imply perfect bliss, but more like perfect fit: corresponding to a child's idea of an ideal form of life. I do not mean that the Neverland is *every* child's idea of paradise, only that being a child's paradise is, so to speak, the *principle* of the island. The specifics, as with other aspects of the story, belong to the author (though I do not think they are entirely idiosyncratic) and his period (though by no means are they all passé). (See also note 16.)

47. *Peter and Wendy*, p. 136; *Peter Pan*, pp. 105-6 (act 2, scene 1); *Peter and Wendy*, p. 132; *Peter Pan*, p. 105 (act 2, scene 1).

48. *Peter and Wendy*, pp. 221,105,74,77.

49. *Peter and Wendy*, p. 98; *Peter Pan*, p. 90 (act 1, scene 1). Trying to tackle the metaphysics of the Neverland is tricky. Even trickier is trying to work out the precise relationship between the island, the mainland, and the grown-up world. The latter two are not, I think, quite identical; but I tend to slip into treating them as if they were, and this will have to do.

50. Or a land you lose: "We too have been there; we can still hear the sound of the surf, though we shall land no more" (*Peter and Wendy*, p. 74).

51. *Peter and Wendy*, p. 110.

52. All except Peter, for whom "make-believe and true were exactly the same thing" (*Peter and Wendy*, p. 128. See also p. 135). They would be, since the distinction does not apply to him: he is neither one nor the other. It is tempting to

think that, if not real, he must be pretend. But that is a misconception. It is more accurate to say that we must pretend to pretend that he exists. Even more accurately, I can no longer tell whether I am saying something intelligible or just pretending to do so — such is the spell cast by Peter Pan.

53. Again, except for Peter: "Make-believe was so real to him that during a meal of it you could see him getting rounder" (*Peter and Wendy*, p. 135).

54. *Peter and Wendy*, pp. 130-1; *Peter Pan*, pp. 115-6 (act 2, scene 1).

55. The allusion is to Ariel's song: "Full fathom five thy father lies; / Of his bones are coral made; / Those are pearls that were his eyes; / Nothing of him that doth fade / But doth suffer a sea-change / Into something rich and strange" (*The Tempest*, act I, scene 2). It does not seem wrong to hear echoes of this song — nor of Prospero's magical island and "brave new world" — when speaking of the Neverland. Moreover, the aerial Peter has several of Ariel's attributes. (He has some of Prospero's too, as will soon emerge.)

56. *Peter and Wendy*, p. 105. Young children often have to stretch their bodies and crane their necks when they want to see something novel and interesting; hence the description of the children standing "on tiptoe in the air," when in fact they have a clear view of the island beneath them. Flamingos are given to standing on one leg, the other leg being withdrawn into their bodies; hence Michael's flamingo with the broken leg. These descriptions illustrate Barrie's ability to convey a child's-eye view of things.

57. *Peter and Wendy*, p. 112; *Peter Pan*, p. 105 (act 2, scene 1); *Peter and Wendy*, p. 202. As Hook discerns, Peter is Pan. Pan was a Greek god of woods and pastures, player of pipes and practical jokes, playmate of nymphs, son of Hermes — the fleet-footed winged god and travelers' guide. The traces of Peter's pedigree are everywhere in the story. He is Peter Pan, son of Pan, grandson of Hermes.

58. *Peter and Wendy*, pp. 93, 97, 112.

59. Note that the lost boys also return to the mainland, where they are adopted by Mr. and Mrs. Darling, and, like Wendy, John, and Michael, grow up, turning into respectable citizens and losing their ability to fly. Tootles becomes a judge, Slightly becomes a lord (*Peter and Wendy*, pp. 215-6, 220). Only Peter remains on the Neverland, together with his cast of characters.

60. *Peter and Wendy*, p. 218.

61. This line of reasoning might make it seem as if Wendy "risks all" for children everywhere, not just for herself; for surely, *all* children stand to lose their childhood if Peter is no longer Pan. However, Neverland logic does not necessarily work along straight lines. So far, I have been speaking of the Neverland in the singular, as a unique island or world. This is how the story, for the most part, has it too. But initially, the novel refers to "the Neverlands" in the plural: "Of course the Neverlands vary a good deal" (*Peter and Wendy*, p. 74). The text indicates that there is a different Neverland for every child; "but on the whole the Neverlands have a family resemblance." You would think, however, that the Neverlands must do more than *resemble* each other; they must be one and the same island. If there is more than one, which is the home

of Peter Pan? Or does each have its own Peter Pan? Assuming the Darling children fly to the same island, whose Neverland is it, and which Peter takes them there? How could *all* the children recognize the island when they see it for the first time? And, stranger still perhaps, how could each of them pick out features from *each other's* Neverland (pp. 105-6)? The obvious solution to these conundrums is this: There is just one Neverland, and it has a family resemblance to itself. This solution to the quantitative problem affords me a basis for arguing that Wendy "risks all" for herself only, not for the children of the world. The argument is simple. If Wendy were to win Peter's hand, Peter would no longer be Pan; if Peter were no longer Pan, the Neverland would cease to exist; but the Neverland resembles itself; therefore, it itself would continue to exist; but it itself cannot exist unless Peter is Pan; therefore, Peter would continue to be Pan, and children would continue to be children. Q.E.D.

    62. *Peter and Wendy*, pp. 70-71, 99.

    63. Keeping the image in mind is not enough; we have to apply it in a given case. This — the application of the double-sided concept of the child — is problematic, and will vary significantly from case to case according to such variables as the age and maturity of the child, the circumstances, and so on. This essay does not aim to provide any help with applying the image; it only aims to provide the image.

    64. Jane Rubenstein has emphasized to me the second of these two points — that Peter would keep Wendy from *ever* growing up; hence her need to leave the Neverland eventually. This sheds light, I think, on the fact that she is resolved to return to the mainland, in defiance of Peter's will, and that her resolve prevails (*Peter and Wendy*, pp. 167- 71).

    65. The Preamble to the UNCRC does, however, note that according to the United Nations Universal Declaration of Human Rights (1948), "childhood is entitled to special care and attention." The United Nations Declaration of the Rights of the Child (1959) goes further in proclaiming "a happy childhood" as part of the "end" which its provisions serve (*Blackstone's*, p. 51).

    66. *Peter Pan*, p. 151 (act 5, scene 2); *Peter and Wendy*, pp. 225, 223.

Chapter 3

United Nations Convention on the Rights of the Child: Developing International Norms to Create a New World for Children

Cynthia Price Cohen

Rights of the Child: Conceptualization

The two closing decades of the twentieth century witnessed a dramatic alteration in the worldview of children. After centuries of being dismissed, ignored, manipulated and looked upon as "objects," children were finally granted legal recognition as "persons." Worldwide focus shifted from negotiations over the types of services to be provided for children,[1] to struggles over how to develop a framework that would allow for active child participation in civil society.[2]

It should not be assumed that the shift in child status from "object" to "person" happened virtually overnight. On the contrary, these developments took place over time and in a somewhat haphazard fashion. In the United States, the first child rights seeds were planted at the national level in the mid-nineteenth century, with the establishment of institutions for children who were orphans or who were blind or deaf. This "child-caring" movement was the impetus behind the creation of special legal procedures for juvenile delinquents and legislation prohibiting child labor.

The "child-caring" movement got its start internationally through the League of Nations in response to the events of World War I. The

International Labour Organisation (ILO) can be credited with the first legally binding treaties protecting children. Beginning in 1919, the ILO adopted a series of Conventions that prohibited children from engaging in specific types of hazardous work.[3] Shortly thereafter, Eglantyne Jebb, founder of the Save the Children International Union,[4] undertook the drafting of a declaration protecting children's rights. Known as the Declaration of Geneva, Ms. Jebb persuaded the League of Nations to adopt it in 1924.[5]

While this short declaration provided a concise list of things that society "owed to the child" and established the notion that children should have certain types of "rights," these were not the types of rights that adults take for granted. They were not rights to "do" or to "act" independently as individuals; instead they were rights to "receive" in the form of things that should be done for and to the child — or what some governments refer to as "entitlements." To understand what was lacking one must look at the Declaration of Geneva in light of the broader context of human rights in general.

The worldwide human rights movement, which began after the child rights movement, was an outgrowth of World War II. Article 1 of the Charter of the United Nations lists among its purposes the promotion and encouragement of "respect for human rights and for fundamental freedoms for all." These words were given meaning in 1948, with the adoption of the Universal Declaration of Human Rights.[6] In other words, the international child rights movement and the international human rights movement can be seen as proceeding along two separate but parallel tracks, both with the goal of promoting human dignity.

The Universal Declaration (like the Declaration of Geneva) was not legally binding, but provided the foundation for numerous legally binding human rights treaties.[7] The most significant of these were the International Covenant on Civil and Political Rights (1966) and the International Covenant on Economic, Social and Cultural Rights (1966).[8] Although both of these treaties were based on the Universal Declaration, because of contemporaneous political forces it was impossible for all of these rights to be protected in a single treaty. Western nations, such as the United States, disagreed with the notion that education and social security were "rights," while the Soviet Union and other Eastern Bloc countries objected to freedom of speech and religion as rights. Interestingly, while many other human rights treaties were drafted during the next quarter century, it was not until the rights of children were put into treaty form that these two sets of rights were finally united into a single legally binding instrument. In fact, the United Nations Convention on the Rights of the Child (UNCRC) encompasses not only civil-political rights and economic-social-cultural rights, but humanitarian rights as well. It was and is a groundbreaking instrument, not only because it combined all types of human rights, but also because it recognized that children should have the same sort of civil and political rights that are guaranteed to adults.

Just as children had been the objects of concern after the First World War, the Second World War brought about a new wave of interest in their well-being. This interest first manifested itself in the establishment of the United Nations Children's Emergency Fund (UNICEF)[9] during the 1940s and later with the adoption of the United Nations Declaration of the Rights of the Child in 1959. However, like its predecessor the Declaration of Geneva, the 1959 U. N. Declaration used language that reflected the then-prevailing worldview of children as "objects" in need of "services." In other words, notwithstanding the word "rights" in its title, the 1959 Declaration was essentially a "child-caring" instrument that perpetuated systematic denial of the child's individual participation rights.

To celebrate the twentieth anniversary of the 1959 Declaration, and as a method of evaluating the world status of children, the United Nations designated 1979 as the International Year of the Child (IYC). As part of this celebration, the Polish government proposed that the rights of the child be re-defined in a treaty — a Convention on the Rights of the Child. Drafting of the Convention began during IYC, but was not completed until ten years later. The U.N. General Assembly adopted the Convention on the Rights of the Child on November 20, 1989.

The Convention was drafted by a Working Group of the United Nations Commission on Human Rights. During the ten-year drafting period the world image of the child was transformed from that of an "object-recipient of services" to an "individual personality" with the right to act and to express an opinion. This transition took place in bits and pieces. First, the Polish government submitted a model of the Convention that was simply a replication of the 1959 Declaration of the Rights of the Child and had minimal implementation provisions.[10] The Commission on Human Rights rejected this proposal. A second model, written in legally enforceable language, was used as a framework for the Working Group throughout the drafting process. It should be especially noted that in this second model one article broke with past conceptions of the child as a mere recipient of services and recognized the child's individual personality rights. Article 7 of this model stated:

States Parties to the present Convention shall enable the child who is capable of forming his own views the right to express his opinion in matters concerning his own person, and in particular, marriage, choice of occupation, medical treatment, education and recreation.[11]

As the drafting process progressed, all of the original articles in the Polish model were refined and/or expanded. In particular, article 7 gave rise to a whole series of articles ensuring the child's right to freedom of expression, freedom of religion, freedom of association and assembly and the right to privacy.[17] Ultimately, the twenty-article model treaty, which had minimal monitoring processes, became a fifty-four-article treaty with a strong, elaborate and innovative implementation mechanism.

While the child rights convention was ten years in the making, the actual formal drafting time took less than four hundred hours. From its formation in 1979, the Working Group met only one week a year, just prior to the full annual Session of the Commission on Human Rights. However, early in 1988, in order to meet a self-imposed completion deadline of 1989, two two-week sessions were held: one session was used to complete the "first reading" or final version of the Convention's content; the other session finalized the Convention's language through a process known as a "second reading." It should be noted that every session of the Working Group also involved numerous informal meetings and that other informal negotiations took place continuously in between the sessions.

Merely counting the numbers of meeting hours cannot begin to indicate the intense interplay of dramatic and colorful elements that went into creating the UNCRC. First, there was the fact that the Convention was being drafted during the "Cold War" — with the East and West regularly clashing over language and ideas. Second, there were constant shifts in the makeup of the Working Group as delegations joined and withdrew from membership in the Commission on Human Rights, with non-members participating as Observer States.[13] In addition, there were constant shifts in representation within the delegations, with very few maintaining a single representative over a period of years.[14] Third, there was the strong influence of non-governmental organizations (NGOs) which formed a coalition for the express purpose of monitoring the Convention's drafting and influencing its final text. Much of the shift from child as "object" to child as "person" came about as a result of NGO support for the United States' civil-political rights proposals, which added to the tension between the Eastern Bloc and Western delegations.

All of the drafting was done by consensus — meaning that even one dissent would cause a proposal to be dropped from the agenda. No vote was ever taken and the views of Observer States were given equal weight with those of States that were members of the Commission on Human Rights. While NGOs could not directly propose articles to be included in the Convention, they were always able to find a government that would support and submit their proposals.[15]

The role of the NGO coalition in creating the final text of the Convention should not be underestimated. Made up of about thirty organizations with varying interests, they called themselves the NGO Ad Hoc Group on the Drafting of a Convention on the Rights of the Child (NGO Group). The NGO Group met twice yearly to discuss proposed articles and draft alternative wording. They would then submit their recommendations to the Working Group at its next session.[16] Members of the NGO Group were present at all sessions of the Working Group and also met informally with delegates to press their views. One of the most effective and unusual tools in the NGO Group arsenal was the institution of their annual "Pea Soup" parties, which took place on the Thursday night of the drafting week. Held in the apartment of one of the NGOs (who also made the pea soup), its informality did much to break down the traditional wall between government delegations and NGOs.[17] The wording of many articles can be traced directly to NGO initiatives, and to NGO-government collaboration.[18] In recognition of their contributions to the Convention, the Working Group included a special role for NGOs in the Convention's implementation provisions.[19]

Rights of the Child: Realization

The UNCRC has been a record-breaker in every sense of the word:

- On the day of its signing ceremony in 1990, it had the greatest number of signatories of any previous UN human rights treaty.
- Having obtained the required number of ratifications, the Convention went into force in September 1990 — faster than any previous human rights treaty.
- It achieved near universal ratification by 1997, making it the most ratified of all human rights treaties.
- It is the only human rights treaty to combine civil-political, economic-social-cultural and humanitarian rights in a single instrument.

The UNCRC comprises fifty-four articles, as well as a thirteen-paragraph preamble. Of the fifty-four articles, forty-one are "substantive." That is, they elaborate the rights that the treaty is protecting. The remainder of the convention is procedural, with articles 42-45 having to do with its implementation mechanism and articles 46-54 outlining the requirements for its entry into force.

Because there are so many substantive articles, covering so many types of rights, there have been numerous efforts to cluster the articles and categorize them in order to get a quick perspective on the rights that are protected. One of the most popular of these is known as the "three Ps": "provision," "protection" and "participation."[20] Such shorthand does a disservice to the complex content of the Convention and minimizes its full effect on the world vision of the child. Note, however, that even in this shorthand overview, two of the three categories are from the "child-caring" orientation, indicating that while children are now being granted a right to participation, the primary emphasis is still on "care and protection." This gives at least some indication of the conceptual distance that must be traveled before children are truly accepted as equals.

Creating a positive, assertive human rights treaty for children does not assure that those rights will be respected or that the world will soon complete the shift from a "child-caring" perspective to a "child-rights" perspective. As with any legislation, the Convention's language must be interpreted in order to have meaning. This linguistic interpretation arguably comes from two sources: reports of governments that have ratified the Convention and the body that evaluates the extent to which government reports show that they are fulfilling their treaty obligations. The mechanism by which this is accomplished is outlined in articles 43-45. Article 43 sets up a body of ten experts known as the Committee on the Rights of the Child. Article 44 outlines the reporting obligations of nations that have ratified the Convention — known as "States Parties."[21] Article 45 gives the Committee other capacities that are not usually available to such monitoring bodies: 1) it allows the Committee to obtain information from outside sources as to the completeness of a State Party's report; 2) it provides for the Committee to assist the State Party in getting assistance that will help it to better fulfill its treaty obligations; and 3) it enables the Committee to request that special studies be done to broaden its knowledge and expertise.

Committee on the Rights of the Child:
Functions

Members of the first Committee on the Rights of the Child were elected at a meeting of States Parties in 1991. They were chosen on the basis of geographic diversity, but serve in their "personal capacities," not as representatives of the countries of which they are citizens.[22] Committee members serve four-year terms, but half of those first elected "drew straws" to decide which members would serve only two years. Since elections are held every two years, this meant that at least half of the original Committee members would remain after the next election. The Committee began its examination of States Parties' reports in January 1992.

The Committee meets three times each year for a period of four weeks.[23] The first three weeks of each session are devoted to public oral examinations of States Parties' reports. The fourth week is spent in private preparations for its upcoming session. It is during this fourth "pre-sessional" week that the Committee utilizes its article 45 powers to obtain the additional material it needs to be able to adequately evaluate a State Party's report. To accomplish this, it meets with representatives from UNICEF and other interested United Nations bodies, and also holds meetings with representatives of national NGOs from the particular country whose report is being examined.

The reporting process begins two years after ratification with the State Party's submission of an initial report to the Committee on the Rights of the Child detailing the action it has taken to implement the Convention. Once the report is received by the Committee it is translated into the Committee's three working languages (English, French and Spanish) and given a place on the list of States Parties reports to be dealt with in the future — from six to eight reports are covered at each session. The Committee examines the report during its "pre-sessional" meetings and then formulates a "list of issues" to be addressed by the State Party in question. These "issues" — or questions — arise either from information that the Committee feels was not covered by the report in sufficient detail or they may be based on information obtained from outside sources. The list of issues is submitted to the particular State Party, which must answer the issues in writing. These questions often form the basis for some of the questioning at the Committee's oral hearings.

Because of the Convention's many articles, the task of preparing the written report for the Committee on the Rights of the Child can be very complicated. In fact, for some underdeveloped countries that are short on staffing, it can be nearly impossible to do the necessary research to write the reports. To streamline the reporting process, the Committee created a set of *General Guidelines Regarding the Form and Content of Initial Reports (Guidelines)*[24] for submission of State Party reports. The *Guidelines* divide the substantive articles in the Convention into eight sections.[25] At the Committee's request, all States Parties' reports follow the pattern of the *Guidelines*. NGOs and others submitting additional information to the Committee — often in the form of "parallel" reports that mimic those of governments — are also encouraged to follow the *Guidelines*. Section III ("General Principles") is especially important because the Committee has singled out four articles as containing rights that are overriding and applicable to all other articles in the Convention: 2 (non-discrimination), 3 (best interests of the child), 6 (right to life and survival), and 12 (respect for the views of the child).

Committee on the Rights of the Child: Processes

Once the Committee on the Rights of the Child has completed its preliminary review of a State Party's report the next step is the oral examination. Typically, the Committee allots three half-day sessions (nine hours) to this process.[26] The hearings are open to the public and are generally attended by national NGOs from the country whose report is being examined and by members of the NGO Group, who actively work to help national NGOs communicate with the Committee. It should be noted that the UNCRC has two unique requirements for States Parties: 1) under article 42 they must make "principles and provisions of the Convention widely known … to adults and children alike" and 2) under article 44 (6) they must also make their reports "widely available to the public in their own counrties." What this means in reality is that civil society — usually through NGOs — is empowered to ensure that the States Parties report truthfully on the conditions in their countries.

Typically, a State Party will send a delegation of several persons to the oral examination of their report. The delegation is ordinarily made up of representatives from various ministries that will have the requisite expertise to answer whatever questions the Committee might pose. The examination takes the form of a "constructive dialogue." That is, the Committee asks questions and the State Party's representative responds. At the conclusion of the final session, each Committee member makes a comment about the State Party's report, commending progress and encouraging improvements. The Committee then submits these comments to the U.N. General Assembly in the form of *Concluding Observations*, which appear in each formal report of its activities that the Committee submits to the General Assembly. The State Party is then required to repeat this process again in five years. There are no sanctions for noncompliance — only public scrutiny, which can be very effective since no country wants to become known as a treaty violator.

It should be remembered that the United Nations is an organization of sovereign nations and therefore there are legal constraints on the types of actions that can be taken to penalize a non-complying government. Additionally, any nation that has become a State Party has voluntarily agreed to uphold the Convention's standards and, in fact, desires to make these standards a reality in their country. As a consequence, the Committee sees its role as that of a guide and facilitator of compliance, since under article 45 it can provide assistance to countries that are having difficulty meeting their State Party obligations.[27]

Committee on the Rights of the Child: General Discussion Days

At the time that the Committee drafted the *General Guidelines*, it also drafted its *Provisional Rules of Procedure*. While the *Rules of Procedure* are mainly concerned with such matters as choice of officers and other similar rules, the Committee saw fit to include one unique provision: the establishment of a special day for "general discussion." This General Discussion Day has become an annual event that takes place at the Committee's fall session. At this open session, NGOs, U.N. bodies and others with expertise in the particular subject that has been chosen for that day's discussion are invited to present information to the Committee that will enhance its members' understanding of the situation of children in the world. The information gathered from the General Discussion Day is published in the Committee's report to the General Assembly.[28] Since this process was inaugurated in 1992, General Discussion Day topics have included: children in armed conflict; economic exploitation of children; the girl child; children with disabilities; children and the family; and, most recently, children and violence.

Committee on the Rights of the Child:
Jurisprudence

The jurisprudence of the Committee on the Rights of the Child is slowly being developed. Although the text of the Convention might seem to be self-evident in its requirements, it was deliberately written in the sort of "constitutive" language that allows for interpretation and that would make it possible for the widest number of countries to embrace its norms. Discovering the true meaning of the Convention requires that real people apply it to a real set of circumstances. In this process, first the language of the Convention is interpreted and applied by the State Party. Then the Committee reviews this interpretation and evaluates the extent to which it reasonably reflects the Convention's intent. At the present time, the Committee's jurisprudence — its interpretation of the Convention — is to be found only by analysis of its *Concluding Observations*. Taken as a whole, even though they might be reflecting on a variety of national situations, the *Concluding Observations* can act as a guide for understanding the Committee's general interpretation of the Convention.

All United Nations human rights treaties are monitored by treaty bodies of experts, similar to the Committee on the Rights of the Child. Some of these, the Human Rights Committee in particular, have issued a series of "General Comments" on individual articles in which they have synthesized the content of their *Concluding Observations* into an interpretive guide for States Parties. The Committee on the Rights of the Child has only recently begun this process and issued the first of its "General Comments" in 2001. For this occasion, the Committee chose to interpret the language of the first paragraph of article 29 on the purpose of education. It has been rumored that the Committee will next turn its attention to article 12 (the child's right to express his or her views) with that "General Comment" to be published in 2002. As for the Committee's interpretation of other articles, it is a matter of having to check each of the *Concluding Observations* separately.[29]

What is truly exciting about the electronic information age is that documentation of all of the above-mentioned Committee processes is available on the website of the U.N. High Commissioner for Human Rights. A researcher can get the full text of every State Party report, as well as the Committee's *Concluding Observations* on the report. Best of all, one can look at the *Summary Records* of the oral examination and discover exactly what questions were asked and how the State Party replied.[30]

Rights of the Child: Actualization

As might be expected, the introduction of a set of complex, innovative child rights norms onto the world scene and into the laws of every State Party has had a gigantic ripple effect. This has been felt on the international level by the move to create still more legal instruments protecting children's rights, by the reorganization of existing child rights bodies, and by the establishment of special offices and world conferences to address violations of children's rights. At the national level, every State Party has been forced to reevaluate its system of support for children. This, in turn, has become a powerful tool for child advocates to use in pushing their governments to do more for children.

International Action: New Child Rights Treaties

Since the U.N. General Assembly adopted the Convention on the Rights of the Child in 1989, other child-focused treaties have been adopted by international organizations.

The Organization of African Unity adopted the Charter on the Rights and Welfare of the African Child in July 1990.[31] The text of this Charter more or less replicates the UNCRC, in that its articles tend to protect the same rights, but with a different order and a specific slant reflecting an African emphasis. For example, the Charter devotes all of article 21 to abolition of traditional practices "prejudicial to the health or life of the child," while this prohibition — which is primarily aimed at eliminating female genital mutilation — appears only in a single paragraph of the Convention's article on health.[32] Interestingly, the OAU Charter also singles out "child marriage" as such a harmful practice.[33]

Shortly after the adoption of the UNCRC, the Hague Conference on Private International Law began the process of drafting a treaty that would make it possible to actualize the Convention's article 21 on intercountry adoption. Without clear procedures, it would be difficult for this article to become a reality and the door would be left open to abusive practices. The purpose of the Hague Convention on the Protection of Children and Cooperation in Respect of Intercountry Adoption (1993) was: 1) to set out rules to be followed by both "sending" and "receiving" nations where a transboundary adoption was to be carried out; and 2) to ensure that the adoption would be legal and would not be undertaken for private gain.

The original draft of the Hague Convention used language focusing on the parents and supporting their efforts to adopt a child. However, due to the strong influence of the UNCRC, the final text of the Hague Convention is decidedly child-focused (as is reflected in the treaty's final title) and now reads as supporting the child's right to a family — not the family's right to a child. It also provides for the child to have a voice in the adoption.[34]

In 1993 the Council of Europe drafted the European Convention on the Exercise of Rights by Children.[35] As a response to the UNCRC, the idea behind the European Convention was to create procedures and an environment that would strengthen the child's right to express his or her views on matters of importance to the child. There were considerable differences of opinion about this treaty and whether it really enhanced the Convention on the Rights of the Child or advanced children's rights. Although a text was finally adopted and ratified by a number of countries, it never became a treaty of any consequence.

Throughout its long history the International Labour Organisation (ILO) has drafted many conventions aimed at eliminating various practices considered harmful to children and young people. After more than a half century of adopting specialized treaties, in 1973 the ILO adopted the Convention Concerning the Minimum Age for Admission to Employment (ILO Convention No. 138) — a blanket treaty covering all types of work and seeking to end all child labor by setting a minimum age of fifteen or in some special cases age fourteen.[36] Despite the fact that Convention No. 138 was ratified by 115 nations, it did not stamp out child labor, probably because it was too difficult to enforce — especially in the poorest countries where children often work to help their families survive. In fact, many child advocates argue that, in some circumstances, a total ban on child labor could actually be psychologically harmful to the child. When the failures of Convention No. 138 became obvious, the ILO drafted a new treaty protecting children, Convention No. 182 on the Worst Forms of Child Labour (1999). It prohibits child slavery, sale of children, trafficking, prostitution, drugs and employment that might endanger the safety or morals of a child. Widely accepted across political and cultural lines, it has now been ratified by 106 nations — including the United States.[37]

Often, after a treaty has been finalized, the body that adopted it will conclude that something was missing in the original version or that the treaty was in some way inadequate. To correct this weakness, an "optional protocol" is drafted to fill this gap in the treaty. Technically, even though it relates to an existing treaty, an optional protocol is a separate treaty with a separate ratification process. In the case of the

UNCRC, the Commission on Human Rights drafted two optional protocols, both adopted by the U.N. General Assembly on May 25, 2000: the Optional Protocol to the Convention on the Rights of the Child on the involvement of children in armed conflicts, and the Optional Protocol to the Convention on the Rights of the Child on the sale of children, child prostitution and child pornography. Both of these Optional Protocols had been preceded and accompanied by intense political maneuvering. Both have received the required number of ratifications to enter into force in early 2002.

The Optional Protocol on armed conflict has its roots in the final days of the Convention's drafting, when efforts within the Working Group to raise the minimum age for armed combat to eighteen were blocked by the United States delegation.[38] Subsequent efforts, especially by the Scandinavian governments and bolstered by the Secretary-General's study on children in armed conflict,[39] led to the appointment of Olara Otunnu as Under-Secretary to monitor the use of child soldiers, and ultimately to adoption of the Optional Protocol, which has finally raised the age for combat to eighteen.

The Optional Protocol on the sale of children was preceded by years of study by a Special Rapporteur on the Sale of Children and Child Pornography who had been appointed by the Commission on Human Rights to survey the world situation of sexually exploited children. This eventually led to the 1996 World Congress on the Commercial Sexual Exploitation of Children. The World Congress, held in Stockholm, was sponsored by a coalition of NGOs, the Swedish government and UNICEF. It gave rise to a number of national conferences and regional meetings on child sexual exploitation and led to a Second World Congress in Yokohama in December 2001. The world energy that has been released to protect sexually exploited children has resulted in the quick ratification of this Optional Protocol.

The UNCRC has had an unspoken secondary influence on the text of all child rights treaties that have been drafted since 1990. As exemplified by the Hague Convention's text, possessive personal pronouns are no longer solely in the masculine gender. Very quietly the girl child is being supported through the choice of words. Thanks to the example set by the UNCRC, treaties now use the dual personal possessive pronouns "his or her" and "him and her," rather than only "his" or "him," as had been the pattern of previous human rights treaties.

International Action: Restructuring
United Nations Bodies and NGOs

The almost immediate, near universal acceptance of the UNCRC has had a startling effect on every type of agency dealing with human rights issues, whether it is governmental or nongovernmental. The result is a sharper focus on child rights as a distinct agenda. Many United Nations bodies had never previously given much attention to children as a separate group. For example, throughout its history the United Nations High Commission for Refugees (UNHCR) had never recognized any age differences within the refugee community. With the advent of the UNCRC, the High Commissioner proclaimed that half of the world's refugees are children. The UNHCR, under strong pressure from NGOs, has since instituted special procedures to deal with child refugees. It has also created new strategies for field workers and developed a book on child refugees that is based on implementation of the standards of the Convention.

Similarly, even though, as mentioned above, the International Labour Organisation had long been concerned with child workers, it was motivated by the UNCRC to open an entire new division, concerned exclusively with child labor issues. The International Programme to Eliminate Child Labour, known as IPEC, keeps worldwide statistics on child labor, develops programs and operates anti-child labor projects in sixty countries.[40]

Perhaps the most dramatic change among international bodies has been the complete restructuring of UNICEF to make child rights the focal point of its work. This is especially interesting, considering that UNICEF had been weak in its support of the Convention when it was being drafted and rarely participated in Working Group deliberations. At that time, UNICEF took the position that the rights of children were too sensitive an issue for it to support. Now, the agency has completely revised its position and all of its programs have a child rights basis.[41]

Even the work of the UN General Assembly and Commission on Human Rights have been altered to incorporate special agenda items and resolutions dealing with child rights issues. Each year both the Commission and the General Assembly's Fourth Committee adopt child rights resolutions — with separate emphasis on the rights of the girl child.

Since its establishment in 1985, the Working Group on Indigenous Populations (WGIP), under the umbrella of the Human Rights Commission, has been examining the situation of indigenous people. After years of deliberations, which had led to the drafting of a

Declaration on the Rights of Indigenous Peoples, an International Year for the World's Indigenous People and the designation of a Decade of Indigenous People, the WGIP devoted its 18th Session in 2000 to indigenous children and youth. Preceding this session, ChildRights International Research Institute organized a First International Workshop on Indigenous Children and Youth to provide a forum for exchange of ideas between indigenous peoples and U.N. bodies regarding the needs of indigenous children. The Workshop was such a success that it was repeated again in 2001. Recognizing the importance of children to the future of indigenous people, the 2001 Workshop called for the establishment of a World Coalition on Indigenous Children and Youth to promote and ensure that children and youth will remain an important focal point of the indigenous peoples' movement.[42]

After the General Assembly adopted the UNCRC, the NGO Group, which had worked so effectively during the drafting of the Convention, changed its name to the NGO Group for the Convention on the Rights of the Child and reordered its mandate to correspond with the responsibilities NGOs had been given under article 45. To facilitate this work, the thirty-plus member organizations of the NGO Group created a series of focal points and Sub-Groups to develop expertise in specific areas. At the present time, the NGO Group has the following active Sub-Groups:

- *Sub-Group on the Commission on Human Rights* — follows the work of the Commission and develops recommendations regarding the Commission's annual child rights resolution and recommends new initiatives.

- *Sub-Group on Children in Armed Conflict and Displacement* — works with the UNHCR, other UN bodies and NGOs as a watchdog on armed conflict issues and to promote the Optional Protocol.

- *Sub-Group on Child Labour* — creates materials and brochures to distribute in countries where there is a high incidence of child labor and works with the ILO and other UN bodies to strengthen anti-child labor action.

- *Sub-Group on the Sexual Exploitation of Children* — one of the co-sponsors of the Second World Congress Against the Sexual Exploitation of Children (Yokohama, December, 2001), works to build regional coalitions against sexual exploitation of children, and to promote the Optional Protocol.

- *Task Force on National Child Rights Coalitions* — works to encourage the development of national coalitions and to assist them in getting their information to the Committee on the Rights of the Child. They have created materials to assist national NGOs in these efforts.

The NGO Group continues to hold its traditional twice-yearly meetings that include a discussion of new developments, projects and initiatives, and reports from each of the Sub-Groups. All child rights NGOs have found that the UNCRC has given new power to their work. National organizations, such as Rädda Barnen in Sweden, are beginning to create a child rights presence in the European Union. Other national NGOs are collaborating in drafting "alternative reports" to the Committee on the Rights of the Child regarding their countries' compliance with the Convention's standards. Regional NGOs, such as ECPAT (End Child Prostitution in Asian Tourism), coordinated their efforts with those of other NGOs, governments, and UNICEF to organize two World Congresses against the Sexual Exploitation of Children.[43] Even NGOs whose mandates were not previously associated with children's rights have found that the UNCRC has affected their work. For example, well-known human rights organizations such as Amnesty International and Human Rights Watch have begun to establish special child rights sections within their organizations and to create programs that produce materials and studies on the rights of the child.

International Action: New Targets and New Target Groups

It is not possible to effectively capture the full range of international action being taken on behalf the child. New initiatives seem to be announced almost daily. It is impossible to attend an international child rights meeting anywhere without finding out about a new, previously unknown effort promoting the rights of the child. Programs are being developed both by academic institutions and by NGOs. Centers are being set up for the purpose of training professionals (teachers, psychologists, pediatricians, juvenile justice officers, judges, police, social workers, etc.) and to act as research resources for those in the child rights field. Law schools and other institutions of higher learning are including an international child rights component in their curricula. There has been a virtual explosion of conferences, seminars, and symposia to support, examine, and analyze the rights of the child.

Governments are beginning to appoint children's ombudsmen to ensure that children's rights are respected and that the requisite services are supplied.[44] At all levels of government there is a move to develop "child-friendly" economic policies and to require "child impact" statements as part of any legislation.

The conceptualization and application of child rights also continues to expand, with new targets and new target groups being designated. While there continues to be international concern about child laborers, sexually exploited children, child soldiers, and refugee children, the list of child target groups grows. Children now being given international attention include: the children of migrant workers; children with HIV/AIDS; Roma (Gypsy) children and indigenous children.

Two new developing movements worthy of watching are the "anti-spanking" movement and the "child participation" movement. The "anti-spanking" movement has its roots in Swedish legislation that prohibits parents from using corporal punishment as a type of discipline. Similar laws are being created, either through legislation or judicial fiat, in a growing number of countries. The "anti-spanking" movement has been spearheaded by a British-based organization called EPOCH (End Physical Punishment of Children) which has brought its concerns to the attention of the Committee on the Rights of the Child. Although corporal punishment is not specifically prohibited by the UNCRC, the "anti-spanking movement" has found a sympathetic audience among members of the Committee on the Rights of the Child. Some members agree that, taken as a whole, the Convention contains an implied prohibition against all physical punishment of children, and they have encouraged States Parties to develop "anti-spanking" regulations.

The "child participation" movement is based on a much clearer link to the UNCRC. Article 12 on protection of the child's right to be heard states that "States Parties shall assure to the child who is capable of forming his or her own views the right to express those views freely in all matters affecting the child..." and that "the child shall in particular be provided the opportunity to be heard in any judicial and administrative proceedings affecting the child." However, because the language of article 12 is not explicit in its parameters, it is open to interpretation. As a consequence, it is being used by the "child participation" movement to greatly enlarge the scope of child input into the total social environment — whether that has to do with the design of a playground or a school's curricula. Supporters argue that for the human dignity of children to be respected, children should have a role in shaping everything that affects them. The goal is to assure that no program relating to children is undertaken without instituting a way for children to participate in the decision-making process.

Rights of the Child: Anticipation

Immediately after the General Assembly's adoption of the UNCRC in 1989, its supporters began to take steps to ensure that children's rights would not vanish from the international agenda. Encouraged by UNICEF, a number of countries joined in a call to hold a World Summit for Children. Heads of state and high-level governmental officials from more than eighty countries attended this highly successful meeting held in New York, September 30-October 2, 1990. It concluded with the signing of a World Declaration on the Survival, Protection and Development of Children.[45]

Ten years later, the U.N. General Assembly voted to schedule a Special Session on children to assess the degree to which nations had succeeded in fulfilling the goals of the World Summit Declaration and to lay out goals for the coming decade. Preparations for the United Nations General Assembly Special Session (UNGASS), which was scheduled for September 19-21, 2001, were begun in May of 2000 with a series of four Preparatory Committee meetings that included the drafting of an "outcome document" for UNGASS, entitled "A World Fit for Children." Governments and NGOs attended the "Prepcom" meetings — each of which lasted a week. NGO participation was particularly strong. Not only did many governments include NGOs in their delegations, but also a coalition of NGOs organized a Child Rights Caucus "to ensure that a strong voice for children's rights, implementation of the UN Convention on the Rights of the Child and rights-based approaches were present in the preparations for the Special Session on Children." One of the Caucus' main activities was the drafting of alternative language for the UNGASS outcome document.[46] There was a major difference between the role of NGOs in the UNGASS preparations and the situation of NGOs at the 1990 World Summit. NGOs had little, if any, input into the World Summit Declaration and they were not invited to participate in the celebratory events. In contrast, NGOs were not only active in every aspect of the Prepcoms, but also were expected to participate in UNGASS.

Negotiations over the UNGASS outcome document were complicated and inconclusive. In addition to the Prepcom meetings, there were numerous smaller expert meetings to work on its text. Yet, only weeks before the scheduled UNGASS meetings there was still no agreement on a final draft and close to half of the proposed language was in dispute. The September 11th terrorist attack on New York's World Trade Center brought all outcome document negotiations to an abrupt halt and UNGASS was postponed indefinitely. Still, even without UNGASS, much can be learned about child rights progress by comparing the World Summit and its Declaration with expectations for UNGASS and its draft outcome document.

During the planning stage for the World Summit, there were only a few States Parties to the UNCRC and the notion that children were holders of legally enforceable rights was quite new and uncertain. Considering that the motivation for the World Summit was to prevent the rights of children from being forgotten, it was totally unexpected that the Convention would already have obtained enough ratifications to go into force before the actual convening of the World Summit.[47] However, this obvious trend toward support for child rights was not enough to overcome the old pattern of "child-caring" sentimentality about the children. The World Summit Declaration opens with a good example of this orientation:

> The children of the world are innocent, vulnerable and dependent. They are also curious, active and full of hope. Their time should be one of joy and peace, of playing, learning and growing. Their future should be shaped in harmony and co-operation. Their lives should mature, as they broaden their perspectives and gain new experiences.[48]

The entire document is drafted in the "child-caring" mode. The rights of children are only mentioned in regard to their survival, protection and development and the sentimental tenor of the entire World Summit Declaration is typified by its closing paragraph: "We do this not only for the present generation, but for all generations to come. There can be no task nobler than giving every child a better future."[49]

The differences between the World Summit Declaration and the draft version of "A World Fit for Children" are striking. Due in part to the near universal ratification of the UNCRC, the world is more comfortable with the idea that children have legally recognizable human rights. This new attitude is apparent in the second paragraph of the draft UNGASS outcome document as it reviews developments since the 1990 World Summit:

> Millions of young lives have been saved, more children than ever are in school, *more children are actively involved in decisions concerning*

their lives and important treaties have been concluded to protect children (author's emphasis).[50]

Note the practical, non-sentimental view of the child and reference to the concept of child participation.

Perhaps the most remarkable difference between these two documents is their general approach to children's issues. Gone are the flowery, sentimental phrases of the World Summit Declaration and in their place is language showing that children are being taken seriously. This is evident in the section on "Review of Progress and Lessons Learned" in which the draft UNGASS outcome document affirms that:

> The experience of the past decade has confirmed that the needs and rights of children must be a priority in all development efforts. There are many key lessons: change is possible — and children's rights are an effective rallying point; policies must address both immediate factors affecting or excluding groups of children and wider and deeper causes of inadequate protection and rights violations; vertical approaches and targeted interventions that achieve rapid successes need to be pursued, with due attention to sustainability and participatory processes; and efforts should build on children's own resilience and strength. Multisectoral programmes focusing on early childhood and support to families, especially in high-risk conditions, merit special support because they provide lasting benefits for child growth, development and protection.[51]

In the future, NGOs, including those organizations run by children and young people, will be playing a major part in promoting and realizing the rights of the child. Children, as individuals worthy of respect for their human dignity, can no longer be ignored or overlooked. The past decade has brought about major changes in the way the world views children. Hopefully, the end of the next decade will find children exercising their newly recognized right of participation as a force for world peace.

Notes

1. The work of UNICEF during the period between the child-caring movement and the child rights movement is characteristic of the attitudes of the time. Prior to the worldwide ratifications of the United Nations Convention on the Rights of the Child, UNICEF's mandate focused on the health of young children in the form of oral rehydration and immunization. Since then, UNICEF has become a leading voice in support of child rights. See Rebecca Rios-Kohn, "The Impact of the Convention on the Rights of the Child on UNICEF's Mission," *Transnational Law and Contemporary Problems* 6 (Fall 1996), pp. 287-308.

2. As of this writing there is a proliferation of projects that are seeking to define and implement the child's right to participation. In particular, there is a major world conference on child participation planned for spring 2003 and tentatively scheduled for Bangkok.

3. The International Labour Organisation has periodically enlarged the scope of treaties prohibiting child labor. For a concise summary of the work of ILO related to children, see Philip E. Veerman, *The Rights of the Child and the Changing Image of Childhood* (Dordrecht, Boston, London: Martinus Nijhoff Publishers, 1992), pp. 309-17, 373-74, 416-23.

4. The Save the Children International Union was the precursor of what is now the International Save the Children Alliance — a network of "Save the Children" organizations all over the world.

5. The Declaration of Geneva is reprinted in Maria Rita Saulle and Flaminia Kojanec, eds., *The Rights of the Child: International Instruments* (Irving-on-Hudson, N.Y.: Transnational Publishers, 1995), p. 3.

6. P. R. Ghandhi, ed., *Blackstone's International Human Rights Documents,* 2nd edition (London: Blackstone Press, 2000), pp. 14, 21-25.

7. International declarations can be viewed as an example of world consensus on a particular topic. They carry enormous moral weight, but have no mechanism for implementation or ratification by the drafting parties. On the other hand, treaties (i.e., Conventions and Covenants, etc.) have an implementation mechanism and are legally binding on ratifying nations.

8. Ghandhi, *Blackstone's International,* pp. 63-87.

9. Although UNICEF is now known as the United Nations Children's Fund, it continues to use its original abbreviation.

10. Proposed text to the Commission on Human Rights for a United Nations Convention on the Rights of the Child, see U.N. Doc. E/CN.4/1292 (1978) submitted by Poland.

11. U.N. Doc. E/CN.4/1349 (1979) Article 7 was subsequently revised by the Working Group and the revised version appears in the Convention as article 12, commonly called the "child's right to participation" or "respect for the views of the child."

12. Although the United States proposed these articles, as of this writing it is one of only two countries in the world that has not ratified the Convention — the other being Somalia.

13. For a detailed overview of the drafting process, see Cynthia Price Cohen, "Drafting of the United Nations Convention on the Rights of the Child: Challenge and Achievements" in Eugeen Verhellen, ed., *Understanding Children's Rights* (Gent, Belgium: Children's Rights Centre, 1996).

14. Countries having the same representative over a period of years were Austria, Finland, the Netherlands, Norway and the United Kingdom.

15. Although the NGOs could not vote against an article, had they strongly opposed any language it would have been possible to find a government to break the consensus on their behalf.

16. The NGO Group also hosted pre-sessional meetings for governments to inform them of their recommendations in advance of the Working Group.

17. Simone Ek, head of Rädda Barnen International (the now-defunct Geneva branch of Rädda Barnen, Save the Children Sweden) hosted the Pea Soup parties.

18. On many occasions NGOs would draft and propose articles, which governments would then schedule for discussion. Some examples of these include articles: 28 (2); 37 (a); and 39 among others. In addition, the language of probably half of the articles was influenced by NGO recommendations. When there were disagreements, NGOs acted as a buffer between the East and West.

19. The phrase "other competent bodies" in article 45 was intended to mean nongovernmental organizations.

20. Sharon Detrick, ed., *The United Nations Convention on the Rights of the Child: A Guide to the "Travaux Préparatoires,"* (Dordrecht, Boston, London: Martinus Nijhoff Publishers, 1992), p. 27.

21. Technically, the term States Parties indicates those nations that have agreed to become legally bound by a treaty — in this case the Convention on the Rights of the Child. While the majority of States Parties have become States Parties through ratification (meaning that they have first signed and subsequently submitted their instrument of ratification to the United Nations) they can also become States Parties through accession (deposit without prior signature) or through Succession (accepting the obligations of a former government after a separation from the original State Party — as in Yugoslavia).

22. The first Committee members came from Portugal, Peru, Barbados, Sweden, Philippines, Egypt, Zimbabwe, Burkina Faso, the Russian Federation and Brazil.

23. Its meetings are generally held in January, May-June and September-October.

24. Actually, the Committee has drafted two sets of *General Guidelines*: one for submission of initial reports and one for the periodic reports that must follow every five years after the initial reports.

25. I. General Measures of Implementation (articles 4, 42 and 44 (6)); II. Definition of the Child (article 1); III. General Principles (articles 2, 3, 6, and 12); IV. Civil Rights and Freedoms (articles 7, 8, 13, 14, 15, 16, 17, 37 (a)); V. Family Environment and Alternative Care (articles 5, 9, 10, 11, 18 (1), 18 (2), 19, 20, 21, 25, 27 (4), 39); VI. Basic Health and Welfare (articles 6 (2), 18 (3) 23, 24, 26, 27 (1), 27 (2), 27 (3)); VII. Education, Leisure and Cultural Activities (articles 28, 29, 31), and VIII. Children in Especially Difficult Circumstances (articles 22, 30, 32, 33, 34, 35. 36, 37 (a), 37 (b), 37 (c), 37 (d), 38, 39, 40).

26. This has been the rule for most initial reports. However, because of the number of States Parties and the continuous problem of preventing a backlog, the Committee has been considering ways to streamline its processes.

27. For example, where a country is unable to meet the Convention's standards on education or health, the Committee can attempt to provide assistance by NGOs or through various branches of the United Nations.

28. The Committee's report to the General Assembly is also available from the website of the U. N. High Commissioner for Human Rights: <www.unhchr.ch>.

29. See Cynthia Price Cohen and Susan Kilbourne, "Jurisprudence of the Committee on the Rights of the Child: A Guide to Research and Analysis," *Michigan Journal of International Law* 19 (1997), pp. 633ff.

30. See note 28.

31. Reprinted in Veerman, *The Rights of the Child,* pp. 579-97.

32. Article 24, paragraph 3 of the UNCRC.

33. It should also be noted that the Charter differs from the Convention in that it has a special article on the needs of children living under *apartheid.*

34. Hague Convention no. 33. See <www.hcch.net>.

35. ETS no. 160, opened for signature in January 1996, entered into force January 2000. See <http://conventions.coe.int/>.

36. Reprinted in Veerman, *The Rights of the Child,* pp. 484-92.

37. See <www.ilo.org/public/english/standards/ipec/ratification/convention/text.htm>. In fact, the United States, which has a weak record on human rights treaty ratification, was among the first to sign.

38. For the full report of second reading negotiations see U. N. Doc. E/CN.4/1989/48 (1989) reprinted in Saulle and Kojanec, eds., *The Rights of the Child,* pp. 31-188. The deliberations over article 20 (now article 38) can be found in paragraphs 600-622.

The move to raise the international standard for participation in armed combat from the Geneva Convention's age 15 to age 18 was led by the Swedish delegation. There were lengthy debates about the wording of such an article — most of which took place within a small drafting party outside of the Working Group. Ultimately, two versions of paragraph 2 were discussed — a version raising the age to 18 and the version that was ultimately adopted. The United States was the lone hold out against raising the age limit.

The general debate centered over whether the mandate of the Working Group was to move beyond existing international standards or merely hold to these standards. The U.S. took the latter position. One motivation for its position was that at that time the U.S. had recruits who were only 17 and did not want to be forced to change those regulations. Interestingly, the U.S. has since raised the age for participation to 18.

39. Graça Machel, *Impact of Armed Conflict on Children* (United Nations and UNICEF, 1996).

40. No one ever refers to IPEC by its full name, and even the ILO website emphasizes "IPEC." Information about this program can be found on the ILO website: <www.ilo.org>.

41. See Rebeca Rios-Kohn, "The Impact of the Convention."

42. The report of the 2001 International Workshop on Indigenous Children and Youth and information about the World Coalition can be found on the website of the ChildRights Information Network: <www.crin.org>.

43. ECPAT originated in Southeast Asia but now has a network of branches in developed countries as well.

44. Norway appointed the first ombudsman for children, Målfrid Grude Flekkøy. See her book, *A Voice for Children, Speaking Out as Their Ombudsman* (London: UNICEF and Jessica Kingsley Publishers, 1990).

45. Reprinted in Veerman, *The Rights of the Child,* pp. 574-78.

46. "'A World Fit for Children' Alternative NGO Text, September 21, 2001," prepared by the Child Rights Caucus in response to the draft outcome document, as negotiated as of September 7, 2001. See <www.crin.org/docs/resources/publications/CR_Alternative_Sept21.pdf>.

47. The UNCRC entered into force on September 2, 1990 after ratification by 20 states. The World Summit convened September 30, 1990.

48. Veerman, *The Rights of the Child,* p. 574.

49. Veerman, *The Rights of the Child,* p. 578.

50. "A World Fit for Children," Third revised draft outcome document (A.AC.256/CRP.6/Rev.3), Bureau of the Preparatory Committee, June 2001, Declaration, par. 2. See <www.Unicef.org/specialsession/documentation>.

51. "A World Fit for Children," par. 11. At the time of writing, UNGASS is due to convene in May 2002. It will be interesting to see whether the additional time will have had a positive effect on the much-debated text of the outcome document.

Chapter 4

Psychology and the Rights of the Child

Målfrid Grude Flekkøy

On September 1, 2000, children's rights advocates celebrated the tenth anniversary of the coming into force of the United Nations Convention on the Rights of the Child (UNCRC). In spite of the fact that all but two nations in the world (Somalia and the United States) have ratified the Convention, much remains to be done to raise its visibility and to secure its implementation. Psychologists, and developmentalists in particular, have been curiously absent from the discussions before and since the United Nations' adoption of the Convention — in spite of their specialized knowledge about myriad relevant issues. One simple reason may be that we psychologists traditionally have little interest in the law in general, and in international conventions in particular. Nonetheless, the Convention provides us with the opportunity and responsibility not only to abide by its provisions but also to contribute our expertise to its implementation. In fact, the emphasis throughout the Convention on "the best interests of the child" and the "evolving capacities of the child" gives child development experts a potential recognition and status in international law never realized before.

The UNCRC has implications for all professionals who work with children. Those of us who are child psychologists need to consider seriously three main questions. First, what are the key issues, academic and practical, that the UNCRC raises for developmental psychology? Second, how should practitioners deal with these issues? Third, what are the implications for cross-professional collaboration?

In this essay, I shall focus mainly on the first of these three questions, turning briefly to the other two questions in the final section. I shall base my discussion on normal, ordinary, average children.

Although no child is "average" in the sense of being exactly like any other child, most children in the world are alike in the standard kinds of care they need. Only on the basis of what children are normally like is it possible to consider the position of abnormal children or children in abnormal conditions. Furthermore, we must view children positively, seeing them as "equal value" humans possessing special qualities of their own, whether they are two, four, six, or twelve years old, rather than seeing them negatively as lacking qualities and as "not yet adults." This is particularly important for participation rights (such as freedom of expression and association), which are perhaps the most controversial group of rights identified in the UNCRC.

To a developmental psychologist the concepts in the Convention that stand out as commanding special interest and presenting a special challenge are the keystone concepts of "the best interests of the child" and "the evolving capacities of the child." Sound interpretation and clear understanding of the articles of the UNCRC rests upon these all-important concepts. They also directly affect the implementation of the Convention. However, while the importance of both concepts is obvious, it is not always obvious how they apply within different groups of rights embodied in the Convention. It may, for instance, seem obvious that survival in itself is in the best interest of the child, and that consequently the child should have the right to live. But it is not necessarily obvious which living conditions are in the child's best interests. And yet, as the late James Grant, Executive Director of UNICEF from 1980 to his death in 1995, often pointed out, survival has little value if the life of the child is meaningless, if the child lives under conditions detrimental to his or her development, or if the life of the future adult were to have no meaning. Similar points may be made in connection with protection rights (the right of the child to be protected against harm and abuse). Again, it seems obvious that it is in the child's best interest to be protected against harm. But whereas in most cases it is not very difficult to define *physical* harm, it is far more difficult to reach a consensus about what constitutes *mental* or *emotional* harm — types of harm which may be even more detrimental to the child's possibilities for development.

As these examples indicate, the articles of the Convention must always be considered together; they interact and they are interdependent. This point is also illustrated by the fact that it is necessary to balance protection rights, participation rights, and development rights (the rights of the child to develop his or her abilities). Like adults, children from birth onwards should, in principle, enjoy every kind of right (with a few exceptions). The fact remains, however, that children need more protection and more guidance than adults do. No one denies that, in general, children should be protected and guided, but numerous questions arise when we try to determine how far this should limit the child's right to autonomy and self-expression. How shall the child exercise these participation rights, and in relation to whom? What kinds of information should the child receive, from whom, and at which age? When and how should children give opinions? Should children be protected from having to make certain sorts of decisions? When and in relation to what kinds of situations should the child be relieved of any obligation to form and express an opinion? And so on.

Based on detailed knowledge about the real competence of children, it should be possible to protect them when necessary, without *over*protecting them. Some advocates, however, believe that it is not children that need protection, but their rights. They think that children should not be treated differently from adults in this respect.[1] It should not be forgotten, however, that protection of children is not a form of discrimination: *all* people need protection at some point or other in their lives and in a variety of difficult situations. Equally, the fact that children are dependent is not a reason to deny their participation rights. In the first place, everyone is dependent on other people at least some of the time, without thereby losing such rights. In the second place, even when adults are totally dependent on others, their autonomy can be provided for, based on their inherent dignity as human beings. Dependent or not, the participation rights of adults are subject to restrictions, bearing in mind the rights of others and the needs of the community. The same applies to children.

The central point is this: the fact that children are immature is not, in itself, a valid argument for restricting their participation rights. However, children have the right to be protected; and this consideration might legitimately lead to such a restriction. This brings me to the principle of "the best interests of the child."

The Best Interests of the Child

In the UNCRC, the principle of "the best interests of the child" underlies the right of the child to protection and care. Furthermore, the principle is invoked to determine the extent to which, and the degree to which, children possess many other rights, and to justify or support actions arising under the Convention. It clearly makes the interest of the child more important than the interests of adults. However, "The central importance of the best interest principle within the [UNCRC] framework does not mean that its interpretation or application is in any way straightforward or uncontroversial. Paradoxically, the greater the agreement as to its centrality, the greater the diversity of approaches advocated in its application."[2] I shall review the factors that give rise to these difficulties, commenting on the implications for child psychologists and children's rights advocates.

Some of the problems with the principle stem from its indeterminate and open-ended character. It is not clear what the outcome will be, in a given situation, of applying the principle, because the criteria for "best interests" are not clearly defined. Cultural and personal values will influence the content of a plan of action based on the principle. Therefore, it can be used to justify even quite opposite outcomes. To some extent, we can clarify the way the principle should be applied by viewing it in the context of the Convention as a whole. However, even taken as a whole, the Convention does not and cannot provide any definitive statement of how the best interest of a child would best be served in a given situation. The implications of the principle will vary over time and from one society with its cultural, social and traditional values and realities to another, and also according to the situation and the age, maturity and experiences of the individual child or the group of children concerned.

Furthermore, article 3 states, "In all actions concerning children…the best interests of the child shall be *a* primary consideration" (emphasis added). In other articles and in other international instruments the principle appears as *the* primary consideration, but generally in contexts with a narrower range of possible situations, such as adoption or custody.[3] As noted by the group that drafted the Convention, there are situations in which competing interests of "justice and society at large should be of at least equal, if not greater, importance than the interests of the child" and "an approach which gave paramountcy to the children's best interests could not be justified in all of the situations to which the article might apply." Alston concludes, "the best interests principle is to be applied by all decision makers, whether public or private, when acting in any matter concerning children. The weight to be given to the principle may vary according to the circumstances, although at the very least it must be an important or primary consideration in all such matters."[4] As children's rights advocates, we might also conclude that when the action proposed is not in "the best interests of the child," the decision-maker must prove why other actions are preferable, and why the "best interest" action is impossible or unfeasible.

This leads to the question of how to determine what action is in the best interest of the child. Such determinations should be based on knowledge of how children of different ages are affected by various possible actions, which would seem to indicate that child development professionals should be essential players in such assessments. However, matters are not that simple. It would be useful if there were, amongst professionals, a general agreement based on long-term, cross-cultural research, about the whole range of cause-and-effect relationships applicable to any individual child at any particular age. Unfortunately, there are no such "global recipes" for determining the right action. The situation is complicated further when we bring in the participation rights of the child: the idea that the individual child, as he or she matures, has the right to have a voice in decisions that concern him or her. The child's immediate wish or opinion might well be self-destructive. Moreover, in the longer run, the child's own preferences might not serve his or her best interest; in which case the adults who care for the child would have to bring into the picture a consideration of the child's future.

In this connection, it needs to be emphasized that the question of what is in the child's best interest changes over time: what is applicable at one age level or developmental stage is not necessarily applicable later (or earlier) in life. At each point in time, decisions must be based on the knowledge we have about the child's basic needs and developmental level, in the culture in which he or she lives. Furthermore, as previously noted, often it is not sufficient to look exclusively at what would be best for the child at the present time; we must consider what would be better in the long run, with an eye on the potential adult, the adult the child could become. Even when this is attempted, there are several difficulties. For one thing, it may be very difficult, not to say impossible, to know what a particular child would consider to be in his or her best interest when looking back, as an adult, at the present time — or indeed any point of time between then and now. The principle of "future consent" — that we should take into account the consent that a child would give in the future as an adult — is therefore questionable at best. A second difficulty is that the world is changing so quickly that it may be hard, not to say impossible, to assess realistically how a hypothetical situation in the present will affect the potential adult. In this connection, as in other connections, there may also be conflicts between what the child perceives as being in his or her best interest and what is so perceived by the adults who care for the child. The latter, moreover, might well disagree amongst themselves, even violently.

In spite of an increasing body of knowledge about child development, family dynamics, and societal impacts on the family and the child, we rely largely on guesswork much of the time when predicting how children will be affected by the way we treat them. Hopefully, the likelihood of making the right choices is very high; but the fact remains that for any individual child there is no control group. Our knowledge of children and how they are affected is often based on research into the experiences of groups, but the degree of fit to each individual child will never be perfect. Furthermore, personal factors, such as lack of knowledge on the part of the parent, ulterior motives camouflaging the real reasons, or subconscious motives of the appraiser, can compromise our ability to make good judgments about what is or what is not in "the best interests of the child." This might be an area of particular responsibility for psychologists, especially those with experience of how subconscious motivation may cause incomplete or skewed perception or understanding. (Supervision of colleagues and other co-workers can help uncover "blind spots" and clarify these issues.) More comparative research on the role of personal factors across cultures is needed. However, while such research might be helpful, it can hardly provide universal answers to the difficult issues that arise in different cultural contexts.

The Evolving Capacities of the Child

Earlier I indicated that it is necessary to balance the different kinds of rights identified in the UNCRC, notably protection and participation rights. It is perhaps in this connection that the principle of the evolving capacities of the child is most pertinent. We have to decide such questions as when, how, and in relation to whom the child should have the right to information, to make choices, to voice opinions, to participate in decision-making, and to take full responsibility for decisions. Our answers to these questions will depend on a realistic consideration of the child's capacities and competence. As mentioned earlier, no actual child is "average"; and even if general knowledge about children can be a helpful guide, we need to evaluate each child individually.

The noun "competence" has its counterparts in "competent" (meaning adept, efficient, qualified, skilled, expert, and proficient) and in the somewhat wider term "capable" (which in addition means able, accomplished, skillful, apt, intelligent, and smart). Competence is not an "all or nothing" quality; it develops gradually, particularly if the child has opportunities to try out budding skills. A child does not always have a *general* level of competence. Rather, a child may be competent in one area, but not in another, and may be competent to take on *part* of a given task, but not the whole. I should like to emphasize also that while the words "competence," "competent" and capable" may cover some of the same qualities as "intelligent" does, they imply abilities that are more than merely cognitive.

During the last ten to fifteen years, there has been an increasing interest within the fields of psychology and education in the importance of competence and in the level of competence children possess. This new interest is based on recent research that has clearly indicated that the competence of very small children has been grossly underestimated. For instance, twenty-five years ago we believed that babies showed no sign of social behavior until they were three to four months old. Now we know that babies react socially, e.g., by imitating, when they are only a few days old. Empathy was not expected until the child was five or six years old. Now we know that prosocial behavior and empathy are capacities found in children from the age of two or three. From the neonate's simple expression of needs to the simple choices possible even in the first year of life, from everyday situations in the family to decision-making in the community, the child is capable of exercising various rights, including the right to state opinions, make choices, participate in decision-making, and gradually to take over responsibility for himself or herself and others. Thus, as the child gets older and more mature, he or she is less in need of protection when it comes to making simple choices in everyday situations.

However, when choices are more complicated, such as choosing between medical alternatives, the situation is more difficult, not only due to the complexity involved, but also because children generally have less experience with these kinds of circumstances and their consequences. The type of choice that has been researched in laboratory conditions has often been exactly of this kind, where the subjects are middle-class children from industrialized societies. In spite of the obvious need for more research, the results so far seem to indicate that by age fifteen there is no reason on the basis of competence to deny minors rights of self-determination, at least in making decisions about treatment.[5] Moreover, in the laboratory situation, nine-year-olds tend to reach the same conclusions as the teenagers. We do not know, but there may be reason to speculate that, provided the situation is familiar to them and that the alternatives are made clear in language they can understand, even younger children might be more competent to give consent and make choices than expected. Overprotection can be as limiting as underprotection, while a good balance leads to healthy development. When a child has the experience of being competent, this leads to feelings of achievement, accomplishment and self-respect.

Sheer faith in the competence of children can provide a positive foundation for working with children and for affirming their rights. But we do not have to rely on faith alone. New research highlights the fact that we constantly need to re-evaluate the "truisms" that often serve as the basis of our knowledge; otherwise we run the risk of underestimating children. There are various pitfalls uncovered by new research, and we need to be continually aware of them. One pitfall lies in using "normal development" as a frame of reference. This can lead child developmentalists to focus on children who have departed in some way from the norm. Their emphasis may fall on weaknesses in contrast to strengths. They may, for example, highlight the vulnerability of the child in terms of possible traumas, or focus on difficulties with either the child or the parents or the feedback system between them.

Similarly, an interest in comparing the normal with the abnormal might lead to a research emphasis on *differences*: differences between "normal" and "abnormal" children, between children and adults, or between children on different age-levels or in different cultures. If so, similarities may be disregarded or downplayed. Young children have distinctive ways of doing the same things as older children or adults do. Consequently, adult observers may have an incomplete picture of what young children are capable of, or an insufficient understanding of the situation in which they can achieve at least partial mastery. Carol Gilligan, in reevaluating the Kohlberg studies of moral judgments of eleven-year-old children, found that by adding a new line of interpretation, it became possible to see development where previously development was not discerned. Furthermore, Gilligan suggests "[I]t immediately becomes clear that the interviewer's problem in hearing Amy's response stems from the fact that Amy is answering a different question from the one the interviewer thought had been posed." Gilligan's conclusion uncovers one of the pitfalls into which researchers can fall:

> In the interviewer's failure to imagine a response not dreamed of in Kohlberg's moral philosophy lies the failure to hear Amy's question and see the logic in her response, to discern that what from one perspective

appears to be an evasion of the dilemma signifies in other terms a recognition of the problem and a search for a more adequate solution.[6] In other words, the adult's preconception about how the child *should* respond blocks understanding of the child's actual capacity. The question may then be raised: How often, and to what extent, are conclusions about the capacities of children distorted by the observer's preconceptions? Another pitfall is age grouping. It might be better to group children according to their developmental level rather than their age, because descriptions of what children are able to do depend not only upon age, but also on the culture in which they grow up. Many scales of development (e.g., the Gesell scales) have been constructed on the basis of observations of children in Western societies, and some of the scales still in use are fifty years old. The application of Western scales is often not appropriate for measuring children from very different sociocultural backgrounds, even when used by local practitioners, unless they have been trained within their own culture.[7] Also, since some norms have changed over the years, even in cultures for which the instruments were constructed, the scales must be used critically or adjusted to the existing changes. Furthermore, as we have refined our research methodology, our views of the competence of children have changed. (Research on the newborn during the past twenty years is a striking example of this.) Our views will probably continue to change as we continue to refine our methodology.

It is true that grouping children by developmental level will usually coincide, more or less, with grouping them by age, but differences must be expected. Even motor development is not a function of physical maturation alone. Hopi children of Native American Pueblo origins, who were traditionally confined to cradle boards as babies, were not able to walk by themselves until a relatively late age, while African children tend to walk early. Some data might suggest that genetic differences may be responsible for some of the variation, but environment must have some effect too. Thus, here is a case where developmental level varies according to culture. Having said that, there are limits to the possible variation. Even if Baganda children walk at eight months and European children at twelve to fifteen months, no child has been known to walk at birth, or even at six months. A further pitfall for the researcher lies in applying standards that do not fit a given society, or failing to apply standards that do. When we view children from another society who are living in deprived conditions, we might well see them as deficient in skills. But the lack of competency may not be as absolute as we might think. As Karsten Hundeide puts it,

From a normative-evaluative point of view, judged in accordance with standards of a middle-class society, *a pattern of deficiencies* appears, that is to say, cultural differences become cognitive deficits. If, on the other hand, one considers the question of skills more from the point of view of the children's own reality, *a pattern of competencies* highly adaptive to a way of life very different from the life of middle-class children emerges.[8]

Children in vastly different cultural circumstances may simply not need the skills of Western middle-class children, but they may be developing a pattern of skills which is highly adaptive and suited to the challenges they face in their own societies. This also demonstrates how comparisons across societies may fail badly if they are made without consideration of, and adjustment for, the problems children face in different cultures.[9]

We also need to consider what we can learn from other cultures as well as other socio-economic settings.[10] For example, while deploring the fate of the "street child" (the child who lives and works on urban streets), it is nonetheless clear that those street children who manage to survive take on more responsibility for their lives than children in other circumstances do. So, if we believe, as I do, that responsibility and rights go together, we need to ask if children in "non-deprived" settings are being cheated by being deprived of responsibilities. Still, there are "non-deprived" cultures where the "yard children" take responsibility for the "knee children," and the "knee children" for the "lap children," as part of the cultural pattern. In many Western societies, with 1.6 children per family, there are few opportunities for older siblings to take on responsibility for younger ones. Yet even children in such families understand that with rights come responsibility. With the right to go to the movies at age five, for example, there is a responsibility to behave in an appropriate way. Children thrive on responsibility, because it can help them feel wanted and needed. In this connection, clearing up one's own room hardly counts, since it does not make much difference to the other members of the family. It is a challenge for parents to find tasks that are appropriate for children and which give them a sense of responsibility towards others, especially when animals are no longer part of the family and machines do most of the work. One mother told me that her five-year-old loved to scrub potatoes for the family dinner, but it took so long that "if I let him, we wouldn't have dinner until tomorrow." Then she paused and exclaimed, "He could scrub the potatoes for tomorrow!" Not only was her solution practical, enabling her to have potatoes that were ready to boil, it also enabled her child to do something — scrub vegetables for the following day — that contributed to the family. Sometimes children do several hours of work per week, walking dogs, minding babies, cutting lawns, shoveling snow; mostly they do this for neighbors, because neighbors tend to appreciate their help more than their families do.

Children who live in severely deprived circumstances may have mental characteristics that make future adjustment in a changing world difficult. Feuerstein and Klein have described such cognitive characteristics as "episodic grasp of reality," failure to make comparisons, impulsiveness, and lack of goal-directed control.[11] Other researchers have emphasized low achievement motivation, fatalism, and resignation.[12] Conspicuously, most of this research has focused on the negative outcomes of such mental characteristics. However, even here there is another side to the story, and a few researchers have focused on the positive resources many of these children must have developed to be able to survive and adapt to extreme life conditions.[13]

In general, we need to look more closely at how the individual child can gain experience in acting responsibly, while not being obliged to take full responsibility for himself or herself. Rather like having a "learner's license" for driving, the child can be given gradual training, combined with gradually increasing responsibility. This implies an approach that is more individualized, and less tied to the specific age of the child.

One reason why the approach needs to be individualized is that some children are more resilient than others; they seem to manage the most terrible situations better than most. In Norway such children are called "dandelion children," pushing their bright flower up through the asphalt of life. Recent research has tried to identify the factors responsible for such resiliency.[14] Some of these factors seem to be inborn, e.g., above-average intelligence. Other factors depend more on the environment and experiences of the child, e.g., a positive self-image, independence, ability to control impulses, creativity, and especially competence in organizing the world in a systematic way. One factor is the child's experience of a locus of control. This has particular pertinence for the exercise of participation rights, for although the locus of control can be external, more often it is internal: the feeling of having some control over what happens to him or her.

For children to develop a healthy personality, it is important — perhaps even crucial — that they exercise their rights of participation. Magne and T. S. Raundalen and Sybille Escalona have demonstrated that teenagers who have the opportunity to experience the feeling of making a difference in their world, of having an impact on it, are less prone to depression and suicide than other teenagers.[15] Moreover, participation is important for the future of a democratic society. In this connection, we must remember that children need time with their peers, unsupervised by adults. For it is in the company of their equals that children learn the rules for democracy and discover how majority decisions are made amongst equals. This prepares them for the time when they must leave their childhood peer group and meet the conditions for being included in the larger group we call society. In the family home, children simply belong; their status as family members is usually secure regardless of what they do. Though they learn how to solve longstanding conflicts with people they care about (or alternatively to live with those conflicts), they do so within the bosom of the family. In the group of peers, by contrast, membership is not automatic: they must be able to meet the conditions of the group in order to remain within it. In the process, children can develop into adults who are competent to participate as equals in a society of equals.

Consequences for Psychologists

As I mentioned earlier, the emphasis throughout the UNCRC on "the best interests of the child" and the "evolving capacities of the child" potentially gives child development experts recognition and status in international law that they have never had before. Why, then, have developmentalists been so reluctant to join the debate over the Convention, particularly the debate about participation rights?

There may be several reasons for this. Some reasons may apply to other professionals and, for that matter, non-professionals. Thus, the articles that assert participation rights are not as instantly recognizable or acceptable as those that assert the rights to survival, protection and development; they may be more open to subjective interpretation and harder to assess, and thus more difficult to defend. Developmentalists may also be haunted by the same doubts and conflicting feelings that lead other groups of adults to oppose certain provisions. Moreover, like many others, they may confuse the issue of children *having* participation rights with the issue of how, when, where, and in relation to whom these rights are to be *exercised*. But over and above these reasons, child development experts may have a special reason for feeling constrained from entering the debate. Being social scientists, they may be less willing than others to argue for the child's participation rights simply on the grounds of common sense, while at the same time they may be more aware than others of the problems involved in attempting to define and defend such rights on the basis of existing research findings.

Despite their reluctance to join the debate over the UNCRC, the Convention poses important challenges for experts in child development. First, it challenges them to rethink the ways in which they interact with children in therapeutic, research, and educational settings. In particular, given its emphasis on the dignity, integrity, and best interests of the child, the Convention calls upon practitioners to safeguard, promote, and strengthen efforts aimed at realizing these values — or, at a minimum, not to impede such efforts. More fundamentally, developmentalists can help illuminate ways of accomplishing the rights enumerated in the Convention, such that they are consistent with the "evolving capacities," "best interests," and dignity of the child. For although these concepts are difficult to define, psychologists and social scientists concerned with children do have special knowledge that can be helpful to policy makers who are faced with various thorny issues; for example, determining the conditions under which children of different ages may best exercise their participation rights without suffering harm as a consequence.

Second, the Convention challenges child psychologists and other social scientists to use their expertise to help monitor compliance with its provisions.[16] Overall responsibility for monitoring the Convention lies with a committee of experts called the Committee on the Rights of the Child (article 43). The Committee may invite "competent bodies" to provide expert advice on the implementation of the Convention (article 45). It has interpreted this to include individuals as well as nongovernmental organizations. This means that the door is open for the Committee to receive expert information from all sources. Whether or not they are under a legal mandate to do so, psychologists and other social scientists should take seriously their role in evaluating the extent to which local, state, and federal policies are consistent with the provisions of the Convention. They should also be willing, either individually or through their professional organizations, to submit information, offer expert advice, and perhaps meet with the Committee to discuss specific problems.

Third, psychologists may play a critical role in helping children to understand and to express the rights granted them under the Convention. Researchers can play this role by assessing children's *perceptions* of their rights, at different ages and under varied circumstances. What rights do children think they have? What do they think it means to have those rights? Finding answers to questions such as these can assist social scientists and educators in two ways: developing effective means of teaching children about their rights, and facilitating the child's ability to express those rights.

Fourth, we psychologists need to consider the consequences of the Convention for our everyday work. As outlined above, we need comparative, cross-cultural research; and there are enormous challenges here for researchers. For those of us concerned with informing politicians and others, the challenge lies in getting the message across persuasively: that children's rights are important, and that there are specific ways in which these rights can be exercised. In this connection, as well as in connection with research, collaboration and cross-fertilization with other professions is absolutely necessary. We need to work with the medical profession; e.g., in determining what sort of information children need, and what sort of decisions they can make, regarding health issues. We need to work with educators; e.g., to plan how children, starting as young as one year, can exercise more self-determination in educational settings. (In this connection, I find it appalling that while Norwegian children know the rules for democratic decision-making in nursery schools and kindergartens, they need to relearn these rules at age ten. I have always found it curious that student councils or classroom representation does not apply to students under this age.) We need to work with social workers for children in care, and with lawyers to find ways of letting children participate in the court systems. We also need lawyers to help interpret national legislation concerning children and propose amendments to such legislation.

Finally, as clinicians, we need to consider what consequences the Convention has for our professional work with children and their parents. I believe that the child's right to be informed, to voice an opinion, to participate in making decisions, and eventually to make those decisions alone, must lead us to consider seriously the rights of the child in a clinical context. Such rights might include the right to be informed about diagnosis, treatment plans, and prognosis. They might also include the right to know that the clinician is conducting research in which the child is a participant. Moreover, there are issues of confidentiality; for confidentiality not only concerns information obtained *from* or *about* the child client, but also information that should become — or alternatively should *not* become — available to the child. In many countries, charts and files are made available to children, which means that they must be written in ways that children can understand. It may be difficult to find the balance between, on the one hand, the child's right to know about himself or herself, and on the other hand, the need to protect confidential information about others —

such as parents — with whom the child is connected, but the problem cannot responsibly be avoided. Furthermore, children may have a right to participate in making decisions about the treatment they receive. Perhaps this arises particularly when the treatment involves institutionalization or the use of medication. Nor is this point confined to older children. Bearing in mind that the child's participation does not automatically mean that he or she will make the final decision, it is certainly possible (though it may be difficult) to help even a small child to understand what is being offered and to give his or her opinion.

In this essay I have outlined a number of ways in which the UNCRC raises issues that are important for child-related professions, particularly psychologists. I hope I have also made it clear that I see the Convention as an instrument that we can improve and further develop as we work for better conditions for children all over the world. Most important, I see the Convention as a universal tool that we can use to put all children on the agenda — and keep them there.

Notes

1. Eugeen Verhellen, "Children and Participation Rights," in P. L. Heilio, et al., eds., *Politics of Childhood and Children at Risk: Provision - Protection - Participation,* Eurosocial Report 45 (Vienna: European Centre for Social Policy and Research - Childhood Programme, 1993).

2. Philip Alston and Bridget Gilmour-Walsh, "The Best Interest of the Child: Towards a Synthesis of Children's Rights and Cultural Values," Paper presented at the International Symposium on the Convention on the Rights of the Child, Salamanca, Spain, 1996, p. 5. See also, Philip Alston, ed., *The Best Interests of the Child: Reconciling Culture and Human Rights* (Oxford: Clarendon Press, 1994).

3. See for example article 21 in the UNCRC regarding adoption and Article IV.1 in the African Charter on the Rights and Welfare of the Child.

4. Alston and Gilmour-Walsh, pp. 17-18.

5. Thomas Grisso and Tony Vierling, "Minors' Consent to Treatment: A Developmental Perspective," *Professional Psychology* 9 (1978), pp. 412-427; Lois A. Weithorn, "Competency to render informed treatment decisions: A comparison between certain minors and adults," (Ph.D. diss., University of Pittsburgh, 1980); Lois A. Weithorn, "Involving Children in Decisions Affecting their Own Welfare: Guidelines for Professionals," in Gary B. Melton, et al., eds., *Children's Competence to Consent* (New York and London: Plenum Press, 1983).

6. Carol Gilligan, "New Maps of Development: New Visions of Maturity," *American Journal of Orthopsychiatry* 52:2 (1982), pp. 202-206.

7. See for example, Marcelle Geber, "Longitudinal Study and Psycho-motor Development among Baganda Children," in *Proceedings of the International Congress of Applied Psychology, vol. 3: Child and Education* (Copenhagen: Munksgaard, 1962).

8. Karsten Hundeide, *Helping Disadvantaged Children: Psycho-Social Intervention and Aid to Disadvantaged Children in Third World Countries* (Oslo: Sigma Forlag and London: Jessica Kingsley Publisher, 1991), p. 17.

9. See for example: Michael Cole and Jerome Bruner, "Cultural Differences and Inferences about Psychological Processes," *American Psychologist* 26:10 (1971), pp. 867-876.

10. See for example: Karsten Hundeide, "Contrasting Life Worlds: Slum Children and Oslo's Middle-class Children's Worldviews," in *Growing into a Modern World*, Conference Proceedings of the Norwegian Center for Child Research (Trondheim, 1988).

11. Reuven Feuerstein and Pnina S. Klein, "Environmental Variables and Cognitive Development" in Shaul Harel and Nicholas J. Anastasiow, eds., *The At-Risk Infant* (Baltimore: Paul H. Brookes, 1985).

12. Martin E. P. Seligman, *Helplessness: On Depression, Development, and Death* (San Francisco: W. H. Freeman, 1975).

13. William Labov, "The Logic of Non-standard English," in Victor J. Lee, ed., *Language Development*, (New York: J. Wiley and Sons, 1979); Unni Wikan, *Fattigfolk I Kairo* (Oslo, Gyldendal Norsk Forlag, 1976); Hundeide, "Contrasting Life Worlds;" Michael Rutter and Nicola Madge, *Cycles of Depression* (Kingston: Heinemann Educational Books, 1976).

14. Michael Rutter, "Separation Experiences: A new look at an old topic," *Pediatrics* 95:1 (1979), pp. 147-154 and "Psychosocial resilience and protective mechanisms," *American Journal of Orthopsychiatry* 57 (1987), pp. 316-331.

15. Magne Raundalen and T. S. Raundalen, *Barn i atomalderen* (Oslo: Cappelen, 1984); Sybille K. Escalona, "Growing Up with the Threat of Nuclear War: Some indirect effects on personality development," *American Journal of Orthopsychiatry* 52:4 (1982), pp. 600-607.

16. Stuart N. Hart, "From Property to Person Status: Historical Perspective on Children's Rights," *American Psychologist* 46:1 (1991), pp. 53-59; Gary B. Melton, "Socialization in the Global Community," *American Psychologist* 46:1 (1991), pp. 66-71.

Chapter 5

Rights of the Child:
A Philosophical Approach

Rosalind Ekman Ladd

In 1989 the General Assembly of the United Nations adopted the Convention on the Rights of the Child (UNCRC). This focused the attention of member states on the question of children's rights. However, the rights affirmed in this document are diverse. They include, on the one hand, rights to protection and care; for example, article 32 recognizes the right of the child to be protected from "economic exploitation" and from work "that is likely to be hazardous or to interfere with the child's education, or to be harmful to the child's health or...development." On the other hand, the document includes provisions that grant children certain liberties; for example, article 15 recognizes the right of the child to "freedom of association."

The right to protection and care and the right to liberty or self-determination are two distinct kinds of rights; they raise quite different issues and foster very different attitudes and public policy concerning children. Both of these kinds of rights make a strong appeal to those who care about the well-being of children. But there is a sense in which they are not only different but actually come into conflict with one another: If children are to be free to decide things for themselves, how can adults protect them from the harms or mistakes to which their youth and inexperience make them vulnerable? Alternatively, if adults take responsibility for the protection and nurturance of children, doesn't that require that children be limited in their freedom?

"Children's rights," then, is an ambiguous phrase and advocates of children's rights face a practical dilemma, for granting one kind of rights for children seems to be incompatible with granting the other kind of rights. Thus, even the most well-intentioned advocates of children's rights can sometimes be talking at cross purposes. Agreeing that children have rights is no guarantee that people will agree on which kind of rights, nor on what practical steps should be taken to fulfill or ensure their rights. Furthermore, on a more theoretical level, there are those who think that using the language of rights in relation to children is inappropriate, and their arguments must be taken seriously.

To try to sort out these issues, the philosopher asks some basic questions. My focus in this essay will be on three central questions. 1) What kinds of rights should be accorded to children? Because the right to protection and care and the right to self-determination are often incompatible, we must be clear on which we are talking about when we talk about the rights of the child. One way of putting this is to ask: What is the difference between talking about rights exercised *on behalf of* children and rights exercised *by* children themselves? 2) If both kinds of rights should be accorded to children, what should be the balance between them? We can decide this only by looking carefully at the arguments that support each kind of rights. 3) Who should decide for children? Assuming that children cannot decide or provide entirely for themselves, what is the appropriate role in decision-making of child, parents, and state?

It must be admitted that the question of the rights of the child is not a question in the forefront of contemporary philosophy, even among those who turn their attention to applied ethics. Indeed, currently and historically there is a good deal more in the philosophical literature on issues about animal rights, important though they may be, than there is on children's rights. This is changing, however, and issues about children and family are slowly gaining a place in the discipline.[1] This is a step in the right direction, for philosophers do have something to contribute to the public discussion, both on the level of theory and with implications for practice as well.

Those who are actively engaged in elementary and secondary education, pediatric medicine, family and human rights law, and all the various aspects of the social services, need to pause to consider the conceptual questions and to think carefully about the place of children in society and what their place would be in an ideal society. Without a picture of the ideal in mind, practical work will be without direction or justification. Thus, the philosopher is a go-between, bridging the gap between theory and practice, borrowing from the empirical research of the social sciences and offering an analysis of basic concepts, clarification of the underlying questions, and critical evaluation of the logic of arguments.

What Are Rights?

A useful, basic definition of rights is that they are justified claims.[2] Some rights are claims to be given something; for example, the right to health care. These rights are sometimes referred to as welfare rights or positive rights. Other rights make a different kind of claim, namely, not to be interfered with. This is the kind of claim that citizens in a free society can make; for example, freedom of association, freedom of religion, preservation of privacy. Interference with a person's activities is justified, according to the liberal tradition, only when those activities pose harm to others. These rights may be referred to as liberty rights, rights of self-determination, or negative rights.

To make a claim in terms of rights is to make a very strong claim, for rights imply duties. If someone is said to have a right, it is meaningful only if there is someone who can be said to have a duty to fulfill that right. Thus, it is empty rhetoric to say that all children have the right to health care, for example, unless someone — parent, state, or other — has the obligation to provide that health care and is prepared to do so. Negative rights also entail an obligation on the part of others: to respect the autonomy or liberty of that individual.

Thus, if children have rights, then some adults have duties and responsibilities either to supply those things that children have a right to, or to refrain from interfering with those activities children have a right to engage in. Thus, a child's right to food and shelter, which entails the responsibility of some adults to supply it, would be a different kind of right from a child's right to play, which entails that all adults have a duty to allow it.

Discussion about what kinds of rights children have or should have plays itself out in the debate between protectionists and liberationists.[3] Although both are sincerely concerned with the well-being of children, protectionists emphasize the need for adults to provide for the needs and interests of children, something that children cannot do for themselves, and to protect them from unwise decisions that they might make. They emphasize rights exercised *on behalf of* children. Ensuring the protection of children, however, generally comes at the expense of restricting their liberty to make decisions for themselves. Liberationists, on the other hand, emphasize rights exercised *by* children, including freedom from interference. Granting children more self-determination, however, puts them at greater risk than if all decisions were made for them.

Thus, distinguishing between protectionist rights and liberationist rights clarifies the ambiguity in the concept of the rights of the child. The dilemma of how best to advocate for children's well-being develops because there is an inverse relationship between the two kinds of rights: the more protection afforded children, the less liberty they have; the more liberty, the less protection. As an illustration of this: protectionists may advocate for tighter laws against child labor, while liberationists may argue for allowing children to choose to work and earn money. Both, however, frame their arguments in the language of rights.

Many recent feminists and others, however, are challenging the appropriateness of applying the language of rights to family and other intimate relationships.[4] The traditional theories, including those of Immanuel Kant and John Stuart Mill, were developed to govern relationships in the larger society, where people are actual or virtual strangers.[5] In that context, formal rules and claims are needed to set out the conditions under which social, political, and economic affairs can be carried out with justice and fairness. It is typically assumed that humans are motivated by self-interest, and that without the rule of law and morality, as Hobbes so poignantly states it, life would be "solitary, poor, nasty, brutish, and short."[6]

Until quite recently, under American law and that of other Western nations, relationships within a family were not open to scrutiny or censure. The husband/father had wide-ranging power to make all decisions for his family, and wives and children had no recourse to law or even appeal to moral rights. For example, although rape was a punishable crime, rape within marriage was not acknowledged legally and a wife could not bring rape charges against her husband. In regard to children, there were no formal means to protect them against abuse until the establishment of the New York Society for the Prevention of Cruelty to Children in 1875. Wives and children quite literally were the property of their husbands and fathers.[7]

With increased sensitivity in this country to problems of child abuse,[8] and in the 1960s to the rights of women, theorists have begun developing an analysis of the morality of family relationships, and public opinion on this subject has changed. The prevalent view is that family relationships are different in kind from those between strangers, and that the language of rights which is suited to the adversarial relationship of the law courts or that of strangers in business relationships is grossly inappropriate to the nature of friendship and family.

As an alternative, feminist scholars are developing a new moral theory based on caring, trust, or intimacy.[9] The argument is made that we should talk in terms of the obligations or responsibilities of adults to children rather than the rights of children.[10] Generally, one is led to make claims about rights only in situations of conflict. Between family members, for example, there is no need to make claims about rights when things are going well; indeed, going around talking about your rights is likely to produce a hostile atmosphere. If the goal of those who are concerned about children's well-being is to establish strong, supportive and helping relationships between family and child, child and school, etc., then taking a legalistic model and outlining rights and duties may be sending the wrong message.[11]

However, despite these important considerations, I will continue to use the language of rights in this essay. We must deal with the concept of rights because it is the language of the UNCRC and the language of law. It is also true that most of what philosophical literature there is on this topic does talk in terms of the rights of the child.

Balancing Protection Rights versus Self-Determination Rights

In virtually all societies, children and adults are treated differently, are accorded different rights and different degrees of self-determination. This point is brought home in a recent cartoon that shows two children reading the sign on a convenience store door: "Proof of age required for cigarette purchase." One child responds, "The problem here is they're treating us like children."[12]

What are the reasons that would justify offering more protective rights and imposing more restrictions on the liberty rights of children? What reasons could be given to justify the opposite? What are the traditional arguments for not treating children just the same as adults?

Although the history of philosophy has not paid much attention to questions about children, several of the philosophical forefathers of western liberal tradition have made clear that children are excluded from the liberty rights to be granted to adults. For example, John Locke argues that there are good reasons for making children subject to their parents' authority. It would put children at great risk, he thinks, if they could make decisions for themselves:

The Freedom then of Man and Liberty of acting according to his own Will, is grounded on his having Reason...To turn him loose to an unrestrain'd Liberty, before he has Reason to guide him is...to thrust him out amongst Brutes, and abandon him to a state as wretched, and as much beneath that of a Man, as theirs. This is that which puts the Authority into the Parents hands to govern the Minority of their children.[13]

Jeremy Bentham also is concerned to point out the limitations of children that justify the restrictions we put on them:

[T]he feebleness of infancy demands a continual protection. The complete development of [the infant's] physical power takes many years, that of its intellectual faculties is still lower...Too sensitive to present impulses, too negligent of the future, such a being must be kept under an authority more immediate than that of the laws...[14]

And finally, Mill, the staunchest defender of the right of adults to determine their own best interests, makes explicit his reasons for saying that children should be treated differently from adults:

It is perhaps hardly necessary to say that this doctrine [that one should never interfere with another person's freedom simply for his own good] is meant to apply only to human beings in the maturity of their faculties. We are not speaking of children, or of young persons below the age which the law may fix as that of manhood or womanhood. Those who are still in a state to require being taken care of by others, must be protected against their own actions as well as against external injury.[15]

While it is well recognized that chronological age is only an artificial mechanism for drawing the line between children and adults, the legacy of Locke, Bentham, and Mill is still with us. Legislators who reversed the decision for dropping the age of legal drinking from twenty-one to eighteen did so for the protection of teenage drivers as well as the safety of others, and those cities which have enacted curfew laws for teens cite their safety as an important consideration.

In the contemporary literature, a number of philosophers make assumptions about the inadequacies of children, either their inability to protect themselves from harm or their lack of full reasoning power, which may lead to making unwise decisions for themselves. Other forms of the argument make generalizations about children's inability to defer gratification and their susceptibility to peer pressure. All in all, these arguments ground the justification for protection rights and the limits on liberty rights for children on their physical, cognitive, and psychological limitations. I refer to these arguments as the arguments from incompetency.

Arguments from the incompetency of children take several forms. The American philosopher, Laura Purdy, argues against equal rights for children on purely practical grounds: children need to be taught self-control and morality and thus need to be under the guidance of adults.[16] Lainie Ross argues that children's decisions are based on limited experience and are not yet part of a life plan; thus they need a "protected period" in which to develop the habits that will facilitate their long-term autonomy.[17] On slightly different grounds, the British philosopher Judith Hughes argues that children are not necessarily lacking in reason, as Locke, Bentham, and Mill seem to have assumed; but that exercising liberty rights is a burden, and a protectionist stance toward children is justified to save them from the heavy burden of taking responsibility for their decisions.[18]

While these arguments are certainly persuasive and sensible, they tend to paint all children with the same brush and gloss over some important differences. Note, for example, how Bentham refers to all children as infants. We really need to distinguish true infants, who cannot do anything for themselves, from school-age children who may, as we will see, reason quite well and have a well-developed sense of self and their own values. And then there are adolescents, who vary greatly in maturity but are, in fact, approaching adulthood and in earlier periods of history were given adult-like responsibilities, if not liberties.

Another important point to notice is that competency is task-specific. This means that the same person may be quite competent in decision-making about one thing but utterly incompetent in a different area of decision-making. For example, a child who has been brought up on a farm will be unlikely to have the "street smarts" to take care of himself in downtown Chicago; but an urban youth can feel quite scared and not know how to act if he finds himself in a field full of cows.

Other, more serious challenges to the incompetency argument come from the studies of social scientists, especially social psychologists, who test the actual decision-making competencies of children. One study that should persuade us to consider carefully before judging that children cannot make wise decisions is in the area of medical decision-making. Conducted by Lois Weithorn and S.B. Campbell, the study presented in age-appropriate language to four different age groups, ranging from eight years old to adults, a choice between several different medical treatments for a particular condition. All the groups, even the young children, made the same choices that the group of doctors chose as most appropriate. The only exception was a group of young adolescents who avoided the choice that would have changed body image, an issue of heightened concern at that age. Although the younger children could not articulate their reasoning as clearly as the older adolescents and adults, their choices demonstrated that their reason was sufficient to understand the consequences of the different choices, the costs and benefits, and to apply that understanding to their own case.[19] Other studies suggest similar conclusions.[20] On the basis of empirical studies such as this, the American Pediatric Association has revised its recommendations about informed consent to say, "Pediatricians should not necessarily treat children as rational, autonomous decision makers, but they should give serious consideration to each patient's developing capacities for participating in decision-making, including rationality and autonomy."[21]

If we have difficulty trying to decide the proper balance of protectionist versus liberationist rights — and we do —, at the heart of that difficulty is the attempt to distinguish child from adult simply on the basis of chronological age. One response is the creation of the legal categories of emancipated minor and mature minor. An emancipated minor is someone under the age of eighteen who has gone to court to have her or his legal status changed from minor to adult. This releases the minor from the restrictions of childhood and confers all the rights and duties of adulthood. Emancipation is granted if it can be shown that the minor is not living with parents and has independent income. Emancipation is automatic without court involvement if the minor marries or becomes a member of the armed forces. A few states also recognize the status of mature minor upon recommendation of a physician. This allows the minor to consent to medical treatment independently, without parental consent.[22] These categories reflect the fact that there are very great individual differences in maturity and in competencies; awarding adult status simply on the basis of age cannot take these differences into account.

An alternative approach, using a competency-based criterion, is suggested by a study of the historical Abenaki Native American culture.[23] In the traditional Abenaki culture, adolescent boys were awarded adult status and allowed to marry only when they proved they were successful hunters and could provide food for a family. Although it is often objected that such a system of individualized skills-testing would be expensive and cumbersome to implement in a complex industrialized society, it is the system that we universally employ to grant to young people the privilege of driving automobiles, and it could be extended to other activities as well. Those who pass the competency test would be given greater rights to self-determination in that particular area and be relieved of some or all protectionist restrictions.[24]

Who Should Decide?

I turn now to a second kind of argument typically given against the extension of liberty rights to children, namely, the argument based on the rights of parents. If parents have absolute authority to decide for children up to the time of legal majority, then children and adolescents cannot have the right to decide for themselves.

There are a number of ways to argue in favor of parents making decisions for children. One presumption, which operates in many states in this country, is that biological parents have a special bond with their own children, ordinarily are the best protectors, and thus that children should remain under the jurisdiction of biological parents whenever possible. This presumption, however, is clearly reminiscent of the idea that children are the property of their parents (their fathers), and for this reason alone may be questioned.

Another assumption is that parents — biological or adoptive — make the best decision-makers for their children because they know their children best and they have the best interests of the child at heart. This assumption, however, is rebutted by the high incidence of child abuse and neglect by parents.

A third argument, developed by the philosopher Ferdinand Schoeman, defends the privacy of the family from state intervention on the grounds that privacy is required as a condition of the intimacy of family relationships, and intimacy constitutes an important value in life.[25]

These are widely accepted arguments; but against these considerations is the recognition that the state has a legitimate interest in having healthy, well-educated future citizens, and that the state should stand *in loco parentis*, not only when parents cannot fulfill their obligations but even at times against parents' wishes, when the well-being of children is at stake. The controversial issue of court-ordered blood transfusions for the children of Jehovah's Witnesses when the parents have refused consent is an illustration of this principle.

The most telling argument which justifies the state's active involvement in the lives of children rests on what philosophers call the vagaries of the "natural lottery."[26] Children do not choose the family into which they are born and families vary so much in what they can give to children — in terms not only of financial support and material goods, but also emotional security, intellectual challenge, exposure to the arts, and cultural heritage. Because of these differences, children's opportunities to grow and learn to the best of their abilities are not equal. If all decisions about children's well-being are left to individual families, then the inequalities are multiplied.

State intervention in the form of compulsory education, required vaccination, and mandated medical treatment in the case of life-threatening illness help to compensate for the inequalities, inadequacies, or idiosyncrasies of private families; but much more could and perhaps should be done to provide the opportunities for each child to develop as fully as possible.

The philosopher Joel Feinberg has developed another moral argument that defends restrictions on parental decision-making. He argues that families should not be allowed to decide for children in ways that cut off the possibility of an "open future" for them, that is, the possibility of their making real choices about the kind of life they want to live when they are adults. He is critical of a court decision that would allow the Amish to restrict their children from continuing education past elementary school.[27]

Related to the principles involved in the Amish case are other laws which grant parents exemption from charges of child abuse or neglect if their actions are based on religious or cultural values. Respect for religious and cultural diversity, so important within a pluralistic society, seems to be in conflict with laws and practices that guarantee protective and liberty rights to children. This is an unresolved issue presently, and we need to work on developing clearer public policy about how to balance families' religious and cultural identity as expressed in children's upbringing versus the power of the state to intervene for the good of the child.

Based on Feinberg's principle of maintaining an open future for each child, we might try to develop consensus on the following basic points. Parents should not have the right to impose extremely restrictive limits on education which would leave children prepared for only one possible role in life. They should not be able to refuse medical treatment for children that puts them at risk of death or serious debilitating illness, even for religious or cultural reasons. Parents should not be able to send young children to work instead of school. And children should not be given in marriage while they are still children and without their consent.

While it is reasonable to expect that parents will want to convey their own values and customs to their children and fashion a style of life that is uniquely their own, there are basic protections and liberties that belong to the child and to the adult he or she will become, independent of the family. We need not go as far as Plato would, to advocate that children be brought up directly by the state and not even know who their own parents are;[28] but if our primary concern is for the welfare of the child, then setting limits on the decisions that parents can make for their children does not seem unwarranted.

Conclusion

Analyzing what we mean by "children's rights" clearly does not in itself settle the questions of the extent to which children should have rights or what kind of rights they should have. This exercise, however, helps clarify the issues and makes the nature of the debate more transparent. Those who are truly concerned for the well-being of children must participate in open, free discussion, and only from that can good policy develop. It is the role of philosophical analysis to ensure that the discussion is enlightened as well as impassioned.

Notes

1. Books by philosophers on the rights of children include: William Aiken and Hugh La Follette, eds., *Whose Child? Children's Rights, Parental Authority, and State Power* (Totowa, NJ: Rowman and Littlefield, 1980); David Archard, *Children: Rights and Childhood* (London: Routledge, 1993); Bertram Bandman, *Children's Right to Freedom, Care and Enlightenment* (New York: Garland, 1999); Jeffrey Blustein, *Parents and Children: The Ethics of the Family* (Oxford: Oxford University Press, 1982); Howard Cohen, *Equal Rights for Children* (Totowa, NJ: Littlefield, Adams, 1980); Lainie Friedman, *Children, Families, and Health Care Decision-Making* (Oxford: Clarendon Press, 1998); Loretta Kopleman and John Moskop, eds., *Children and Health Care* (Dordrecht: Kluwer, 1989); Rosalind Ekman Ladd, ed., *Children's Rights Re-Visioned: Philosophical Readings* (Belmont, CA: Wadsworth, 1996); Ruth Macklin and Willard Gaylin, eds., *Who Speaks for the Child?* (New York: Plenum, 1982); Onora O'Neill and William Ruddick, eds., *Having Children: Philosophical and Legal Reflections on Parenthood* (Oxford: Oxford University Press, 1979); Laura Purdy, *In Their Best Interest?* (Ithaca: Cornell University Press, 1992).

Books on family include: Laurence D. Houlgate, ed., *Morals, Marriage, and Parenthood: An Introduction to Family Ethics* (Belmont, CA: Wadsworth, 1999); Diana Meyers, Kenneth Kipnis, and Cornelius Murphy, eds., *Kindred Matters: Rethinking the Philosophy of the Family* (Ithaca: Cornell University

Press, 1993); Hilde Lindemann Nelson, ed., *Feminism and Families* (London: Routledge, 1997); Geoffrey Scarre, ed., *Children, Parents and Politics* (Cambridge: Cambridge University Press, 1989).

2. Joel Feinberg, quoted in Lawrence M. Hinman, *Ethics: A Pluralistic Approach to Moral Theory* (Fort Worth: Harcourt Brace, 1998), p. 245.

3. See Aiken and La Follette, eds., *Whose Child?*, and Joseph Hawes, *The Children's Rights Movement: A History of Advocacy and Protection* (Boston: Twayne Publishers, 1991).

4. See for example: Onora O'Neill, "Children's Rights and Children's Lives," and Mary Midgley, "Rights Talk will not Sort out Child Abuse," both in Ladd, ed., *Children's Rights Re-Visioned*.

5. For a good overview of the ethical theories of Mill and Kant, see Hinman, *Ethics*.

6. Thomas Hobbes, *Leviathan*, ed. Edwin Curley (Indianapolis: Hackett, 1994), p. 76.

7. See Hawes, *The Children's Rights Movement*, and Mary Ann Mason, *From Father's Property to Children's Rights* (New York: Columbia University Press, 1994).

8. Ruth S. and C. Henry Kemp, *Child Abuse* (Cambridge: Harvard University Press, 1978).

9. Caring: see Carol Gilligan, *In A Different Voice* (Cambridge: Harvard University Press, 1982), and Nel Noddings, *Caring: A Feminine Approach to Ethics and Moral Education* (Berkeley: University of California Press, 1984). Trust: see Annette Baier, "Trust and Antitrust," *Ethics* 96:2 (January 1986), pp. 231-260. Intimacy: see Ferdinand Schoeman, "Rights of Children, Rights of Parents, and the Moral Basis of the Family," *Ethics* 91:1 (October 1980), pp. 6-19.

10. O'Neill, "Children's Rights and Children's Lives," and Mary Midgley, "Rights Talk Will Not Sort Out Child Abuse," both in Ladd, ed., *Children's Rights Re-Visioned*.

11. Martha Minow, "Rights for the Next Generation: A Feminist Approach to Children's Rights," *Harvard Women's Law Journal* 9 (Spring 1986), pp. 1-24.

12. Toles, Universal Press Syndicate, *The Buffalo News*, 1997.

13. John Locke, "Paternal Power, from *The Second Treatise of Civil Government*," in O'Neill and Ruddick, eds., *Having Children*.

14. Jeremy Bentham, *Theory of Legislation* (Boston: 1840), vol. I, p. 248.

15. John Stuart Mill, *On Liberty*, Alburey Castell, ed. (New York: Appleton-Century-Croft, 1947), p. 10.

16. Laura Purdy, *In Their Best Interest?*

17. Lainie Ross, "Health Care Decision-Making by Children: Is It in Their Best Interest?", *Hastings Center Report* (1997), pp. 11-12.

18. Judith Hughes, "The Philosopher's Child," in Morwenna Griffiths and Margaret Whitford, eds., *Feminist Perspectives in Philosophy* (Bloomington: Indiana University Press, 1988).

19. Lois Weithorn and Susan B. Campbell, "The Competency of Children and Adolescents to Make Informed Treatment Decisions," *Child Development* 53:4 (1982), pp. 1589-1598.

20. For a comprehensive review of the literature on this topic, see Dan Brock, "Children's Competence for Health Care Decision-Making," in Kopleman and Moskop, eds., *Children and Health Care*.

21. See American Academy of Pediatrics Committee on Bioethics, "Informed Consent, Parental Permission, and Assent in Pediatric Practice," *Pediatrics*, 1995, p. 315.

22. Martin Guggenheim and Alan Sussman, *The Rights of Young People* (Toronto: Bantam Books, 1985).

23. Rosalind Ekman Ladd, "The Concept of the Child in Abenaki Tradition" (unpublished manuscript).

24. A different approach, using "borrowed capacities" of adults who act as agents for children, is proposed by Howard Cohen in *Equal Rights for Children*.

25. Schoeman, "Rights of Children."

26. This concept is based on John Rawls, *Theory of Justice* (Cambridge: Harvard University Press, 1971).

27. Joel Feinberg, "The Child's Right to an Open Future," in Aiken and LaFollette, eds., *Whose Child?*

28. Plato, *The Republic*, Book V, 457d.

Chapter 6

The Promise of Rights for Children: Best Interests and Evolving Capacities

Christina M. Bellon

In contemporary philosophy, significant disagreement exists about the proper function of rights. Some theorists argue that rights ought to protect important interests, while others argue that rights ought to protect individual choice.[1] Depending on the view one holds, one may or may not take children to be appropriate right-holders. Assuming the protected choices model, children only rarely achieve right-holder status because of their as yet underdeveloped capacities for autonomy and for making choices. Children, generally characterized as lacking these capacities, are thereby considered appropriately lacking the rights associated with them. Assuming the protected interests model, children more readily achieve right-holder status because of the importance of some of their basic interests and their vulnerability to threats of harm or neglect.

In this essay, I argue that children ought to have rights with both sorts of function. To make this argument, I draw upon the United Nations Convention on the Rights of the Child (UNCRC) and its use of the concepts of best interests and evolving capacities. Consideration of the evolving capacities of the child allows us to recognize the value of protecting children's choices just as the best interests criterion allows us to recognize the value of protecting children's interests. Doing so, however, requires a rejection of "either/or" thinking about the capacity for choice. It also requires flexibility in protecting children's interests against, or at the expense of, securing children's liberty and self-determination.[2]

The Philosophical Value
of the Convention

The UNCRC is a useful resource for philosophical inquiry into children's rights. Three features of the document stand out: 1) it has received near global political and moral acceptance; 2) it employs two important principles for justifying children's rights, paying special attention to children's self-determination rights (which include rights of participation, conscience, association, and access to information); and, 3) it presents rights as consistent, not conflicting, with values not typically associated with conceptions of rights.

The importance of the near universal acceptance of this document ought not to be ignored.[3] Philosophers spend considerable effort attempting to identify universal principles and norms. The pursuit of universal principles is advanced, I believe, by consideration of near universally accepted principles. Without conflating validity with acceptance, I think much can be gleaned from philosophical explorations of accepted moral principles.[4] The UNCRC offers us some means of identifying near universally accepted moral principles available to justify children's rights. Let us consider what the document offers by way of justificatory principles of rights, how these inform the content of rights for children, and what it suggests about the relation between rights and other values.

In the UNCRC, we find that the substantive content and operation of children's rights are informed by considerations of children's important interests against harms, abuse and neglect, and by considerations of children's capacity for liberty and self-determination as well.[5] The content of some of these rights includes provision of a name and identity, freedom of movement and travel, the provision of an education and medical care, of opportunities for leisure and rest, of opportunities for cultural participation, access to information, freedom of religious belief and conscience, and protection from physical, mental, and sexual abuse and exploitation. It also includes protections against specific threats to which only some children may be vulnerable, such as the provision of fair proceedings for children who come before the criminal law, provision of special education for children with disabilities, and protection from exploitation of various sorts for child refugees and children in war.

An analysis of these and other rights found in the document indicates the justificatory use of two principles, which inform the content and guide the operation of rights for children.[6] The first, perhaps most obvious, principle requires that children's important interests in security and nurture ought to be protected according to their unique vulnerabilities and needs. This is often referred to as the best interests principle, since it requires that norms governing our relations with children ought to secure the best interests of the child according to the threats the child faces and according to the vulnerabilities peculiar to the child. This principle requires that the child's best interests, or welfare, receive primary consideration in deliberations and actions that affect children. The second, and seemingly opposed, principle requires that children's developing capacities for choice, independent thought, and self-directed action ought to be respected. We may call this the evolving capacities principle, since it requires that norms governing our interactions with children secure for them the possibility of developing these capacities, which includes respect for children's exercise of these capacities in matters pertaining to themselves.

The UNCRC also yields insight into the relation between rights and other values. The responsibilities of parents and the integrity of the family and community are linked to rights in a supportive and reinforcing way. Children are neither self-sufficient nor independent and autonomous individuals. Rather, they are necessarily dependent (to varying degrees) on other individuals and whole communities for their survival and for enjoying the benefits their rights provide. Hence, the values of community, of caring, of interdependence, of social progress, and of cultural integrity, rank high among the values that inform the content and operation of children's rights. Rather than presenting rights as being incompatible with and as conflicting with such values, the UNCRC correctly construes these as mutually supporting.[7]

For example, the assessment of whether any particular course of action would promote the best interest of the child in a divorce proceeding requires consideration of the family structure, the quality of the relationship between the child and each parent, the relative importance of maintaining familial ties with both parents and extended family for the identity formation of the child, and other matters. Assessing the best interest of the child in this way is not simply a pragmatic consideration of which parent ought to have what sort of custody, but it reflects concern for the importance of family, of community, and of the social environment in which the child currently exists and will exist in the future. The operation of the child's rights in a parental divorce proceeding would be difficult to effect without consideration of such values. Indeed, it would be difficult to construe what the child's welfare would amount to without consideration of these complementary values.

Just as the child must be understood as enmeshed in relationships characterized by values of this sort, so, as among the more important norms that ought to guide us in our relations with children, rights must also be understood as both constrained and supported by such values. An adequate conception of rights for children must be responsive to the parameters such values create. But, this is not to say that rights ought not to be used to challenge such parameters, when it is necessary to do so for the sake of the child. Rather, this recognizes that rights are not the only norms of import in matters relevant to children, and that they do not exist and function from within a normative vacuum.[8]

The Principle of Best Interests

The principle of the best interests of the child provides moral justification for the protective rights of children. It does so by appealing to children's important interests, and requires that these be secured from less important interests. Since rights are among the best means available for identifying and securing important interests, the best interest principle can be construed to support children's rights. Doing so, however, presupposes that a distinction can be drawn between important interests, which can be secured as rights, and less important interests, which can be secured through other means. The best interest principle offers moral reasons for constraining the actions of some (or all) people with regard to children and provides a means for balancing apparently conflicting important interests.[9]

The rights justified by appeal to the best interests of children may be referred to as protective rights. The function of these is twofold. First, they guard against threats and vulnerabilities typical of childhood. Among such threats are the infliction of physical, emotional, and mental harms, neglect and abuse, enslavement, torture and murder, and various forms of political or legal corruption (denial of trial, denial of citizenship, discriminatory allocation of public or governmental services, etc.). Second, protective rights secure some minimal provision of goods necessary to the subsistence, health, development, and overall well-being of children.[10] Where children cannot do so for themselves, someone must provide such goods as food, clothing, shelter, health and medical services, and some basic education. They also require leisure time and rest from work or studies, and a name and nationality. Together these important interests in security and subsistence justify the existence of protective rights for children. The value these secure and promote is the overall well-being of the child.[11]

Some of these interests, and the values they imply, also justify the existence of, and inform the content and operation of, rights for adults. Where they do so, they should likewise justify rights for children. Perhaps more so, since children are generally less capable of protecting their own interests than otherwise similarly situated adults. Children's relative weakness and vulnerability to identifiable threats, however, entitles them to the special protective force of certain rights that are generally regarded as inappropriate to adults. Since the language of rights is among the strongest normative languages we have, we have reason to use such language in the effort to secure important interests for those who cannot do so themselves.[12]

The best interest principle is not limited only to those aspects of a child's well-being in the current or short term, but includes a child's long term well-being and the interests which promote it. Among these long term interests are the development of social and moral sentiments and sociability, building a sense of self upon a relatively secure and stable foundational identity, and developing into an autonomous moral being.[13] These also include an interest in living a good life. A child's short term interests frequently have to be balanced against her or his long term interests, and vice versa.

For example, it is not unusual to find a situation in which a child's short term interest in being removed from an abusive home appears to conflict with his long term interest in forming a stable identity as a member of a particular family with a particular set of parents and siblings. Likewise, we may find a situation in which a child's short term interest in receiving psychiatric treatment for early onset schizophrenia in a residential facility may interfere with her long term interest in receiving a good education through regular school attendance and classroom participation. These interests must be balanced where their mutual satisfaction is difficult. They may have to be prioritized where their mutual satisfaction is impossible. The best interest principle, together with the background values identified earlier, help to establish some balance or some prioritization of interests: first, by forcing the distinction between long and short term well-being; second, by requiring a distinction to be drawn between important and less important interests; and third, by requiring that any action or cessation of actions regarding the child promote the child's well-being (both long and short term, insofar as possible).[14]

To continue the example, a child's interest in not being abused physically, sexually, and emotionally, is not independent of his ability to form a stable and secure identity as a member of a particular family, with a particular set of parents and siblings. Rather, much psychological evidence shows that among the traumatic effects of childhood abuse is the difficulty in forming a stable and secure identity with which the adult-child can be comfortable. If this research is accurate, then the child's long and short term interests are interwoven in such a way that the abuse must be stopped and the identity formation must be allowed to continue. A child's best interests can then be served by taking such action as is necessary to stop the abuse with minimal interruption of family life and minimal disruption of familial associations.

Contrary to the approach taken by some social service agencies in the United States, this speaks against removing *the child* from an abusive home, and speaks in favor of removing *the abuser*, if he or she can be identified with certainty. If this is not possible, then, supposing that the child is abused by many of the members of the household, the child may be removed; but contact with the family (both nuclear and extended) ought to continue in such a way that the child is both protected from further abuse and in a position to develop non-abusive familial connections. If this is not possible, for lack of social resources or other important reasons, then the child's long term interest in forming an identity around kinship ties may be sacrificed to his interest in not being abused in the short term, and not threatening his long term interest in forming a stable and secure identity around other associational ties.

The best interest principle also allows us to balance children's important interests against the important interests of others. This balancing is precisely what occurs in decisions regarding the custody of a child where the interests of a parent in maintaining her relationship with her child conflicts with her ability to keep the child safe and fed. Or, it may arise in decisions regarding the course of medical treatment for a child where the religious beliefs of parents conflict with the best available medical opinion. Requirements to act in the best interests of the child impose on parents, doctors, judges, and others a requirement to make these sorts of balancing assessments.[15]

The principle of the best interests of the child, however, does not do all the justificatory work. It addresses the existence, content, and operation of protective rights. Self-determination rights, which are frequently portrayed as conflicting with protective rights, are justifiable by appeal to the children's developing capacities for exercising liberty and for controlling the circumstances under which their interests are secured.[16]

The Principle of Evolving Capacities

Consideration of this other sort of right requires a discussion of the evolving capacities of the child and of the justificatory role of the principle of evolving capacities.[17] The following claims are integral to an appreciation of the evolving capacities approach to recognizing children's liberty and self-determination rights: 1) children develop cognitive and moral capacities in regard to diverse areas and aspects of life at different times and to differing degrees of maturity; 2) children develop their moral sensibilities, as they do their critical cognitive skills and their physical abilities, through active learning and participation in guided activities.

Observation of children from infancy to adolescence reveals an interesting developmental pattern. Very young children may become quite expert at some tasks, utilizing complex mental and motor skills. For example, a young child who is learning to play the game of hide-and-seek is required to know how to count (high enough so other children have time to hide), to discern locations in the neighborhood where a child can hide, to spy another child without being seen (by deception or stealth), to assess when to run for home before the other child does. This game, like others, also requires the child to understand the nature of rules, to act in conformity with them, and to discern violations of the rules. This presupposes a fairly high level of appreciation for fairness in competition (to win the game) and fairness in sharing (to have fun together). All of these tasks presuppose capacities for normative judgment and for moral decision-making within the context of the game.

Another example may be found in a situation in which a toddler offers his toy to another crying toddler who has lost his own. This demonstration of concern for the suffering child requires, on the one hand, an ability to discern discomfort or distress, to identify a possible source of the distress, to identify a possible means for alleviating the distress, and the moral sense to respond to the crying toddler on his own.[18] A child may demonstrate such cognitive and moral capacities well before he is able to tie a knot, or read a book, or prepare a meal. By their actions in some arenas (e.g., successful game playing, or successful playmate selection, or responding morally to others), children can demonstrate a high level of development of right-related agency capacities (e.g., rule recognition and compliance, a willingness to act, obligation identification).

It is also true, however, that young children lack competence in assessing their own interests, prioritizing among competing interests, and choosing between conflicting interests. Young children are notorious for their seeming shortsightedness about their own interests. A child might believe it to be fully reasonable and not at all detrimental to her health to have a desert of ice-cream every night, or that never doing her school lessons will not damage her future educational and employment opportunities.[19] Children with such beliefs demonstrate a failure to distinguish between wishes and well-being, between desires and interests. This problem is not peculiar to children, though the consequences of such incompetence, both for themselves and for others, may be more grave.[20]

Some philosophers have argued that the inability to distinguish interests from desires, to forgo the satisfaction of short-term interests for the sake of long-term interests, and to recognize when some interests intractably conflict, is a significant moral shortfall. Given such moral incapacity, the argument continues, such beings ought not to have self-determination or liberty securing rights. This argument does not necessarily hold against children specifically or singularly. Rather, anyone, adults included, without these abilities will be incapable of acting in a self-determining way. Allowing such individuals to have rights that protect choice or self-determination would afford such beings the normative resources to harm themselves and others, and this would amount to a failure to comply with rights that secure to those same individuals their own well-being.

For centuries, this has been the lot of individuals with mental limitations, of children, and of whole peoples once thought to be primitive or infantile. Nearly all of the major works in political philosophy since the Enlightenment have maintained that those who lack the ability to assess their own interests are also incapable of self-determination, and that appropriately they should be deprived of liberty and self-determination rights.[21] The ability to assess one's own interests is implicit in the very conception of rationality that informs these works. On this conception, a being who willfully or ignorantly acts against its own interests, or is unwilling or unable to determine its own interests, cannot be rational; such beings act without the benefit of reason. Since many of the early conceptions of rights were strongly tied to self-determination, liberty, and reason, the arguments concluded that any being unable to act with reason would necessarily lack rights. The assumption underlying this position is that the ability to recognize and to act in accordance with one's interests is held all or none, not in degrees. It follows, then, that liberty and self-determination rights would only be held in similar "all or none" fashion, rather than in degrees according to one's capacities.[22] Variations on this argument still surface in contemporary discussions of children's rights, though the roots in early political conceptions of rights are rarely recognized or admitted.[23]

It may well be the case that a child excels at chess or hide-and-seek, but is miserable at making decisions about whether to take a class in French or in math, or about whether it is appropriate to play now or to study. But it is also quite appropriate to expect that the child will come to develop the ability to make good educational choices and good choices about the use of time and of liberty when having to balance desires against obligations to oneself or to others.

The important point here is that children *come to develop* capacities for decision-making and for exercising liberties through guidance and practice. Just as a child learns to read or gather roots by actively participating in these endeavors with adults or older children, so too a child learns what is right and wrong, acceptable or unacceptable, by active participation in the moral community. Among the most important capacities a child ought to develop is the capacity to recognize her interests, to prioritize them, and to balance competing interests (both other interests of her own and those of other persons). For the development of these abilities, however, she needs careful and considerate assistance by those persons who have some concern that her best interests are met, and who are able to assess the possible consequences of meeting or not meeting certain of her short-term interests for the sake of certain long term interests, and vice versa.[24]

Each of these points is evident in article 5 of the UNCRC, which reads:

> States Parties shall respect *the responsibilities, rights and duties of parents* or, where applicable, the members of the extended family or community as provided for by local custom, legal guardians or other persons legally responsible for the child, *to provide, in a manner consistent with the evolving capacities of the child, appropriate direction and guidance in the exercise by the child of the rights* recognized in the present Convention. (emphases added)

Article 5 marks the first and most definitive appearance in the document of the concept of evolving capacities. From it we have a sense of the child as a fundamentally social being, embedded to some degree in social, cultural, and legal relations with other people. These people ought not only to be in a position to provide for the child and to secure her welfare-based protective rights; they ought also to be in a position to direct and guide the child in using the rights which the

UNCRC stipulates she ought to have. Since rights constrain the actions of others to the advantage of the right-holder, these adults are charged with the responsibility to teach a child to navigate the moral domain by helping her to use her rights well. Such teaching necessitates a child's participation in assessments of her interests, in identifying the relevant moral facts in various situations and circumstances, and in making moral judgments about matters that directly affect her.

A child can use her protective rights to secure for herself her own future well-being or some short-term interest she perceives to be important. She may also use rights to secure for herself the enjoyment of some liberty. Article 5 charges relevant others (parents, teachers, doctors, judges, and others) to assist the child in the use and enjoyment of both sorts of rights. This entails helping a child by complying with or enforcing her protective right against some threat. It also entails assisting a child to make good decisions and to exercise her liberty in an environment that supports further development of decision-making capacities and further good exercise of liberties; that is, providing a protected environment in which the child can develop generally and in which she can practice making decisions, making judgments, and using her liberties effectively and wisely.[25] Assistance will likely also be necessary in the form of protecting a child's liberty or self-determination rights from the interfering or impeding actions of others.

With the principle of evolving capacities, we recognize that children *come to have* capacities of moral agency, that these capacities develop in the child with the assistance of caring adults, and are enhanced through meaningful participation in matters where children's own interests are at stake. The principle of evolving capacities comprises one of the central criteria in assessments of a child's claim to control over the circumstances in which her interests are at stake. Claims to control are, in most rights theories, tied closely to a being's autonomy. Because liberty and self-determination rights confer on the right-holder some degree of control over specific circumstances, they have structures that permit right-holder operation (exercising, claiming, waiving, transferring, demanding, or not-claiming). Hence, a large part of the justification for having these rights lies in a being's claim to control or influence the relevant circumstances in which that being has a right.[26] A child's claim to the right to control some elements of the circumstances in which she has significant interests at stake can be established by considering the degree to which the child is capable of controlling the given circumstances. In the UNCRC, the principle of evolving capacities requires such an assessment of a child's agency abilities. As such, a child's capacity for self-determination or for exercising some liberty serves as the criterion upon which her claim to control rests. When a child demonstrates the capacity for effective choice in a certain context and with regard to some action or decision, then the child has a claim to some degree of control over that action or decision. The claim holds against those who are in the position of responding to the decision and who are also charged with protecting the child's best interests. Respecting a child's claim to control entails allowing the child to exercise her liberty, to make significant choices, or to direct her affairs, and for others to comply accordingly.

It is important to note, as H.L.A. Hart does in his discussion of liberty-securing rights, that a person need not be capable of total and complete control in order to have a right in the given circumstances.[27] Control admits of degrees. For children, given that their capacities for good decision-making and for self-determination are still developing, total control would be inappropriate. Indeed, it may constitute an injustice to the child, since the result may well damage her own best interests.[28] It may be sufficient to the enjoyment of a liberty right or of a self-determination right for the child to contribute to decisions, say, regarding her education or her place of residence, and for these contributions to be taken seriously by those charged with protecting her best interests. She need not be empowered to make the decision entirely on her own and for herself, especially when she lacks the ability to make such serious decisions.

In this regard, a child's capacity for self-determination must be balanced by considerations of her best interests. Through such balancing, the best interest principle and the evolving capacities principle can be understood to be mutually supporting rather than conflicting. Where a child is able to make effective decisions regarding some aspect of his well-being, and can do so without the assistance or guidance of others, then a more considerable degree of control would be appropriate. In such a case, the child's self-determination right (say, to make the decision to continue or not with his formal education) requires that the child's choice be respected, protected, and complied with. In this way, the child's enjoyment of his right to determine the direction of his own education is secured. His liberty and his autonomy are secured. In such a situation, as is more typically the case for adults, the child would have this right even if using it is deemed by others (guardians, teachers, doctors, etc.) to run counter to his own best interests, in the long or in the short term. Where a child lacks this degree of development of the relevant capacities, then his degree of control over the circumstances ought to be less, accordingly. Acting in accordance with the principle of best interests requires balancing the child's wishes against his best interests as assessed by those persons who do have the relevant capacities, the relevant experience, and the relevant information about possible long and short term consequences.[29]

The Promise of Rights
for Children

Rights protect interests or protect choices by constraining the actions of other people to the benefit of the right-holder. But other normative tools also impose constraints on the actions of others. For example, a requirement to maximize utility places constraints on people's actions by prohibiting acts that reduce utility.

Rights are distinguished from other action-constraining norms by the following three additional attributes: they are high-priority, mandatory, and fully individuated.[30] All rights contain, at least, a claim to that which the right secures (i.e., a liberty, a determinate object, or a protective action). That a right is a high-priority constraint means that failure to comply will in itself constitute a wrong. The wrong that results from the violation of a right is additional to the other possible harms that may result from denying what is owed. When the interest or liberty at stake is important enough to generate a right, then compliance is mandatory. The duty imposed by a right is mandatory in the sense that any competing claims or considerations must be of even higher priority than the protected interest or liberty in order to override the right. The weight of a competing interest (or liberty) must be greater than the weight of the protected interest (or liberty).[31]

Proper individuation of rights requires that the interest or liberty at stake belongs to some specifiable being. Some person, A, has a claim to X. But individuation also requires that a duty-bearer, the one who must comply with the right in question, be specified. That is, some person, A, has a claim to X *and* A holds it against some other person, B. What a right would do is to secure A's interests in X by providing A control over the circumstances by limiting what B may legitimately do to comply. B cannot arbitrarily waive A's claim to X, she cannot avoid doing or providing X without wronging A in the process. This element of control is considered, by some philosophers, to be necessary for proper individuation of the right, and to reinforce the mandatory quality of the duty rights impose. If, for a right to exist, it must secure some high-priority interest or liberty, must impose mandatory duties on others, *and* be fully individuated in this way, where full individuation necessitates control on the part of the right-holder, then children could not have rights so long as they lack the capacity to control the circumstance in which others must comply with their claim.

However, it is not clear that in the absence of the additional criterion of control we do not already have adequate individuation. Indeed, many of our most prized legal and moral rights meet only the first two criteria (securing high-priority interests or liberties and imposing mandatory duties on others), yet we consistently and accurately refer to them as rights, though they confer no control on those who hold them. For example, the various parts of due process rights (to be informed of charges, to receive legal counsel), the right not to be killed or tortured, the right not to be deprived of property, the right not to be raped or kidnapped, or even the right to inherit from a benefactor, are all rights that require no specific exercise on the part of those who possess them. That is, these rights exist and impose duties on others apart from any acts of claiming, waiving, or demanding by the right-holder. These rights are justified, simply, by the specific interests of specifiable people. When arrested, I have an interest in being informed of the charges, in having an attorney present and in not being made to incriminate myself. I, as most other people, have an interest in not being tortured, killed, raped, or abducted. These acts are all specifiable threats to my (or anyone's) well-being and liberty which, if committed, would seriously impede my ability to live a minimally decent life. In short, these rights do not necessarily secure for the right-holder any control over the circumstances, though they are adequately individuated (i.e., *I* have this claim against *you* and *everyone*).

What does all this mean, in light of the foregoing discussion of best interests and evolving capacities? Consider the following example. A child has a high priority interest at stake in being provided with enough food to survive without significant harm to her health, welfare, and further growth and development. Because of this great need, and its relation to important factors such as physical and mental well-being, this interest can be protected in the form of a right to being provided with adequate food. This interest is of such high priority that any competing interests or considerations must be more weighty before the child's right can justifiably be denied. The duty it imposes is also mandatory, since the preservation of life and promotion of physical and mental well-being are very important goals. If rights do anything, they ought to secure these values against all threats. That the duty here is mandatory means that the child's parent or guardian, and any other persons on whom the duty bears, must comply. Failure to comply would be a violation of the child's right and would constitute a wrong in addition to any other wrongs that result from the failure to comply.

Those rights that pertain to a child's well-being are principally comprised of a claim-immunity pair.[32] Their structure consists of the core claim to the provision of some good or protection against some harm, plus an immunity from arbitrary changes to the child's claim. The right imposes non-optional binding duties which constrain the actions of relevant others in the interests of the child. The immunity also imposes a disability on others to prevent alterations in the child's claim either to attempt to avoid the duty altogether or to avoid certain of the constraints imposed. A child's welfare interests thereby generate rights of a sort that do not require right-holder operation and control. Hence, they do not presuppose capacities for moral agency. Accordingly, even infants and very young children have rights in the case that they have important welfare interests.

Returning to the example, suppose the child's parent could earn more money from selling the food allotted to the child and that she would use this money to purchase bandages and medicine for a severe cut to her own leg. Would her health interest in having bandages and medicine for her wound override (outweigh) her child's right to food? We can answer this by considering whether the lack of bandages and medicine is on a par with the lack of food for her child. Without adequate food, the child will suffer from malnutrition and perhaps become vulnerable to life-threatening illness. If other means are available (other items that can be sold or traded for the bandages) then these must be pursued. In this instance, the mother's interest in selling her child's rations for medical supplies does not outweigh her child's claim to the food. Indeed, the child's right imposes a disability on the parent, and thereby restricts the scope of the mother's competing claim: she may not secure her interests in healing her wounded leg by depriving her child of needed food. She cannot deny the child food without this constituting a violation of the child's right. The child's right, then, requires provision of the food and prohibits her mother from denying it in order to sell it for other goods or medicine. Consideration of her competing claim, while not insignificant in itself, is not sufficient to override the child's claim.

In the case that no alternative means exist for the mother to obtain what she needs to heal her leg, consideration of the long-term interests of the child and the mother reveal that these seemingly conflicting interests converge. The long-term interests of the child in continuing to have her mother able to provide for them both and the interests of the mother in healing her wound converge on the mother's long-term health. An untreated wound could result in greater infection, amputation, or death, leaving the child prematurely independent or otherwise vulnerable to other persons. In this case, securing the mother's interest in healing her wounded leg contributes to further securing the child's long-term interests in overall good health. The child's right may well be "sacrificed" to the interests of the mother. But this is a misleading way of characterizing the situation. A child's right to adequate food can be better secured if, in this case, some food meant for the child can be traded for medical supplies for her mother.

As is apparent, such rights do not confer control over the situation on the right-holder; they do allow the respondent to the right (i.e., the duty-bearer) to choose the means by which she fulfils her duty. For example, an infant's right to be provided with nourishment leaves the duty-bearer unconstrained in the means by which she complies. She may feed the child animal flesh or vegetables or a nutritional supplement. This choice is independent of the child's right. Her compliance with the right, however, is not optional. The child's wishes regarding how or whether compliance is achieved become relevant when the child has a claim to control over the circumstances in which she has a right. At this point, a claim to control is generated by the child's capacity for autonomous moral agency in the given circumstances. Where a child has the cognitive and moral abilities to assess her interests, and to make reasoned judgments as to the likely effect of her actions on herself and others, a child has a claim to some degree of control over the circumstances in which her interests are at stake.[33] A child has a claim to control over the circumstances in which her welfare interests, as well as her self-determination interests, are at stake proportional to her ability to contribute. The child's capacity for autonomy includes her ability to assess her own current and future interests, how these interests should or should not be met, and what further ends would be served by doing so or not.

Returning to our example, suppose the child is capable of recognizing her mother's need for medical supplies and the way in which her interests and her mother's converge on her mother's health. In light of these abilities, the child has a claim to some degree of control over the circumstances. She has a claim against her mother that her mother hear her assessment of the situation, to make a contribution to resolving the seeming conflict of interests. She may choose to forgo some food, remain hungry, and agree to let her mother sell her rations in exchange for medicine. Or she may know of some other means for securing either food for herself or medicine for her mother. Or she may assert her right to the food and remind her mother of her duty to provide.[34] However the child contributes to the situation, whatever form her exercise of her right takes, she must be recognized to have a moral claim to contribute to the resolution of the situation as she develops the cognitive and moral ability to do so. Her participation in determining how or whether her mother must comply must also be recognized and respected.

In short, the principle of evolving capacities requires that we assess a child's ability to contribute to situations in which her interests are at stake and to participate in decision-making relevant to her life, and that we respect the contribution she makes. It also requires that we recognize and respect the value of liberty for children and secure for them some appropriate degree of liberty and self-determination.

The two principles together — best interests and evolving capacities — require that we treat children as whole beings, whose well-being is shaped in large part by our decisions and actions toward them, and by the decisions and actions children make for themselves. The choices a person makes today greatly affect the interests she finds herself with later on. This applies to children as well as to adults. Rights, insofar as they protect both our interests and our liberty by constraining the actions of others in relevant ways, cannot neglect the dynamic relation between our past, present, and future interests and the various avenues for autonomous action available at each temporal junction.[35] In standard theoretical accounts of rights, those which take the adult case as normative, the right-related concepts of welfare and autonomy imply fully developed cognitive and moral abilities of the right-holder. Non-normal adults and children are relegated to the margins because they do not meet this presumption of full moral agency. Their capacities either are no longer present, never were present, or are not yet present. That children can be understood to have rights is in large part a result of recognizing that rights function in at least these two possible ways: to protect interests and to protect liberty and self-determination. It is also, in part, a result of recognizing that we come to have claims to control over our normative relations with others gradually, with guidance, and with increasing practice. This recognition is reflected in the UNCRC's interconnected reliance upon the best interests principle and the principle of evolving capacities.

Conclusion

In this essay I have tried to show how children's developing moral capacities have a crucial place in establishing children's rights to liberty and self-determination. While the essay does not develop a complete conceptual framework within which a theory of children's rights can be fully articulated, it does at least allow us to identify certain necessary elements of any adequate theory of rights for children.

I hope to have shown that rights may readily and non-controversially be understood to have two distinct yet related functions: to secure a being's important interests, and to secure a being's liberty and autonomy. I hope also to have given sufficient reason for recognizing that children have rights of both sorts. The important contribution of the UNCRC to the philosophy of children's rights comes in its adoption of two crucial principles: the best interests of the child and the evolving capacities of the child. Both of these principles serve well to justify recognition of both children's protective rights and their rights of self-determination and liberty.

Notes

1. For a concise and accurate overview of this rift in rights theory literature, see the introductory chapter of L.W. Sumner, *The Moral Foundation of Rights* (Oxford: Clarendon, 1987). This debate takes various forms, and is also known as the dispute between the interest-thesis and the will-thesis, or as the dispute between well-being and control (or autonomy). Advocates of the former frequently employ a consequentialist or axiological justification of rights, while the latter frequently employ some variation on deontic or positivist justifications.

2. It should be noted that I do not intend to resolve the existing dispute about the proper conception and function of rights. Elsewhere, I have attempted to argue the case that rights function both to protect choices and to protect important interests: see my "A Vindication of the Rights of Children" (Ph.D. diss., University of Colorado, Boulder, 1998). The two are not incompatible. However, even on such a combined view, some rights function principally to protect interests, other rights function to protect choices, while yet some others function in both ways. For example, the right to sue in court is a legal right that functions both to protect an individual's autonomy against violations or interferences by others, and to protect an individual's interests in attaining her or his preferred ends or well-being.

3. We ought, however, to be careful of overstating the philosophical significance of the near universal acceptance of this document and of the rights it contains. Universal acceptance does not equal universal validity. Many practices, while near universally accepted, have been shown to be universally false. Consider the near universal, though morally repugnant, practice of slavery, or of war. We also need to be careful of overstating the acceptance of any moral justifications that can be read into or gleaned from the document. Rights are still regarded with suspicion from the perspective of non-Western, non-Enlightenment traditions. And while members of such traditions and of the cultures in which they thrive might accept and implement the UNCRC, they may not necessarily be doing so because they have accepted the moral reasoning or principles reflected in the document.

4. Here, I have in mind something along the lines of Rawls' overlapping consensus. The greater the overlap of values between disparate individuals and communities, the greater the confidence with which we can assume the universal quality of these values. There is a danger here, though. For example, at one time human individuals and whole societies overlapped considerably on the legitimacy of slavery. Overlapping consensus on the value of holding human beings as property, however, would likely not be found today. For more on the use of this heuristic device in deliberations about justice see, John Rawls, *Political Liberalism* (New York: Columbia University Press, 1993), pp. 78, 140.

5. A point of clarification must be made about interests. By stating that children *have an interest in* X or Y, I do not mean to claim that children *are interested in*, desire to have, want or prefer X or Y. Rather, what I, and most philosophers mean by the statement is that X or Y contributes to the child's well-being, is an aspect of their welfare, or otherwise is valued for them to have or do, even if it is not presently desired or preferred by them. The child may not want, desire, or prefer X or Y, but nonetheless X or Y may still be in her interest to have or do. For further elaboration on the distinction between interests (understood as needs) and preferences, see David Braybrooke, *Meeting Needs* (Princeton: Princeton University Press, 1987), pp 199-204. Also see Raz's distinction between "taking an interest in X" and "X being in one's interest," in Joseph Raz, *The Morality of Freedom* (Oxford: Oxford University Press, 1986), pp. 188-91.

6. It must also be noted that this Convention draws on the principle of dignity. The preamble reveals the priority of the equal dignity of the child and, while this underlies some of the rights found in the document, it is not unique to considerations of children's rights. Here, I am after those principles which directly and uniquely support children having and enjoying rights. Each of the human rights oriented Conventions and Charters issued by the United Nations draws on the principle of equal dignity. On the role of dignity in justifications of rights, see, for example, Joel Feinberg, "The Nature and Value of Rights,"

Journal of Value Inquiry 4 (1970), pp. 243-57; and, Alan Gewirth, *Human Rights: Essays in Justification and Applications* (Chicago: University of Chicago Press, 1982).

7. This view of rights, as sources and progenitors of conflict with values of relationship and community, is characteristic of authors who promote the rejection of rights language and rights-informed social policy. An excellent example of this position is found in Mary Glendon's *Rights Talk: The Impoverishment of Political Discourse* (New York: The Free Press, 1991).

8. This claim is well argued by Martha Minow in an insightful article proposing that rights can augment and support relationships rather than just create or reinforce normative and emotional distance between people. See, "Rights for the Next Generation: A Feminist Approach to Children's Rights," *Harvard Women's Law Journal* 9 (1986), 1-24.

9. In a very insightful article, George Rainbolt argues that all rights can be structured as a claim-immunity pair that constrains the actions of others. The central function of a right, on Rainbolt's model, is the imposition of a binding constraint on others. Hence a claim (to that which is the object of the right) and an immunity (from having one's claim dismissed, altered or transferred) are both necessary and sufficient to have a right. See, "Rights as Normative Constraints on Others," *Philosophy and Phenomenological Research* 53:1 (March 1993), pp. 93-111. This general characterization of the function of rights could, conceivably, incorporate both functions I have identified above. On this account, what distinguishes rights from other norms that constrain actions is the way in which rights do it — by imposing mandatory duties and normative impediments to avoiding one's duties.

10. What is needed to secure a minimal provision of such goods may vary from place to place and from child to child, but a baseline minimum of nutrition, for example, can be ascertained with relative certainty. Children's physiological requirements for vitamins, minerals, protein, and calories is well established. I follow Henry Shue in depicting the provision of subsistence goods, by right, as a minimum. Falling below the minimum results in an increased likelihood of harms such as malnutrition, developmental delay, illness. These ill effects are preventable if the minimum is provided. The principal function of rights, according to Shue, is to secure this minimum standard of nutrition, shelter, and clothing. See Henry Shue, *Basic Rights: Subsistence, Affluence, and U.S. Foreign Policy* (Princeton: Princeton University Press, 1996), p.vi.

11. This language implies a consequentialist approach to justifying protective rights for children. Of the possible theoretical approaches, I think a consequentialist view is capable of justifying protective rights. Indeed, it may be that such protective rights are the only sort of rights that can be justified in consequentialist terms. I am not necessarily wedded to a consequentialist approach, however. A good case can be made for taking recognition and

enforcement of protective rights to entail respect for and acceptance of the value of children's well-being, their equal moral status, their human dignity, or whatever other value is held, regardless of the consequences of doing so.

12. On the normative strength of rights language, coupled with an argument for the limited use of such language, see Mary Glendon, *Rights Talk*, pp. 3-12. Also see L.W. Sumner's discussion of the various approaches to providing a moral justification of rights and the concomitant search for the normative force of rights language, in *The Moral Foundation of Rights*, pp. 15-18.

13. Most theories of justice assume that adults will have developed these, and other, listed capacities when claiming that the people of a just society will have to know what is fair or what equality requires. Further, such capacities are presupposed when adults are taken to assume certain social roles necessary to the functioning of a well-ordered and just society. For example, citizen, family member, and co-operating economic participant, all presuppose some degree of sociability, identity development, and moral sensibility. No mention need yet be made about the content of the identity, and the social character and moral sense (i.e., Celtic or Indian cultural identity, supporter of welfare reform or of universal healthcare, defender of utilitarian moral principle over the Kantian alternative, etc.), but that a child must develop some of each to assume her or his role in a just society seems clear. See Braybrooke, *Meeting Needs*, pp. 48-9, and Rawls, *Political Liberalism*, pp. 18-22.

14. This is the approach taken by the Supreme Court in its ruling that a child's need for psychiatric care must be balanced against the child's interest in fairness and due process. See *Parham v. J.R*, 442 US 584 (1979).

15. This balancing of interests approach is common in legal settings where judges must attempt to find solutions to a wide variety of conflicts involving children. However, it should not be limited to the deliberations and actions of officials. Parents and extended family ought also to employ such balancing measures in their deliberations and actions regarding the children in their care. Likewise for other individuals whose public or personal undertakings affect children.

16. For a thoughtful and insightful portrayal of the potential for conflict between children's protective rights and their liberty and self-determination rights, see Laura Purdy, *In Their Best Interests? The Case Against Equal Rights for Children* (Ithaca: Cornell University Press, 1993), pp. 124-149.

17. At least one commentator on the Convention's use of the term "evolving capacities" has chosen to infer an Eriksonian view of child development, though this is not the only interpretation possible. See James Garbarino, "The Child's Evolving Capacities," in *Children's Rights in America*, eds. Cynthia Price Cohen and Howard A. Davidson (Washington DC: American Bar Association Press, 1990), pp. 19-32. In the children's psychological development literature considerable debate exists as to the adequacy of evolutionary models to appreciate the dynamic and dialectical

nature of children's cognitive development within their social and ecological surroundings. See Jean Piaget, "Advances in child and adolescent psychology;" L.S. Vygotsky, "Genesis of the higher mental functions;" and, B. Rogoff, M. Gauvain, and S. Ellis, "Development viewed in its cultural context," in *Learning to Think: A Reader*, eds. Paul Light, Sue Sheldon, and Martin Woodhead (London: Routledge, 1991). It is important to note also that John Eekelaar employs a similar view of the dynamism of the relation between a child's interests and her capacities to affect those interests through meaningful choices and projects undertaken by the child. He does not, however, discuss the Convention's use of the concept of evolving capacities. See, Eekelaar, "The Interests of the Child and the Child's Wishes: The Role of Dynamic Self-determinism," *International Journal of Law and the Family* 8 (1994), pp. 42-61. I understand the concept of evolving capacities, as used in the Convention, to imply a more dynamic development of capacities and skills than the more rigid evolutionary models allow.

18. A similar example is used by Hoffman in his discussion of the moral acumen of very young children. See, Martin L. Hoffman, "Empathy, Role Taking, Guilt, and Development of Altruistic Motives," in *Moral Development and Behavior*, ed. Thomas Likona (New York: Holt, Rinehart and Winston, 1976), p. 129; and as discussed in Gareth Matthews, *The Philosophy of Childhood* (Cambridge: Harvard University Press, 1994), pp. 57-8.

19. This example stems from a discussion with my then six-year-old niece about what variety of rights she takes herself to have. A right to dessert every night was among the top five on her list. After some discussion of the positive and negative implications of having this right enforced, she was willing to concede that her right may only be to dessert at least two nights per week. I could not shake her from the view that this might not be a right at all. This example also illustrates the importance of guiding young children in their understanding and use of rights language and its place in moral thinking and acting.

20. Consider the number of young college students each year who either drink themselves to death at the prompting of peers or for other reasons, who become alcoholic and fail out of school, or who engage in spontaneous yet risky sexual behavior only to contract HIV or to become pregnant. The seeming inability to prioritize interests or to distinguish interests from desires is a serious one for humans of all ages. The problem may be more acute for young children, since they lack experience and lack the cognitive and emotional resources that may help them to overcome the possible negative consequences of satisfying short-term interests over long-term interests. This informs a more general problem for moral philosophy which has received considerable attention in consequentialist discussions of the distinctions between desires, preferences, needs, and welfare. See for example, Braybrooke, *Meeting Needs*.

21. One notable pre-Enlightenment example is found in Aristotle's political writings. See, Aristotle, *The Politics*, tr. William Ellis (New York: Prometheus

Books, 1986). For representative examples, see Thomas Hobbes, *Leviathan*, ed. Edwin Curley (Indianapolis: Hackett, 1994), chap. XVI "On Persons, Authors, and Things Personated"; John Locke, *Second Treatise of Government*, ed. C.B. Macpherson (Indianapolis: Hackett, 1980); Jean-Jacques Rousseau, *On the Social Contract*, tr. Donald A. Cress (Indianapolis: Hackett, 1987); Thomas Paine, "The Rights of Man," in *The Writings of Thomas Paine*, vol. 2, ed. M.D. Conway (New York: Knickerbocker, 1894); Mary Wollstonecraft, *A Vindication of the Rights of Women* (Peterborough, Ontario: Broadview Press, 1997).

22. A contemporary exception to this "all or none" view of liberty rights is found in Carl Wellman's discussion of partial rights for those persons, children and mentally infirm alike, who have some capacity for choice or control. See Carl Wellman, *Real Rights* (Oxford: Oxford University Press, 1995). It should be noted, though, that these partial rights are not full rights and are not, in Wellman's account, on a par with full or real rights, the possession of which requires a fully developed capacity for moral agency and choice.

23. In contrast with other areas of contemporary philosophy, feminist political criticism does correlate the lack of rights for some beings to historical discussions of reason and morality. The examples are many, including the following ground-breaking analyses: Alison Jaggar, *Feminist Politics and Human Nature* (New York: Rowman & Allanheld, 1983); Carole Pateman, *The Sexual Contract* (Stanford: Stanford University Press, 1988); and Susan Moller Okin, *Women in Western Political Thought* (Princeton: Princeton University Press, 1979). Much of the discussion that follows in this essay is inspired by the analyses found in these texts.

24. It should be noted that the person or persons best able to guide a child in these ways need not necessarily be partial to her or care overly much for her. I see no reason why this sort of guidance cannot be provided by an impartial individual who has no particular emotional or kinship ties or feelings for the child. For a controversial argument for the normative limitations of care for children, and the ways this can impede parental decision-making, see Howard Cohen, *Equal Rights for Children* (Totowa, NJ: Rowman and Littlefield, 1980).

25. Purdy suggests that provision of a protected sphere for practicing moral activity requires only the recognition and enforcement of protective rights, not a similar recognition and protection of liberty rights. See her discussion of enabling virtues and of human development, *In Their Best Interests?*, pp. 45-7, and 87-123, respectively. I argue that this also requires the recognition of children's liberty rights.

26. A central figure on this side of the rights debate is Carl Wellman, who maintains that the definition of both a legal and a moral right is a norm that confers control or dominion over the circumstances of one party over the interests of another. Accordingly, rights must be structured so as to allow for operation (powers and liberties being core elements of any right) and function

so as to confer control on the right-holder (by protecting right-holder autonomy and liberty interests). See, most recently, *Real Rights*, pp. 107-8.

27. H.L.A. Hart, "Bentham on Legal Rights," in *Oxford Essays in Jurisprudence*, Second Series, ed. A.W.B. Simpson (Oxford: Clarendon, 1973), p. 192, nn. 85, 86.

28. Laura Purdy discusses this point in her larger argument against children having liberty rights all together. See *In Their Best Interests?*, pp. 124-49.

29. While I have not discussed the relevance of information to children's use of rights, it must be noted that children who are capable of making decisions often fail to make good ones because they lack necessary information. This is especially the case with information about other possibilities, additional options, and possible consequences of choices or actions. A child presented with a choice of peas or broccoli may be quite able to choose between them and to act on his choice with resolve. But he may be fully unaware of other options — Brussels sprouts, for example. If he were aware of this other option, he may well have selected it from among the expanded set. Insufficient information of this sort can have more serious repercussions when the situation itself is more important than deciding about vegetables. Consider, for example, a child who grudgingly eats veal because it is presented as the food option in his family. His ignorance about a vegetarian option may significantly affect his future moral relations with his family, with animals, and his own self-image. The problem of limited information is often overlooked in discussions of children's self-determination and agency.

30. These are among the key criteria used to distinguish rights from other important norms, such as goals, utility, or virtue. For a clarification and further supporting argumentation for maintaining the distinction between other norms and rights, see James W. Nickle, *Making Sense of Human Rights* (Berkeley: University of California Press, 1986), pp. 24-32.

31. Among the more vexing conceptual problems of rights is the seeming preponderance of conflicting rights, when one mandatory duty conflicts with another of equal normative weight. It may be possible to rank rights, as many human rights and other rights declarations often attempt to do. But where two or more rights exist, each imposing contradictory mandatory duties on respective respondents, moral (or legal) judgment would have to be used to adjudicate between the rights and the corresponding duties to be performed, unless some legitimate basis for ranking conflicting rights — which is no easy task — can be found. There may well be no right-related reasons on which to base this judgment, however, and this requires that background supporting norms and values be identified. This is no less the case for children's rights when these conflict with the legitimate rights of other beings, or other of the child's rights. It is my impression, however, that fewer rights actually conflict in this way than is popularly believed. What is most important to limit the occurrence of conflict is proper identification of the scope and content of the

rights at issue. For example, a parent's right to raise his child is often presented as conflicting with a child's right to be protected from parental abuse. The state, as respondent to both, has a duty to act to protect the child, which often involves sacrificing compliance with the privacy and liberty rights of the parent. This situation seems not to be one of conflicting rights, properly understood. A parent's right to privacy and liberty to raise his child expressly excludes the abuse of the child in the process. The child's right against abuse restricts the scope of the parent's right by imposing limits on the means by which the parent can exercise his right to raise his child.

32. This language is taken from Wesley Hohfeld, *Fundamental Legal Conceptions* (New Haven: Yale University Press, 1913). Hohfeld identifies eight fundamental legal concepts which are ordered into four correlative pairs: claim/duty, liberty/no-right, power/liability, and immunity/disability. A "claim-immunity pair" would involve four of Hohfeld's concepts: claim/duty and immunity/disability. Such rights would grant a claim and immunity to the right-holder and impose a corresponding duty and disability on the respondent.

33. Wellman comes to a similar conclusion in his argument in support of the recognition of partial rights, which are scaled in scope according to the right-holder's capacity for moral autonomy. See *Real Rights*, pp. 125-32.

34. This last possibility may indicate the child's as yet not well developed ability to assess her own interests in light of the important interests of others; especially lacking may be the ability to adequately identify her own long-term interests in her mother's health. If this is the case, then the child's control over the circumstances may correspondingly be limited.

35. On the interconnection of autonomy with well-being, and on uses of liberty and meeting interests, see the following accounts of rights that appeal to "life plans" or "rational pursuit of well-being": Loren Lomasky, *Persons, Rights and the Moral Community* (Oxford: Oxford University Press, 1987); Gewirth, *Human Rights*; Raz, *The Morality of Freedom*. With regard to children, see Eekelaar, "The Interests of the Child and the Child's Wishes."

Chapter 7

Creating the Child, Constructing the State: *People v. Turner*, 1870[1]

David S. Tanenhaus

Children have had a difficult time finding a suitable home in modern American law. They remain, as Martha Minow has observed, "the paradigmatic group excluded from traditional liberal rights" because "children for the most part still stand in official relationship to their parents under law, rather than assuming the position of autonomous individuals."[2] In this essay, I explore this perennial problem of situating children in a liberal legal order by examining its origins in the aftermath of the Civil War, when Americans questioned what exactly liberty would mean in "the world the War made" and attempted to construct a modern liberal order around the constitutional rights of autonomous individuals.[3] The war, by abolishing chattel slavery, had triggered a "revolutionary era in constitutionalism," in which ideas about liberty, dependence and governance were all up for grabs.[4] One of the central tensions in this fashioning of the liberal state concerned the seemingly intractable contradiction between radical individualism and traditional assumptions about the "natural" dependence of children. Ultimately, out of this era emerged two visions of children's rights, which were used by children's advocates not only to define the place of children in American law, but also to delineate the role of the state in American life. One vision focused on the universal needs of children and paved the way for the creation of specialized juvenile courts at the turn of the century; the other championed the rights of parents and children and limited state action through a rights-based critique of experiments in state paternalism.

In this essay, I use the case of *People v. Turner*, a controversial 1870 decision of the Illinois Supreme Court, as a lens through which we can see the first flowering of children's rights during the bright, although brief, days of Radical Reconstruction.[5] This case reveals that the history of children's rights has been episodic and that we must pay particular attention to specific moments in order to appreciate its complexity.[6] Otherwise, historical accounts will substitute cultural consensus where conflict raged, and we are in danger of overlooking losing arguments, which, like dissenting opinions, were central to the process by which the majority wrote their ideas into law and history.[7]

Scholars have long known about *Turner* because the case extended due process protections to minors and called into question the constitutionality of paternalistic state action. Although *Turner* was the first children's rights case to achieve national prominence after the Civil War, scholars have had a difficult time fitting this case into the history of juvenile justice because it disrupts conventional narratives that trace the evolution and expansion of state power over children from the establishment of houses of refuge in the 1820s to the creation of juvenile courts at the turn of the twentieth century. In such narratives, *Turner*, if mentioned, becomes an inconvenient detour on the otherwise straight road from the building of asylums and institutions in Jacksonian American to the campaigns for socialized justice in the Progressive Era.[8]

This essay contends that we must reconstruct the cultural and legal conflicts over the relationship of the child to the state in order to better understand the precise relationship of children's rights to conceptions of state power. As the history of *Turner* reveals, legal thinkers created the two prevailing modern visions of children's rights at the same time that they created the liberal state. This simultaneous process suggests that it is neither realistic nor advisable to discuss children's rights without also exploring their relationship to state power. Indeed, it is my argument that modern conceptions of the child and the state grew up together and remain inseparable.

The Case of *People v. Turner*

Unfortunately, no evidence survives that can tell us exactly why on September 9, 1870, fourteen-year-old Daniel O'Connell was arrested and brought by a magistrate before the Cook County Superior Court. The magistrate charged Daniel with being "destitute of proper parental care."[9] The judge found the boy "to be a proper subject for commitment to the [Chicago] Reform School," which the common council had established fifteen years earlier in an effort to solve the city's juvenile delinquency problem.[10] Thus, without a trial by jury, Daniel O'Connell was committed to the reform school and Robert Turner, the superintendent of the school, now had custody and control over Daniel until he turned twenty-one.[11]

Commitment entailed incarceration for an indeterminate period because the children were disciplined by a system of rewards and punishments. Through good behavior, a boy could work his way up a ladder of seven "families" of boys, each one sporting a different color uniform to designate its members. Once a boy reached the top, he was given a "ticket of leave" and allowed, if he chose, to find work elsewhere. According to the superintendent, a boy could "grade out in six months," but the average stay at the school was closer to eighteen months.[12] Some boys, however, stayed on for years. Thus, Daniel would have to spend at least six months at the school, and could possibly be there for seven years.

At the school, Daniel was placed in congregate care with approximately thirty boys. Together they compromised a "family," which was under the supervision of a house mother and father. Daniel's new "family" members were a mix of dependent and delinquent children. The majority had confessed to petty larceny, vagrancy, homelessness, or incorrigibility.[13] Daniel's day now began with a drum beat awakening him every morning at 5:30. Religious services, work, school, meals, singing, general exercises, and a bedtime prayer at 7:30 completed his day.

The reform school had come under fire in the postbellum period. Opponents argued that it was a juvenile prison, not a school. Catholics were also upset that the boys were receiving Protestant religious instruction. In fact, during the year prior to Daniel's commitment, the Illinois Supreme Court had freed sixteen boys by writs of *habeas corpus* from the school.[14] On November 12, 1870 Michael O'Connell exercised this option when he filed for this writ to free his son.[15] In his application for the writ, the father informed the court that, to make ends meet, he needed the four dollars a week that his son earned in a local tobacco factory. Apparently, Daniel had been working in the factory for the past eighteen months.[16] Six days later, the high court issued the writ demanding that Turner produce Daniel "forthwith" so that the court could "then and there consider of him."[17]

The timing of the case was fortuitous because the justices were sitting in Chicago for this session making it possible for Michael

O'Connell to bring his case to court. The timing was also symbolic because Michael O'Connell filed for the writ of *habeas corpus* to free his son right after election day, when in a spirit of celebration, black men in Chicago had voted for the first time since the passage of the 15th Amendment.[18] As a local paper observed, "It was a holiday for them...The denizens of Fifth avenue and Sherman street arose early yesterday, jumped into their sleekest harnesses, and rushed to the polls to deposit their ballots. Many brought their wives and sweethearts to see them vote."[19]

William T. Butler, the local attorney who represented the O'Connells, contrasted the newfound freedom of the African Americans with the Irish boy's loss of liberty. He declared that Daniel was trapped in a prison because the school knew "no intermission! No rejoining of the family circle at noon or night! No Saturdays of Emancipation! No Sunday without Enthrallment!" Moreover, Daniel was in a state of "involuntary servitude" that denied him the "privileges and immunities" of citizenship.[20] Butler added that if this had been done to an African or Chinese child we could "expect to hear the alarms of the 14th Amendment to the Federal Constitution resound about our ears."[21] Why were these bells not sounding for Daniel? he asked. Butler's playing of the race card suggested how problematic it now would be to treat "white" children as slaves.[22]

The arrest of Daniel in September had occurred less than a month after the new state constitution went into effect. Butler was thus also able to use Daniel's case to question whether its civil rights provision, which guaranteed that "no person shall be deprived of life, liberty or property without due process," applied to minors.[23] Accordingly, the case could be used to determine how expansive the definition of "liberty" would be in the postbellum world.

The existence of a new constitution coupled with the burst of rights-consciousness in the wake of the Civil War also provided Butler with an opportunity to challenge the leading legal precedent *Ex Parte Crouse* (1838). In this antebellum case, the Pennsylvania Supreme Court had denied a petition for a writ of *habeas corpus* to free Mary Ann Crouse, a minor, from the Philadelphia House of Refuge.[24] In *Crouse*, the Pennsylvania court had asked, "[M]ay not the natural parents, when unequal to the task of education, or unworthy of it, be superseded by the *parens patriae*, or common guardian of the community?"[25] Working within the common law vision of a well-regulated society, the justices had added: "the public has a paramount interest in the virtue and knowledge of its members, and that, of strict right, the business of education belongs to it."[26] As William Novak has shown, such reasoning emphasized the social nature of human beings and their connections to local communities. In such a world, the first maxim of the common law, *salus populi suprema lex est* (the welfare of the people is the supreme law), granted local officials vast power to regulate private actions for the common good.[27] Determining that the House of Refuge was "not a prison, but a school" where "reformation, and not punishment" was the goal, the Pennsylvania court rejected the petitioner's claim that the commitment and detention of Mary Ann without a trial by jury had violated the state's Bill of Rights.

I.N. Stiles, the city attorney who represented the Chicago Reform School in *Turner*, based his case on *Ex Parte Crouse*. Moreover, he asserted that Daniel had never possessed liberty because minors had no such rights under the law. "In or out of the Reform School he can make no valid contract, he can bring no suit in the courts to enforce or protect his rights, except through the agency of a next friend," he stated.[28] According to Stiles, "the law assumed that a guardian looked out for a minor's well-being," and "that the liberty which the framers of the constitution were so desirous of protecting" did not apply to children.[29]

Butler did not see how this could be. The United States Constitution, he argued, had just been "amended to the very verge of perfection" to guarantee personal freedom. He explained:

> Ten years ago we were told by some people that American liberty was not the right of all persons; but was the exclusive right of those of a certain color, or rather those of no color. And now the learned Counsel for the respondent in their case argue that the liberty of to-day is not the right of "all persons," notwithstanding the very words of the Constitution; but is the exclusive right of persons over and above a certain age.[30]

On behalf of Daniel O'Connell, Butler demanded that it was time to reexamine *Ex Parte Crouse* because the antebellum decision was "rife with principles dangerous to liberty."[31] It would, he concluded, be "better [to] banish the boy at once and give him his liberty elsewhere if the good of society will not permit him to enjoy it here."[32] Butler's argument suggested that the Reconstruction Amendments had ushered in a new era of American constitutionalism, in which all persons, broadly construed, had constitutional rights and that it was necessary for the nation's courts to protect these individual rights.

The attorneys thus presented the justices of the Illinois Supreme Court with two very different conceptions of the relationship of the child to the state. Stiles, representing the Reform School, had made the traditional argument that children had no rights and that boys like Daniel required positive state tutelage, not negative liberty in the form of due process protection against arbitrary state intervention into their lives. Butler, on the other hand, contended that children were persons who had constitutional rights under Illinois law. Thus, at this critical moment in the construction of the American liberal state, Butler envisioned that the state would protect and respect children's rights.

Butler, it turns out, won the case, but his libertarian vision of children's rights did not carry the day. The Illinois Supreme Court based its decision on a combination of parents' rights, the public's interest in preserving family ties and children's rights. Justice Anthony Thornton, a Republican, wrote the unanimous opinion for the court, which carefully balanced these guiding principles. After briefly explaining the facts of the case and the specifics of the reform school legislation, he cautioned "in our solicitude to form youth for the duties of civil life, we should not forget the rights, which inhere both in parents and children."[33] He then described the parent/child relationship, highlighting its reciprocal bonds. "The parent has the right to the care, custody, and assistance of his child," he wrote.[34] To provide for his children the father required power over them, "a power which is an emanation from God," he stressed. The state should not disturb this power "except for the strongest reasons."[35] Implicit was the notion that parental authority helped to beget the obedience essential for a good education and solid upbringing.

The public benefited from preserving family ties, Thornton argued, because they not only bound the father to his family, but also to his workplace. As Amy Dru Stanley has revealed, proponents of free labor assumed that fathers as breadwinners earned enough money to support their families, which allowed their wives and children to remain at home.[36] After the Civil War, Senator Henry Wilson, for instance, explained to a meeting of newly freed people in South Carolina that "freedom does not mean that you are not to work. It means that when you do work you shall have pay for it, to carry home to your wives and children of your love."[37] Now that slavery had been abolished, free men entered the marketplace so that their dependents could remain at home, in a realm supposedly safe from the corrupting influences of commerce.

Although the facts in *Turner* suggested that this ideal of a father supporting his dependents did not always match social reality, Justice Thornton still noted, "in this country, the hope of the child, in respect to education and the future advancement, is mainly dependent upon the father; for this he struggles and toils through life; the desire of its accomplishment operating as one of the most powerful incentives to industry and thrift."[38] He added, "The violent abruption of this relation would not only tend to wither these motives to action, but necessarily, in time, alienate the father's natural affections."[39] Thus, the emotional ties between a father and his family helped to bind society together by encouraging men to labor productively. To sever family ties risked destroying not only the father's "natural affections" for his offspring, but also his desire to work.

Justice Thornton concluded his opinion with a powerful argument about children's rights that focused on children, especially boys, as social actors. He observed that minors actively participated in American society.[40] He agreed, for example, with Butler that "the disability of minors does not make slaves or criminals of them."[41] To drive this point home, Thornton listed a series of legal connections among children and society, including the fact that minors were bound by "an implied contract for necessaries," were "liable for torts," "punishable for crime[s]," paid taxes, constituted "a part of the militia," and had "to endure the hardships and privations of a soldier's life in defence of the constitution and the laws."[42] He added, "the only act, which they are under a legal incapacity to perform, is the appointment of an attorney."[43] He then posed the question: "Can we hold children responsible for crime; liable for their torts; impose onerous burdens on them, and yet deprive them of the enjoyment of liberty, without charge or conviction of crime?"[44]

In Thornton's view, Daniel O'Connell had been imprisoned in a highly arbitrary manner and was now "deprived of a father's care, bereft of home influences, has no freedom of action, is committed for an uncertain time, branded as a prisoner, made subject to the will of others, and thus feels that he is a *slave*."[45] This last point about Daniel's state of mind mattered because "nothing could more contribute to paralyze the youthful energies, crush all noble aspirations, and unfit him for the duties of manhood."[46] Since the father's and the son's rights had been violated and the public's interest in both the father and the son fulfilling the duties of manhood had been jeopardized, the Illinois Supreme Court ordered Daniel O'Connell to be discharged and struck down the provisions of the reform school act that had allowed children who had not been convicted of crimes to be incarcerated.

The significance of *Turner* did not end with Daniel's departure from the Chicago Reform School.[47] The court's broad interpretation of "all men" to include children clearly demonstrated that as the liberal state was created it was not only possible to imagine granting constitutional rights to minors, but that that possibility had become the law in Illinois. Furthermore, Justice Thornton's opinion also reached a national legal audience in 1871 when Isaac Redfield, the eminent jurist and Chief Justice of the Vermont Supreme Court, endorsed *Turner* in the *American Law Register*, an influential case reporter. Redfield used the decision to challenge allegedly benevolent laws passed to protect children. *Turner*, in his view, would help to prevent reformers from using the state to erect "an empire, superior both in character and power to any other, ancient or modern" through "legislative moral reform and compulsory popular education."[48] Redfield argued that the *Turner* decision, by "striking a fatal blow at the very foundation of their entire superstructure," would prevent reformers from "mould[ing] so vast an empire as this, composed of such diverse nationalities, and such discordant religious and political opinions, into one homogeneous compound of purity and perfection."[49] The decision would thus advance liberty "among the children of white parents, as well as those of a more somber hue."[50] Catholic children, for instance, Redfield declared, could now no longer "be driven into a Protestant school, and made to read the Protestant version of the Holy Scriptures."[51] Redfield's ringing endorsement of *Turner* forced supporters of reforms aimed at minors, such as compulsory school attendance laws, to come to terms with the decision. No longer could they simply rely upon the reasoning of *Crouse* to justify state paternalism. They would have to make a convincing case explaining *why* children required the protection of the state, instead of protection from the state.

In Illinois, *Turner* remained the law of the land until 1882, when the state's supreme court reconsidered the consequences of its earlier decision and decided to embrace the doctrine of *parens patriae* and allow the General Assembly to establish a publicly-subsidized system of industrial schools for dependent girls. This retreat from *Turner* has led historians to conclude that the controversial decision had no "lasting influence on the course of law" in Illinois or elsewhere.[52] In fact, Steven Schlossman even speculated in his path-breaking book *Love and the American Delinquent* that the justices of the Illinois Supreme Court must have felt "considerable embarrassment" about the decision and they were looking for an opportunity to overturn it.[53]

The Implications of *Turner*

This interpretation of the legacy of *Turner*, however, obscures three important points that I would like to make by way of conclusion. First, central to the repudiation of *Turner* were the specifics of the relevant late-nineteenth-century cases. In Illinois, these cases — *Petition of Ferrier* and *County of McLean v. Laura B. Humphreys* — involved very young girls (ages 9 and 7) who did not have viable families.[54] These girls were, in effect, poster children for dependency, unlike Daniel O'Connell, who could be seen as a fairly typical young man working to help his family to survive hard times. In these later cases, it was quite possible that these young girls might die without state assistance. Their cases pushed the logic of post-Civil War liberalism to an extreme: Could a seven-year-old or nine-year-old child, especially a girl, be considered an autonomous individual with personal liberty?

The Illinois General Assembly passed the Industrial Schools Act to restore to the state some of its power over dependent children that had been stripped away by the Supreme Court in *Turner*.[55] The new law, which was based upon a Wisconsin statute, established a procedure for triggering state action to bring "dependent" girls into county courts. Any "responsible person," who had lived in the county for a year, could petition to have the court "inquire into the dependency of any female infant then within the county."[56] The petitioner was required to provide the names of the child's parents or guardian, show why they were not fit to have custody, and take an oath to verify these claims.[57] Once the petition was filed, the clerk of the court would issue a writ to the sheriff to bring the girl before the court. Other procedural safeguards were also included to appease the Supreme Court, including the requirement that notice of the hearing had to be given to the parents or guardians if they were in the county at the time.[58] The hearing would take place in open court before a six-member jury. In addition, if the girl did not have a counsel, the court would appoint one for her.

If the jury found a girl to be "dependent," then the judge could commit her to an industrial school, preferably to one within the county if such an institution existed.[59] Any seven or more residents of Illinois, as long as the majority were women, could, with the consent of the governor, establish a tax-exempt industrial school for girls under the state's incorporation laws.[60] This requirement that the majority of the board be women reflected the maternalist assumption that women by nature were suited to be the primary caretakers of young children.

In the *Ferrier* case, the mentally unstable mother of a nine-year-old girl had tried to hang her daughter Winifred and then herself.[61] At the dependency hearing, Winifred testified: "I love papa; I don't know whether I love mama; I have tried to do as they wanted; I am not a bad girl; I try to be good; I do sometimes run away; my mother tried to hang me and then tried to hang herself; I am afraid of her; I know of this industrial school and want to go there."[62] The girl's father, neighbors, and a physician also testified that they believed that the girl should be committed to the South Evanston Industrial School. A six-man jury heard the case and determined that Winifred was a "dependent girl."

The Illinois Supreme Court declared that the procedures for hearing dependency cases established by the Industrial School Law did not violate the state constitution.[63] Justice Sheldon writing for the court in *Ferrier* applauded the "anxious provision" that the legislation "made for the due protection of all just rights."[64] Moreover, he declared that the South Evanston Industrial School was actually a school, not a prison.[65] This critical distinction allowed the court to conceptualize the Industrial Schools Act not as a part of the *criminal* law, but rather as belonging to "the same character of jurisdiction exercised by the court of chancery over the persons and property of infants, having foundation in the prerogative of the Crown, flowing from its general power and duty, as *parens patriae*, to protect those who have no other lawful protector."[66] This reasoning meant that cases brought under the Industrial Schools Act had only to follow chancery procedures, not the more stringent criminal ones.[67]

This interpretation opened up the possibility for treating *all* children's cases in a similar fashion. In the 1890s, when legal reformers scoured through the case law searching to find openings that would allow for children's cases to be handled in a special manner, they would seize upon this interpretation of *parens patriae* as the legal justification for the establishment of a children's court. Justice Sheldon also drew a distinction between "natural" and "civil" rights that further opened up the possibility of treating all children as a class. He explained that children did not have absolute liberty, but should instead be classified as "dependent" or "helpless" individuals who needed to be in a controlled, hierarchical relationship such as "parent and child, guardian and ward, [or] teacher and scholar."[68] This broad language classified children as social beings with civil rights, whose limits were "restrained by human laws (and no further) as is necessary and expedient for the general welfare."[69] This understanding of the social nature of human existence was, of course, not new. It had served as the foundation for American governance from the revolution until the rise of post-Civil War liberalism.[70] The emerging liberal legal order was replacing this vision of a well-regulated society with a new emphasis on individual rights.[71] Justice Sheldon, in this case, retained the older notion of civil rights because he could not conceive of young girls as autonomous individuals with constitutional rights that needed to be protected at all costs. Government's responsibility, he believed, was to ensure that these girls were in a safe, structured setting like an industrial school or a respectable family.

Progressive child savers used cases such as *Ferrier* and *McLean*, that involved young girls with nowhere to turn, to establish the doctrinal foundation for the juvenile court. This reliance upon cases involving dependent girls to build the juvenile court was somewhat ironic because these specialized courts over the course of the twentieth century heard many more cases involving delinquent boys than either delinquent or dependent girls. Despite juvenile courts focusing their efforts on delinquent boys, child savers would continue to cite the nineteenth-century cases involving young dependent girls to sustain the legitimacy of these courts over the course of the twentieth century.[72] Thus, defenders of juvenile justice used legal principles established well before the creation of juvenile courts to defend their subsequent practices.

Second, the lasting significance of *Turner* becomes more apparent once we realize that juvenile courts were controversial institutions from their creation at the turn of the twentieth century. Opponents of the Cook County Juvenile Court, the world's first and foremost children's court, would use *Turner* in their campaigns to delegitimize this new experiment in state paternalism. For example, William H. Dunn, a Chicago manufacturer and opponent of the Juvenile Court, even managed to cut off its funding right before America's entry into the First World War.[73] Periodically, critics of juvenile justice would rediscover *Turner* and incorporate the case into their arguments that arbitrary state power is a constant threat to individual liberty. Such legal arguments were the precursor to *In Re Gault* (1967), the famous case in which the United States Supreme Court granted children in juvenile courts limited due process rights, including the right to notice, counsel, confrontation, cross-examination of witnesses, and the privilege against self-incrimination.[74] This victory for children's rights in *Gault*, as Barry Feld and Christopher Manfredi have argued, triggered the process of rethinking the relationship of the child and the state, which contributed to the recriminalization of juvenile justice.[75] As Feld has argued, "by emphasizing criminal procedure regularity, the [Supreme] Court shifted juvenile court's focus from 'real needs' to 'criminal deeds' and effectively altered delinquency proceedings from an inquiry about social welfare into a criminal prosecution."[76] Although children received select constitutional rights from decisions like *Gault*, they may have ended up exchanging positive liberty in the form of social services and programs for these limited due process protections. Scholars are still assessing what the true costs of this exchange were.[77]

Third, an argument might be made that the idea of parental rights expressed in *Turner* is also a source for today's parental rights movement and that an exploration into children's rights might also uncover a lost tradition of parental rights. For example, congressional supporters of recent parental rights bills have cited *Pierce v. Society of Sisters*, a 1924 United States Supreme Court decision that declared an Oregon law unconstitutional. The law attempted to remove Catholic children from parochial schools by requiring parents and guardians of children between eight and sixteen years of age to send their children to public schools. The lawyers who represented the Society of Sisters, a corporation established in 1880 "with the power to care for orphans, educate and instruct youth, [and] establish and maintain academies or schools," cited *Turner* to support their argument that the Oregon law infringed upon the liberty of parents.[78] In the spirit of *Turner,* the Supreme Court declared, "the child is not the mere creature of the State" and struck down the law.[79] Isaac Redfield would have been pleased. We need to know more, however, about use of parental rights to curtail child-saving legislation before we can know for certain whether today's concerns about state paternalism are part of a longer historical tradition whose roots lay in "the world the war made."

We must remember, in any case, that modern conceptions of children's rights and the liberal state developed together and have been mutually constitutive. In the past, rethinking the idea of children's rights forced Americans to rethink the role of the state in American life. The repudiation of *Turner*, for example, paved the way not only for the creation of juvenile courts, but also laid the foundation for the American welfare state.[80] In the 1910s, juvenile courts were expanded to administer the first mothers' pensions (cash disbursements to single mothers with dependent children), the precursor to the federal Aid to Dependent Children program (later Aid to Families with Dependent Children). Proponents of child welfare, by highlighting the needs of dependent children, had helped to establish these home-based family preservation programs. As we begin exploring the rights of the child for the twenty-first century, we must not forget this lesson about the political uses of the concept of child dependency as building blocks in past state building. We must keep in mind that we need to think not only about future children, but must also imagine what kind of state we should construct for them.

Notes

1. Many years ago, I presented the first draft of this essay at the Social History Workshop at the University of Chicago and would like to thank all the participants, especially Andrew Cohen, Kathy Conzen, Elizabeth Dale, Chad Heap, Betsy Mendelsohn, Susan Radomsky, Mark Schmeller and Michael Willrich, for their useful comments. I am also grateful for the invaluable editorial suggestions of my late wife Jenifer Stenfors and my colleague Paul Werth. Finally, I would like to thank Brenn Sarata and the editors, Kathleen Alaimo and Brian Klug, for their help in expanding this essay.

2. Martha Minow, *Making All the Difference: Inclusion, Exclusion, and American Law* (Ithaca: Cornell University Press, 1990), p. 283.

3. In a January 3, 1877 letter to Reuben Benjamin, Chief Justice Sidney Breese of the Illinois Supreme Court stated that "we must live in the world the War made." Eric Foner used this phrase as the organizing principle for the first chapter of *Reconstruction: America's Unfinished Revolution, 1863-1877* (New York: Harper & Row, 1988), pp. 1-34. On the creation of the American liberal state, see William J. Novak, *The People's Welfare: Law and Regulation in Nineteenth-Century America* (Chapel Hill: University of North Carolina Press, 1996), pp. 235-248.

4. Robert Kaczorowski, "Revolutionary Constitutionalism in the Era of the Civil War and Reconstruction," *New York University Law Review* 61 (November 1986), pp. 863-940. A growing historiography concerned with "the problem of freedom in the age of emancipation" has revealed the critical role played by legal ideas in this process of social and political reconstruction, a process which often ended up reproducing categories of dependency along racial, class, and gender "fault" lines. An excellent example of this scholarship is Amy Dru Stanley, "Beggars Can't Be Choosers: Compulsion and Contract in Postbellum America," *Journal of American History* (March 1992), pp. 1265-1293.

5. *People v. Turner*, 55 Ill. 280 (1870). The opinion was reprinted in 8 *American Reports*, 645 (1870), and in 19 *American Law Register*, 367 (1871). The famous jurist Isaac F. Redfield wrote a comment for its reprinting in the *American Law Register*. All subsequent citations will be to this version.

6. Hendrik Hartog's exciting work on marriage, which he presented to the Comparative Legal History Workshop at the University of Chicago, has helped me to appreciate the episodic nature of family law. See Hendrik Hartog, *Man and Wife in America: A History* (Cambridge, MA: Harvard University Press, 2000). Linda Kerber's recent work on citizenship has also revealed a similar pattern in the history of citizenship. See, e.g., Linda Kerber, "The Paradox of Women's Citizenship in the Early Republic: The Case of *Martin vs. Massachusetts*, 1805," *The American Historical Review* 97 (April 1992), pp. 349-378 and Kerber, *No Constitutional Rights to Be Ladies: Women and the Obligations of Citizenship* (New York: Hill & Wang, 1998).

7. See, e.g., Martha Minow, "'Forming Underneath Everything That Grows': Toward a History of Family Law," *Wisconsin Law Review* (1985), pp. 819-897.

8. See, e.g., Sanford J. Fox, "Juvenile Justice Reform: An Historical Perspective," 22 *Stanford Law Review* (June 1970), pp. 1216-1221; Douglas R. Rendleman, *"Parens Patriae*: From Chancery to the Juvenile Court," *South Carolina Law Review* 23 (1971), pp. 233-236; Steven L. Schlossman, *Love and the American Delinquent: The Theory and Practice of "Progressive" Juvenile Justice, 1825-1920* (Chicago: University of Chicago Press, 1977), pp. 8-17; Christopher P. Manfredi, *The Supreme Court and Juvenile Justice* (Lawrence: University of Kansas Press, 1998), pp. 24-28; and Barry C. Feld, *Bad Kids: Race and the Transformation of the Juvenile Court* (New York: Oxford University Press, 1999), pp. 48-57.

9. This information comes from the brief and argument of the relator, William T. Butler, filed 23 November 1870, n.p. Case file 16742, State Archives, Springfield, Illinois. [hereafter cited as Butler's brief].

10. This quotation is from the brief by I.N. Stiles, the City Attorney and counsel for the Chicago Reform School, filed 23 November 1870, 1. Case file #16742 [hereafter cited as Stiles' brief]. For a short history of the school see Joan Gittens, *Poor Relations: The Children of the State in Illinois, 1818-1990* (Urbana: University of Illinois Press, 1994), pp. 90-104. Copies of the annual reports of the school are at the Chicago Historical Society [CHS]. For the development of houses of refuge in the Jacksonian Era see David J. Rothman, *The Discovery of the Asylum: Social Order and Disorder in the New Republic* (Boston: Little & Brown, 1971; 2nd ed, 1990). Cf. Gustave de Beaumont and Alexis de Tocqueville, *On the Penitentiary System in the United States and Its Application in France*, trans. by Francis Lieber, (1833; Carbondale: Southern Illinois University Press, 1964), pp. 136-158. On "the domestification of the house of refuges" see Steven L. Schlossman, *Love and the American Delinquent*, chap. 3.

11. The power of the Board of Guardians of the school ranged widely. According to section 10 of the statute, all boys committed "shall be kept, disciplined, instructed, employed and governed, under the direction of the board of guardians of said school, until he be either reformed and discharged, or be bound out by said guardians, or until he shall have arrived at the age of twenty-one years; and said guardians are hereby clothed with the sole authority to discharge any boy or boys from said reform school, who have heretofore been or may hereafter be legally committed thereto; and such power shall rest solely with said board of guardians and with no other persons or body politic or corporate; but it shall be the duty of said board of guardians, and they shall have the power, to return any boy to the court, police justices or other authorities, ordering or directing said boy to be committed, when, in the judgment of said guardians, they may decree said boy an improper subject for their care and management, or who shall be found incorrigible, or whose continuance in the school they may deem prejudicial to the management and discipline thereof, or who, in their judgment, ought to be removed from such school for any cause; and in such case, said court, police

justice or other authorities, shall have power, and are required, to proceed as they might have done, had they not ordered the commitment to such school."

12. *Twelfth Annual Report* (1868), p. 51.

13. *Chicago Reform School Annual Reports, 1866-1872* (Chicago, 1872). The information comes from the *Sixteenth Annual Report* (1872), p. 14. [Hereafter all citations will be to a specific annual report.]

14. *Fourteenth Annual Report* (1870), p. 6.

15. Daniel O'Connell appropriately enough shared the same name as "the Great Emancipator" of Irish history. I must thank Paul Townend for pointing out the significance of Daniel's name to Irish-Americans in this period.

16. Petition for *Habeas Corpus*, issued 12 Nov. 1870, n.p. Case file 16742.

17. Writ of *Habeas Corpus*, filed 18 Nov. 1870, n.p. Case file 16742.

18. *The Chicago Times*, November 9, 1870, p. 1.

19. Ibid.

20. Butler's brief, n.p.

21. Ibid.

22. Scholars of "whiteness" have written about the process by which the Irish became "white." Recent scholarship has also examined the process of racial marking in an attempt to explain how racist thought and practice have been reproduced and reconfigured in American history. For an introduction to this scholarship, see Thomas Holt, "Marking: Race, Race-making, and the Writing of History," *The American Historical Review* 100 (February 1995), pp. 1-20.

23. The following other constitutional provisions were cited in Butler's brief: "No person shall be deprived of life, liberty or property without due process of law," (Art. II, Sec. II); "The right of trial by jury, as heretofore enjoyed, shall remain inviolate," (Art. II, Sec. 5); "All penalties shall be proportioned to the nature of the offense," (Art. II, Sec. II); "Every person ought to find a certain remedy in the laws for all injuries and wrongs which he may receive in his person, property or reputation," (Art. II, Sec. 19).

24. *Ex Parte Crouse*, 4 Wharton 9 (Pa., 1838). For an excellent discussion of the case see Michael Grossberg, *A Judgment for Solomon: The D'Hauteville Case and Legal Experience in Antebellum America* (New York: Cambridge University Press, 1996), pp. 74-75.

25. *Ex Parte Crouse*, p. 11.

26. Ibid.

27. For a philosophical introduction to the precepts of the "well-regulated society" and an examination of these ideals-in-action, see Novak, *The People's Welfare*.

28. Stiles' brief, p.1.

29. Ibid., p. 2.

30. Butler's brief, n.p.

31. Ibid.

32. Ibid.

33. *People v. Turner*, p. 369.

142   *Children as Equals: Exploring the Rights of the Child*

34. Ibid., p. 369. According to the common law, the father had complete control over the children, although mothers gained considerable rights over the course of the nineteenth century. See Michael Grossberg, *Governing the Hearth: Law and the Family in Nineteenth-Century America* (Chapel Hill: University of North Carolina Press, 1985), pp. 234-281.

35. *People v. Turner*, p. 369.

36. Amy Dru Stanley, *From Bondage to Contract: Wage Labor, Marriage, and the Market in the Age of Slave Emancipation* (New York: Cambridge University Press, 1998),

37. Quoted in Stanley, *From Bondage to Contract*, p. 140.

38. *People v. Turner*, p. 369.

39. Ibid. Thornton was quoting a passage from an anonymous author.

40. Nearly forty per cent of the "men" who fought in the Civil War enlisted before they had reached twenty-one. In Illinois, boys as young as fifteen fought in the war, although their parents had to sign consent forms. This fact suggests how blurry the transition from childhood to adulthood was in the mid-nineteenth century. Did going to war transform an adolescent into a "man"? The narrow legal answer could differ widely from the social responses and treatment of the solider. A possible analogy might be Frederick Douglass's assertion that African Americans needed to fight in the Union army so that they could earn their freedom as a race. Although young people did not act as a group, the decision to go to war was a way to earn "personal freedom" and "emancipation." The first chapter of Stephen Crane's *The Red Badge of Courage* (1895) provides a good fictional account of the psychological burdens associated with enlistment.

41. *People v. Turner*, p. 370.

42. Ibid., pp. 370-371.

43. Ibid., pp. 370-371.

44. Ibid., p. 370.

45. *People v. Turner*, p. 371 (my italics).

46. Ibid.

47. The school closed partially as a result of the court's decision and as a consequence of the Chicago Fire of 1871. See Fox, "Juvenile Justice Reform," pp.1218-1219.

48. *People v. Turner*, p. 372

49. Ibid., pp. 372-373.

50. Ibid., p. 373.

51. Ibid.

52. Fox, "Juvenile Justice Reform," p.1219.

53. Schlossman, *Love and the American Delinquent*, p.14.

54. *Petition of Ferrier* 103 Ill. 367 (1882) and *County of McLean v. Laura B. Humphreys* 104 Ill. 379 (1882). For an extended analysis of these cases see David Spinoza Tanenhaus, "Policing the Child: Juvenile Justice in Chicago, 1870-1925" 2 vols. (Ph.D. diss., University of Chicago, 1997), pp. 85-107.

55. "An Act for Industrial Schools for Girls," *Laws of Illinois* (Springfield, 1879), pp. 309-313.

56. Ibid., p. 309.

57. Ibid., p. 310.

58. Ibid.

59. In 1880, there were only two such schools in the state; one was located in Evanston and the other in Springfield.

60. "An Act for Industrial Schools for Girls," p. 309.

61. Tanenhaus, "Policing the Child," pp. 84-90.

62. Quoted in Ibid., p. 88.

63. *Petition of Ferrier*, p. 367.

64. Ibid., p. 371.

65. Ibid., p. 373. He stated: "The decision in 55 Ill. [*People v. Turner*] as to the reform school, we do not think should be applied to this industrial school."

66. *Petition of Ferrier*, p. 372. The court cited Joseph Story, *Commentaries on Equity Jurisprudence as Administered in England and America* (Boston: Hilliard, Gray, 1836).

67. *Ferrier*, p. 374.

68. Ibid., p. 373.

69. Ibid. Justice Sheldon was quoting from William Blackstone, *Commentaries on the Laws of England*, vol. 1, (1765-1769; Reprint, Chicago: The University of Chicago Press, 1979), p. 125.

70. Novak, *The People's Welfare*.

71. Ibid., pp. 235-248.

72. Bernard Flexner and Reuben Oppenheimer, "The Legal Aspect of the Juvenile Court," 67 *The American Law Review* (1923), pp. 65-96.

73. David S. Tanenhaus, "Rotten to the Core: The Juvenile Court and the Problem of Legitimacy in the Progressive Era," in *A Noble Social Experiment? The First 100 Years of the Cook County Juvenile Court 1899-1999*, ed. Gwen Hoerr McNamee (Chicago: The Chicago Bar Association, 1999), pp. 24-28.

74. *In Re Gault*, 387 U.S. 1 (1967). For a useful analysis of *In Re Gault*, see Manfredi, *The Supreme Court and Juvenile Justice*, pp. 80-129.

75. Ibid., pp. 156-199. Cf. Feld, *Bad Kids*.

76. Feld, *Bad Kids*, p.107.

77. For a good introduction to the literature about the state and future of juvenile justice, see Thomas F. Geraghty and Steven A. Drizin, "Foreword — The Debate Over the Future of Juvenile Courts: Can We Reach Consensus?" 88 *The Journal of Criminal Law and Criminology* (Fall 1997), pp. 1-13.

78. *Pierce v. Society of Sisters*, 268 U.S. 510, 531, 519 (1924).

79. Ibid., p. 535. For more on the legal basis of proposed parental rights bills, see "Array of Opponents Battle Over 'Parental Rights' Bills," *The New York Times*, 1 May 1996, p. 1.

80. For the connection between juvenile courts and the welfare state, see, e.g., Andrew J. Polsky, *The Rise of the Therapeutic State* (Princeton: Princeton

University Press, 1991); Theda Skocpol, *Protecting Soldiers and Mothers: The Political Origins of Social Policy in the United States* (Cambridge, MA: Belknap Press of Harvard University Press, 1992); Linda Gordon, *Pitied But Not Entitled: Single Mothers and the History of Welfare* (New York: The Free Press, 1994); Joanne L. Goodwin, *Gender and the Politics of Welfare Reform: Mother's Pensions in Chicago, 1911-1929* (Chicago: The University of Chicago Press, 1997); and Tanenhaus, "Policing the Child," pp. 276-328.

Chapter 8

A Child-Centered Jurisprudence: Reconciling the Rights of Children and Parents within the Family

Joan M. Smith

One hundred fifty years ago, John Stuart Mill wrote, "[T]he family must be more than a school for obedience. Justly constituted, [it is] the real school of the virtues of freedom, [a] school of sympathy in equality, of living together in love, without power on one side or obedience on the other."[1] The reality, though, for many children is that their family is a microcosm of a patriarchal society which is characterized by competition and hierarchy in which people are used as means to others' ends. In effect, in all too many families, the marketplace is the model for relationships and this model promotes discord and conflicts.

A truly nurturing family fosters opportunities for children to develop and pursue self-fulfillment, and promotes physical and emotional health, motivation, and positive self-esteem. But what happens when family relationships break down and parent and child do not agree? Who should prevail? Can such a family avoid the trauma of bitterly contested custody battles and the drama of a courtroom where child is pitted against parent in a war over legal rights? Philosophically, if we had to choose between children and adults, we might prefer to be a society that makes the child's interests paramount. Yet, while we might aspire to achieve this goal and become a society based on a nurturing family model, the reality is different. Consequently, it behooves us to be concerned with how the interests of parent and child link together in relationships.[2]

This essay argues that ⌐there is an alternative to the marketplace model for family relationships, one in which care, concern, openness, and trust are guiding principles for family law⌐After discussing family rights in the United States and the current state of the law, I will discuss an alternative perspective on the family and a jurisprudence for families with children. Finally, I will describe a practical legal application for resolving family conflicts.

Family Rights Under United States Law

When discussing any legal system, we must remember that the law is more than just a set of rules, procedures, and prohibitions. Law itself is rhetoric and the vision by which community and culture are established, maintained, and transformed.[3] Islamic law, for example, sets the parameters for the relationships between men and women that in many ways define Islamic life. What about United States law? What is the vision that informs the legal system and the rights that exist within it?

Influenced by eighteenth-century discourse concerning an individual's right to life, liberty, and property, jurisprudence in the United States has developed as an individualistic, rights-based legal philosophy that constitutionally protects citizens' private lives.[4] It is universally agreed that rights only protect an individual's self-determination and personal integrity.[5] For example, I have a right to choose how I express my gratitude to a Supreme Being, but not to choose your religious beliefs for you. Similarly, I have a right to choose a vegetarian lifestyle but cannot require the same of my neighbors or even my husband for that matter.

Within this framework, one could argue that it is inconsistent for parents to claim child-rearing rights. As opposed to the right to *have* children, child-rearing "rights" are more like a privilege to authorized control over the life of another, not oneself. Yet,⌐our legal tradition has rationalized this prerogative by treating the child as "an isolated human possession"[6] and has ignored the interdependency of family relationships. Unfortunately, the legal system in the United States does not yet encourage families to adopt those behaviors toward each other that are the foundation of a secure and loving home, for example, a respect for each individual's thoughts and feelings regardless of age, or urging children to risk being different and becoming secure in their own independence and autonomy. Rather, enter any family court and you will see disputing parties as legal opponents with litigation that is adversarial and contentious.

When the law is adult-centered, children become marginal figures in the legal system that claims to serve them.[7] Currently, most discussions of family law characterize the relationship between parents and children in terms that stress parental entitlement over responsibility, adult autonomy over family connectedness, and adult self over others.[8] The parents' right to custody and visitation pits parents against each other in custody disputes, without regard for the child's need to establish a relationship with both parents, nor for the specific amount of time this may take for each child/parent couple.

It has been argued that rights theory "fosters selfishness rather than altruism or community mindedness,"[9] that the style of rights arguments tends to promote egotistic instincts among all claimants,[10] and that "thinking in terms of rights...encourages us to think about what constrains us from doing what we want, not what obligates us to do what we ought."[11] So, should we abandon the concept of rights entirely when discussing families? Although some people may think that it would be better to use another terminology to secure for children the lives they deserve, it seems to me, as an attorney, that abandoning rights rhetoric might well undermine many legitimate claims that children have. In addition, they would likely lose their means to redress any grievances, particularly within a legal system that sets claimants against each other as legal adversaries and forces them to make claims in terms that establish their entitlement to the "rights" they seek. Thus, rather than abandoning rights, this essay argues for rights to be extended to children within the family.

In the United States it is commonly understood, in theory and in practice, that family rights are essentially parents' rights. This notion is reflected in the earliest "children's cases," and has been reaffirmed in the last century. Thus, in 1923, the Supreme Court confirmed a fundamental right to establish a home and bring up children,[12] under a substantive due process analysis that protects a person's property from unfair governmental interference. This constitutionally protected property right of parents and guardians has been extended to include the custody, education, and upbringing of children.[13]

In 1944, the Supreme Court, for the first time in a parenting context, addressed a challenge to state action that coupled due process with a claim that the state was prohibiting the free exercise of religion.[14] In allowing a guardian to permit a child to distribute religious tracts in public places, the Court's decision established that the Free Exercise clause protects parents' efforts to indoctrinate and train their children in various religious practices so long as the children are not exposed to particularly grave dangers, even though some lesser harm may befall them.[15] Using this same rationale, our laws permit parents who sincerely object to particular forms of medical treatment on religious grounds to refuse treatment for their children and to avoid state child abuse and neglect laws in so doing.[16] Obviously, such parental rights are not absolute. But while medical treatment will uniformly be ordered where necessary to save the life of a child,[17] courts have divided over the question of whether the state may order medical treatment to avoid grievous injury short of death.[18] Of all fifty states, only Oklahoma expressly limits the scope of exemption on religious grounds, confining it to cases in which there is no danger of permanent physical damage to the child.[19]

In the area of education, states can require children to attend school until they reach a particular age. Parents cannot circumvent this mandate if their only reason for doing so is a purely secular interest in the nurture and education of their children.[20] But, again, it is the Free Exercise clause that enables parents to surmount reasonable state regulation. Amish parents in Wisconsin objected to a law requiring school attendance until the age of sixteen. Accepting the argument that exposure to worldly influence and higher learning would alienate Amish children from God and the life of their church community, the court in *Wisconsin v. Yoder* extended the right of religious parents to determine their own behavior in accordance with their beliefs. The court ruled that religious parents have a liberty to control the lives and minds of their children; to keep their children to themselves, isolated from outside influences; and to make their children the type of persons they want them to be in light of their (the parents') own religious beliefs. We do not know what the children's wishes were, as their voices were not heard and were not considered.[21] Such cases highlight the way in which children are used as a conduit for the religious expression, cultural identity, and aspirations of their parents.

Parental rights can usurp some rights that children may ordinarily have. Parents can commit their children to state mental facilities without formal adversary proceedings, thus circumscribing the child's due process rights.[22] Parents are subject to only minimal state requirements when establishing religious schools or home schooling because the state is not empowered to save a child from his or her parents by ensuring the child's growth toward intellectual autonomy.[23] Biological parents, whether married or not, have an equal privacy interest in having contact with and caring for their children.[24] But our jurisprudence is silent with respect to the child's interest in maintaining his or her connection to certain biological, actual, or perceived parental relationships. Federal courts are split on the right of the child to create and maintain sibling relationships. Nevertheless, many states have encouraged the continuation of such affiliations by expanding custody and visitation statutes to include grandparents, great-grandparents, stepparents, and siblings.[25] Unfortunately, foster parents are not yet included in this group even though the Court acknowledges that a deeply loving and interdependent relationship between adults and children in their care may exist in the absence of a blood relationship.[26] Interestingly, some state courts are requiring biological parents to manifest actual nurture and care of the child when considering custody requests[27] and are even allowing children to petition for termination of parental rights for failure to provide such care.[28]

Historically, the status of children, like the status of women in society, was equivalent to that of animals and slaves, and all came under the control of the patriarch of the household. While the subjugation of women and African Americans lost its force with the recognition that their capacities are as great as those of adult white males, children continued to be perceived as naturally suited for governance by others. Fueled by the "child-saving" era during the early part of the twentieth century, the perceived incapacity of childhood was extended to include adolescence. As a result, semi-independent youths who earlier had performed adult economic roles and claimed some personal freedom, found themselves increasingly under the watchful eye of adults.[29] Legally, childhood extends from birth through age eighteen, and children are not considered legally responsible persons. It is notable that the few exceptions to this legal incapacity, such as obtaining a driver's license, are based on the recognition that children's capacities change with age.

In short, in a legal system that is predominantly adult-centered, the status of children within the family is essentially subordinate to that of their parents. However, through the years, there have been those who have argued that children are not merely the chattels of their parents. The legal system has struggled long and hard with finding a rationale that would allow it to mitigate the effects of the possessive and patriarchal model of children as property — a situation which put many children at risk when parental decisions did not foster the child's welfare. What emerged was the legal standard of the best interest of the child — that judicial decisions must further the child's best interest[30] This standard has been criticized as being indeterminate,[31] as allowing white male judges to bring their middle-class biases into custody cases and thereby to favor men over women,[32] and as working against poor and minority families.[33] However, Carl Schneider has concluded that this standard may provide "as reasonable a framework for balancing the advantages of rules and discretion as we are likely to find."[34]

There is no consensus over precisely what should be considered in any specific determination of what is best for a particular child in a particular case. Nevertheless, the standard rightfully retains its place in American law as an expression of the need to keep the interests and perspectives of the child foremost in the minds of adult decision-makers.[35] Barbara Bennett Woodhouse suggests that the cure for the indeterminacy of the best interest standard is not to substitute the interests of the powerful (parents) but rather to take a closer look at the interests of the powerless (children).[36] What these interests are and how they come to be argued to the Court are both undergoing a transformation. This transformation is not unrelated to changes that I shall now describe.

Changing Conditions and
Changing Perspectives

The ideal American family of married man and woman with two biological children living happily in the suburbs is now recognized as mythical. With teen pregnancies, the higher divorce rate, and increasing single-parent adoptions, one-parent families have become more common. The recognition of same-sex unions presents children with two mommies or two daddies who live together happily. Remarriage of divorced or widowed parents produces the blended family of his, hers, and theirs. It may not be possible for the casual observer to identify who the biological parent is; and for most children it is immaterial. Children identify their parents as simply the people they have been told are their mother and father. It is not uncommon for a young child being raised by grandparents to identify the grandmother as mommy, the grandfather as daddy, and the parent as his or her sibling. One way of putting this is to say that children do not require DNA evidence to give credibility to the relationships they form! To some extent, courts are validating children's perceptions of who their parents are. For example, when a man has held himself out as the father of a child for a significant period of time, the court may disallow genetic testing to disprove his paternity and to exonerate him from a support obligation.[37]

Or it may protect the relationship that has developed between children and their unwed fathers.[38]

Perhaps the most important advance under the rubric of children's rights is the opportunity children are increasingly being given to articulate their own interests. The United States legal system has come to regard the child as neither automatically competent nor automatically incompetent. The American Bar Association has promulgated standards of practice for child advocates in abuse and neglect cases which take the position that the lawyer's primary duty is to protect the legal rights of the child client, and therefore the lawyer owes the same duties of undivided loyalty, confidentiality, and competent representation to the child as to an adult client. Insofar as judicial decisions must take into consideration the expressed preferences that the child articulates, child advocates encourage their young clients to participate in the decision-making process in a manner consistent with their capacities, thus giving credence to the child's voice in the judicial process.

When the nations of the world have gathered to consider the place of children in society, they have agreed that children are fully endowed persons possessing basic human rights.[39] The General Assembly of the United Nations unanimously adopted the United Nations Convention on the Rights of the Child (UNCRC) on November 20, 1989 and opened it for signature on January 26, 1990.[40] Sixty-one nations signed the UNCRC that same day. The Convention went into force on September 2, 1990, and by February 1, 1997, 189 nations had become States Parties, making the UNCRC the most rapidly and widely adopted human rights treaty on record. In view of these facts, it is clear that the consensus of the world community is that familial rights should emphasize children's, rather than their parent's, interests.[41] The UNCRC codifies the view of the international community that children have a right to a cultural heritage (article 30); to appropriate parental care that is consistent with the child's evolving capacities (article 5); to non-separation from parents and to contact with both parents when separation is a result of state action (article 9); to family reunification (article 10); to a standard of living adequate for their full development (article 27); to a secondary education (article 28); and to protection from all forms of abuse and neglect (article 51).

Apart from Somalia, which has no recognized formal government and therefore cannot ratify treaties, only the United States has failed to become a State Party of the UNCRC. Historically, the United States has disavowed the influence of international agreements on its own domestic policy. The U.S. Supreme Court has declared that "the standards of other countries and international human rights instruments are essentially irrelevant. As long as there exists an American consensus, courts should not look to other nation's practices."[42] It is not surprising that customary international law as well has been invoked only rarely in United States courts and is unlikely to produce practical results in the immediate future.[43] Does this mean that international policy and expectations have no influence on United States law? To the contrary, the United States was actively involved in the debate over, and drafting of, the UNCRC, and its provisions can influence our thinking about the directions family law should take within the United States.

A Philosophy of the Child-Centered Family

The best environment for the development and growth of a child is within a protective and caring family. As a matter of social and economic policy, the family is regarded as the appropriate institution to provide love, guidance, and the economic and material needs of the child. Intact and functional families are morally grounded in the conviction that they serve children's interests.[44] Parents who accept the responsibility of centering their role round their children interpret the role of parent broadly and flexibly. These parents see children as individuals with their own interests and concerns and identify with them. They encourage children to share their perceptions and help them to learn to express themselves in the broader society. Such parents are satisfied only when the children have turned out well.[45]

In undertaking to view parents' rights from the perspective of children, Woodhouse coined the term "generational justice" to describe a just ordering of relations between adults and children, one that is grounded in and gives normative consequence to children's needs, values, dignity, and experiences, as opposed to the legal tradition of excluding such experience and perception as quintessentially irrational.[46] Justice for all generations means that the caretaker or parent does not own children, but is responsible for their daily nurture and care and for directing their lives to the extent necessary for them to become caring and loving participants in the relationships which are family.

Families come in many shapes and sizes and increasingly may be headed by two parents of the same sex, by stepparents, by foster parents, or by a single parent. Families are not static, but are full of life and vigor, pain and need. The dynamics of the relationships between members of a family unit change as each member experiences his or her own life and shares that experience with the others. To the extent that the adults exhibit an unselfish, loyal, and benevolent concern for each other, the children are promoted in their own growth and development. The love of family members for each other nourishes the child and creates an environment for growth. As adults care for the child, they build relationships and intimacy with each other and within the family unit.[47] Adults in such families understand that their relationships constitute a large part of the self-conception of young children.[48] It is the critical functions of the family — readying the child for school, fixing meals, taking the child to extracurricular activities, accompanying the child to health care appointments, nursing the child when sick, arranging alternate care, counseling and disciplining — rather than its specific configuration that nurtures children.

Social scientists tell us that children regularly need activities with people with whom they can develop a strong, mutual, emotional, and visceral attachment. When the adults who are close to a child are committed to the latter's well-being and development, the child grows intellectually, emotionally, socially, and morally.[49] It is the role and responsibility of parents to foster the growth of the child in all these respects. Furthermore, good parents should be assessed not only on the extent to which they are tangibly involved with their children, but also on their commitment to, and cooperation with, each other. This definition of parenthood within a family system recognizes the fact that children need parents who take responsibility for each other's well-being as well as for that of their children.

Whatever form a family may take, successful care-giving is more easily accomplished in an environment of relationships of mutual care and interdependence. But families cannot fully nurture children in isolation. In the ideal, a wider community of care supports families as well.[50] The old African proverb that it takes a village to raise a child is true today more than ever. Caregivers need other adults to offer additional guidance to their children, to provide time-out, and to encourage and appreciate the relationship of the caregiver and the child. They also need a work environment that recognizes and supports their parenting obligation with family leave policies, flex-time, and liberal policies toward missed work because of the child's activities or illnesses.

The community contains innumerable resources for the family. The extended family of grandparents and other relatives provides a perspective rooted in the child's cultural history. Neighbors and friends can offer additional attention to each other's children, and a watchful eye when parents are not available. Corporate day care programs combine quality child care with convenience: parent and child travel together to their required daily activities, and they are in close proximity during their separation from each other. Spending time with the families of friends of a different racial or cultural background expands the child's views. Adult participation in community sports or service programs allows parents to care for every child by providing safe, secure activities beyond their own doorstep. Religious organizations provide families with a moral perspective and support against social injustices.

While many concerns have been expressed about the effect of domestic violence upon children, little research has been done to determine the best way to nurture them through such trauma. Often immediate removal from the home environment seems to be the only option. Yet, being separated from the non-abusive, victimized parent may further traumatize the child. Moreover, the violence, hostility, poverty, and neglect suffered by the non-abusive caregiver can have a deleterious effect on children. Consequently, social and political policy must address these problems with an eye toward children's total well-being, and with a view to encouraging their healthy development.

Responsible parenthood is an obligation that arises because a child has been brought into existence. Any authority that parents exercise in speaking and acting for a dependent child is not vested in them automatically; it is earned by dint of active nurture and care of that child. Precisely how they exercise their authority depends both on what they judge to be in the child's best interests and on the resources available to them through a nurturing community. But further, their authority over the child must be limited by the latter's emerging capacities, for only thus can the dependent child grow into a responsible adult.[51] In short, a philosophy of the child-centered family is one in which each parent is seen as taking responsibility for actively raising their children, rather than possessing proprietary rights over them. In the child-centered family, the needs, experiences, and capacities of children come first.

A Child-Centered Jurisprudence

Disputes involving children and their families raise delicate, complex, and troubling questions of social policy, legal doctrine, and psychological theories of child rearing. Certain practical problems in regulating the behavior of parents toward their children compound the difficulties of dealing with such disputes within the provisions of the law. Nevertheless, there are many ways in which the legal system can refocus family conflicts and give validity and support to the development of the child.

Whenever parties come before the court to resolve family problems, they are best served by having legal counsel to represent them. This is particularly important for children, who may not normally be seen as parties to the proceeding. For example, when parents are pitted against each other in a contested dispute over custody, the child is the hapless victim. By appointing a guardian *ad litem* for the child, the court can more readily assess what the child's needs and experiences are. It should not be presumed that all children have been programmed to hate the non-custodial parent, nor that awarding custody on the basis of a presumed or stated preference of the child will invite continued outrageous antagonistic behavior on the part of parents.[52] Similarly, in dependency cases, the child advocate can help children testify as to whether the proposed plan for termination of parental rights or reunification with the parent is what the child feels will best serve his or her needs. The advocate can also prepare professional testimony that will support the child's position and give credence to the child's position.

A legal system that approaches children developmentally would recognize both the capacity for change within the family and the child's changing capacity. In the prosecution of child sex crimes, children as young as three years of age have been shown to be competent to testify against a perpetrator, yet in family court the same child is often not given any credibility in describing his or her own life. As children develop, their potential — intellectual, physical, and emotional — changes.[53] They must be given the opportunity to exercise their rights in a manner consistent with their capabilities.

It should not be assumed that children do not know what is in their best interest. But advocates might make this assumption unless they get to know their clients. Regardless of age, children can express their relationships with their caregivers, whether in words or "body language" or both. As a child advocate, I frequently make home visits to my clients. On one initial visit to a pre-verbal toddler, I recall watching her playfully avoid her mother's requests to get dressed, and the mother's sympathetic efforts to gain compliance. It was obvious that despite allegations of neglect, this child and her mother were connected in a positive way.

Advocates for children must listen carefully to the perceptions and wishes of the child in dependency, termination, and custody matters, and propose solutions to accommodate the child's needs. Lawyers for older children should assume the same role as they would with an adult client and give credit to the child's voice in the judicial process. The twelve-year-old boy who is despairing for his mother may well be safe returning to her care despite the fact that severe punishment of his younger sister resulted in an abuse proceeding. Perhaps the boy, being older, is better able to protect himself, and can draw on the loving relationship he has with his mother. Each case must be judged on its merits, each child must be heard in his or her own right.

Assuming a child-centered philosophy, it is possible to fashion a jurisprudence that supports families and children. Such a jurisprudence could be influenced by the philosophy underlying the legal systems of continental Europe which, contrary to the United States view,

> have imagined the human person not only as a free, self-sustaining individual, but also as a being defined in part through his or her relations with others. The individual is envisioned as situated within family and community; within the legal and social unit of family, rights are viewed as inseparable from corresponding responsibilities and...[p]ersonal values are regarded as higher than social values, but as rooted in them.[54]

For a child-centered philosophy to work, United States law must be reshaped to reinforce two ends or values: parental dispositions toward generosity and other-directedness, and community responsibility toward supporting families. Expectations for parents must be high; but room should be left for them to accept responsibility for their children in the true sense of the word. In custody matters, parents should be forced to state their claims from the perspective of each parent-child relationship.[55] Judicial decisions should be made after evaluating those claims on the basis of the following considerations. First, the court should take account of the child's report of the parent-child relationship. Second, an assessment should be made as to which connections between parent and child are most important to validate. Third, both parents should be called upon to demonstrate a sense of responsibility for, and commitment to, the quality of the relationship with the child. Furthermore, in my view, the policies of the court should be based on the premise that a continuous history of day-to-day care-giving and interaction is more important to the child than biological parenthood, and that the experience of carrying a baby for nine months and giving it birth establishes a greater connection to the child than does biological fatherhood.

Relationships lie at the heart of our social and individual beings. They should be viewed not as trophies that can be earned, or as commodities subject to barter or exchange, but as opportunities given to us to express who we are.[56] Legal rulings affecting children should all be based on the character and quality of the relationship of caregiver or parent with the child. If the law were to support responsible decision-making in the interests of the child, every courthouse would make mandatory mediation programs available, as well as programs that educate parents about the effects of divorce on children. The role of law in forming the social context within which parents might internalize high ideals for responsibility and voluntarily proceed to act upon them is a tricky one. Nevertheless it is an effort which should be pursued.

A United States legal system founded on a jurisprudence of the child-centered family would emphasize the interests of children. It would recognize their need for affiliation and support, for nurture and care, for respect and encouragement to grow into responsible adults. Such a system would encourage joint decision-making, negotiation, and mediation (except when there is domestic violence or abuse), rather than litigation of disputes, and would require the child's voice to be included in the process. However, while our legal system can encourage behaviors toward each other that are the foundation of a secure and loving home, it cannot mandate them; in the final analysis, the basis for such behaviors lies in responsible relationships within the child-centered family.

Turning Theory into Practice

When those who are involved in the dependency system are genuinely focused on the child, truly remarkable things can happen. The child service agency, child advocate, and parent can work together to support and nurture the healthy development of the child client. I shall close with a brief narrative of a case — one that is still ongoing at the time of writing — which illustrates the point.

I have represented a ten-year-old little girl, who I will call Alicia, in dependency court for the past four years. She entered foster care at age three because of suspected sexual abuse by her father. Being too young to discuss what had happened to her, she acted out the effects of trauma — sexualized play, dislike of being touched, extreme anger and aggression at caregivers and other children, and enuresis and soiling after contact with her father. Her mother has struggled with drug abuse and mental health problems, and several times has relapsed after being rehabilitated.

At the time of writing, the mother has been in a treatment program for a year, and has not taken addictive drugs throughout this period. The family history shows her father incarcerated and under a protection order to stay away from Alicia. Thus she has not seen him since her mother surreptitiously allowed him to visit during family visitation three years ago. Her mother was unable to protect Alicia from abuse and, because of her addiction, has often not been able to meet Alicia's basic needs for food or shelter. As a result, Alicia moved from foster home to foster home. Finally, two years ago, she entered a therapeutic program where she has been able to bond with a stable family who encourages her contact with her mother and siblings.

Federal law now requires plans for children such as Alicia to focus on making arrangements of a permanent nature.[57] Despite her mother's efforts to stay sober, maintain housing, keep steady employment, and visit regularly, she has not taken any initiative in understanding Alicia's emotional needs, participating in her special education plan, or addressing the question of how to resolve Alicia's feelings that she had been abandoned. Any hopes of the mother dealing with her daughter's emotional issues are years away. In view of all this, the mother stated initially, in the midst of discussions about the involuntary termination of her parental rights, that she would relinquish her rights voluntarily. But subsequently she decided to contest the termination and the fact that the goal had been changed to adoption. Alicia herself wanted her foster family to adopt her. Thus, when a new caseworker and new attorneys for both parents were appointed, mother, child, and agency stood in opposition concerning the planning goal and whether the agency should proceed with the termination.

It looked as if the case was headed for a contested hearing, with acknowledged drawbacks for both mother and child, whatever the result. If, on the one hand, Alicia was successful, then she would be alienated from her mother by virtue of having had to testify against her. Moreover, the mother would be marked with having lost one child, thereby being more vulnerable to losing others. If, on the other hand, the mother "won," there was no assurance that reunification would occur any time soon. Rather than march headlong toward a contested hearing, it was agreed to interview parent and child and attempt to negotiate the needs of both. Alicia was adamant that she wanted to be adopted by her foster family. Moreover, since family visits were often stressful for her, Alicia wanted to decide how often she would see her mother. Mother, enlivened by her new attorney, was initially asserting her right to reunification with a newfound vigor. (Unfortunately, father's interest remained undetermined, as his whereabouts could not be ascertained after he left prison, despite efforts by the agency to do so.)

Finally, a face-to-face meeting was arranged to gain unanimity for a plan for Alicia's future. Encouraged by her foster mother, her therapist, and her advocate, Alicia made an impassioned plea, assuring her mother of her love, but imploring her to agree to an adoption. "Giving me up will probably be the hardest thing you'll ever do, but it will show me, more than anything else in the world, how much you love me. My foster mom tells me that her job is to give me roots, or the rules of living, and wings so that when I am ready, I can fly away. I need you to give me wings now, Mom." Alicia continued, "I don't want you to say goodbye. I always want you to be part of my life. I want you to come to my soccer games and to my birthday parties. I want to call you on the phone and tell you how my day has been. I want you to continue loving me."[58]

Although Alicia's mother entered the meeting resolved to maintain the legal relationship with her daughter, Alicia was able to present her own adoption as a wonderful gift that only her mother could give. When her mother learned that a voluntary relinquishment of Alicia would have no bearing on the status of two other children currently in foster care, she was inclined to go along with it.

I wish I could say that Alicia's case was resolved during the first meeting, but unfortunately it was not. Alicia's mother was still wary about the implications of voluntarily relinquishing her parental rights where Alicia was concerned. It took several more meetings, during which Alicia remained steadfast in her position, before her mother finally began to see the situation from Alicia's viewpoint.

She also visited with Alicia and saw the bonds that had grown between her child and the foster family. She witnessed the foster mother's involvement with Alicia's school, her Girl Scout troop, and her soccer team, and acknowledged that Alicia seemed to be much happier with her foster family than she had been with her. At first these visits were a double-edged sword. Although the mother understood that Alicia was living in a safe, secure environment, her own feelings of inadequacy interfered with her ability to make a decision. More recently, however, she has been able to focus on discussions about Alicia's future and what's best for her daughter, rather than seeing a relinquishment as a personal attack on her adeptness as a mother. Additionally, she now understands that if the matter evolves into a court proceeding and her parental rights are involuntarily terminated, she has a greater potential of losing her two children who are in foster care. At the time of writing, there is no question that she is still struggling with her decision. So far, all concerned are willing to give her some more time, albeit limited, to continue informal negotiations rather than run pell-mell into a hearing and risk having her rights terminated involuntarily.

Alicia's case might not be closed. But thus far, it illustrates how the legal system can support the development of the child by approaching conflicts between parents and children on the basis of concern, openness, trust, and negotiation, rather than antagonism and the litigation of disputes. Such an approach not only emphasizes the interests of children, it also grants them a voice in the decision-making process, and holds out the best promise of reconciling the rights of children and parents.

Notes

1. Cited in James MacGregor Burns and Stewart Burns, *A People's Charter: The Pursuit of Rights in America* (New York: Vintage Books, 1991), p. 454.

2. Katherine T. Bartlett, "Re-Expressing Parenthood," *Yale Law Journal* 98 (1988), p. 304.

3. James Boyd White, "Law as Rhetoric, Rhetoric as Law: The Art of Cultural and Communal Life," *University of Chicago Law Review* 52 (1985), pp. 684-702.

4. Roger J. R. Levesque, "International Children's Rights Grow Up: Implications for American Jurisprudence and Domestic Policy," *California Western International Law Journal* 24 (1994), p. 228.

5. James G. Dwyer, "Parent's Religion and Children's Welfare: Debunking the Doctrine of Parent's Rights," *California Law Review* 82 (1994), pp. 1371-1447.

6. Barbara Bennett Woodhouse, "Hatching the Egg: A Child-Centered Perspective on Parents' Rights," *Cardozo Law Review* 14 (1993), p. 1809.

7. Ibid., pp. 1809, 1811-12.

8. Bartlett, "Re-Expressing Parenthood," p. 298.

9. Suzanna Sherry, "An Essay Concerning Toleration," *Minnesota Law Review* 71 (1987), p. 964 cited in Bartlett, "Re-Expressing Parenthood," p. 294.

10. Bartlett, "Re-Expressing Parenthood," p. 312, n. 79.

11. Carl Schneider, "Rights Discourse and Neonatal Euthanasia," *California Law Review* 76 (1988), p. 162-64, quoted in Bartlett, "Re-Expressing Parenthood," p. 298.

12. *Meyer v. Nebraska*, 262 U.S. 390 (1923).

13. *Pierce v. Society of Sisters*, 268 U.S. 510 (1925).

14. *Prince v. Massachusetts*, 321 U.S. 158 (1944).

15. Dwyer, "Parent's Religion and Children's Welfare," p. 1382.

16. Ibid., pp. 1396-97. The United States Department of Health, Education, and Welfare implemented the Child Abuse Prevention and Treatment Act of

1974 that mandated such exemptions. States have effectively limited the scope of these exemptions to non-fatal cases by successfully prosecuting parents under criminal statutes other than their abuse and neglect laws. But this backdoor approach has come under attack on due process grounds and courts have overturned criminal convictions finding that the religious exemptions in neglect laws lead parents to believe that they are free not to seek medical care for their children so that the laws of the state as a whole do not give parents unambiguous or fair notice of their legal duty.

17. *Jehovah's Witnesses v. King County Hospital*, 278 F. Supp. 488 (W.D. Wash. 1967), *aff'd*, 390 U.S. 598 (1968) (mem.).

18. *State v. Miskimens*, 490 N.E. 2d 931 (1984) and *Brown v. Stone*, 378 So 2d 218 (Miss. 1979), *cert. denied*, 449 U.S. 887 (1980).

19. Dwyer, "Parent's Religion and Children's Welfare," p. 1397, n. 97.

20. *Wisconsin v. Yoder*, 406 U.S. 205 (1972).

21. Levesque, "International Children's Rights Grow Up," p. 204.

22. *Parham v. J. R.*, 442 U.S. 584, 603-04 (1979).

23. *New Life Baptist Church Academy v. Town of East Longmeadow*, 666 F. Supp. 293, 318-19 (D. Mass. 1987) *rev'd on other grounds*, 885 F.2d 940 (1st Cir. 1989), *cert. denied*, 494 U.S. 1066 (1990).

24. *Caban v. Mohammed*, 441 U.S. 380 (1979); *Stanley v. Illinois*, 405 U.S. 645 (1972); *Santosky v. Kramer*, 455 U.S. 745 (1982); and *Lear v. Robertson*, 463 U.S. 248 (1983).

25. Gilbert A. Holmes, "The Tie That Binds: The Constitutional Right of Children to Maintain Relationships with Parent-Like Individuals," *Maryland Law Review* 53 (1994), p. 363.

26. *Smith v. Organization of Foster Families for Equality and Reform*, 431 U.S. 816, 844 (1977).

27. *Doe v. Roe (In re Adoption of Doe)*, 543 So. 2d 741 (Fla.), *cert. denied*, 493 U.S. 964 (1989).

28. See for example, Scott A. Cannon, "Finding Their Own 'Place to Be': What Gregory Kingsley's and Kimberly Mays' 'Divorces' From Their Parents Have Done for Children's Rights," *Loyola Law Review* 39 (1994), pp. 837-856.

29. Levesque, "International Children's Rights Grow Up," pp. 199-200.

30. Woodhouse, "Hatching the Egg," p. 1756.

31. See, for example: Andrea Charlow, "Awarding Custody: The Best Interests of the Child and Other Fictions," *Yale Law & Policy Review* 5 (1987), pp. 267-290; Jon Elster, "Solomonic Judgments: Against the Best Interest of the Child," *University of Chicago Law Review* 54 (1987), pp. 12-16; Robert H. Mnookin, "Child Custody Adjudication: Judicial Functions in the Face of Indeterminacy," *Law & Contemporary Problems* 39 (Summer 1975), pp. 257-61.

32. See, for example, Rena K. Uviller, "Father's Rights and Feminism: The Maternal Presumption Revisited," *Harvard Women's Law Journal* 1 (1978), pp. 121-26.

33. See, for example, Joseph Goldstein, Anna Freud, and Albert Solnit, *Before the Best Interests of the Child* (New York: Free Press, 1976), and Michael S. Wald,

"State Intervention on Behalf of 'Neglected' Children: Standards for Removal of Children from Their Homes, Monitoring the Status of Children in Foster Care, and Termination of Parental Rights," *Stanford Law Review* 28 (1976), p. 629, quoted in Bartlett, "Re-Expressing Parenthood," p. 303.

34. Carl E. Schneider, "Discretion, Rules, and Law: Child Custody and the UMDA's Best-Interest Standard," *Michigan Law Review* 89 (1991), p. 2291.

35. Jane Ellis, "The Best Interests of the Child," in *Children's Rights in America: U.N. Convention on the Rights of the Child Compared with United States Law*, eds, Cynthia Price Cohen and Howard A. Davidson (Washington DC: American Bar Association, 1990), p. 4.

36. Woodhouse, "Hatching the Egg," p. 1827.

37. See for example, *Miscovitch v. Miscovitch*, 720 A.2d 764 (Pa.Super. 1998).

38. *Caban v. Mohammed*, 441 U.S. 380 (1979).

39. League of Nations O.J. Spec. Supp. 21 (1924). Children's rights first attracted international attention with the adoption of the Declaration of Geneva (the Geneva Convention) by the Fifth Assembly of the League of Nations. The Declaration emphasized protecting children's basic material needs. It required children to be the first to receive relief in time of distress, to be fed when hungry, helped when sick, reclaimed when delinquent, sheltered when orphaned, and protected against exploitation. Additionally, the child was given affirmative rights including to be put in a position to earn a livelihood and to be brought up so he will devote his (sic) talents to his fellow men. Principles I through IV delineate the special protections afforded to children.

40 The UNCRC resulted from ten years of drafting to embody the values contained in the United Nations Declaration of the Rights of the Child.

41. Levesque, "International Children's Rights Grow Up," p. 195.

42. *Stanford v. Kentucky*, 109 S.Ct. 2969, 2975, n. 1 (1989).

43. Levesque, "International Children's Rights Grow Up," p. 222, quoting Nadine Strossen, "Recent U.S. and International Judicial Protection of Individual Rights: A Comparative Legal Process and Proposed Synthesis," *Hastings Law Journal* 41 (1990), pp. 814-23.

44. Dwyer, "Parent's Religion and Children's Welfare," p. 1378.

45. Bartlett, "Re-Expressing Parenthood," p. 300.

46. Woodhouse, "Hatching the Egg," p. 1752, n.10.

47. Ibid., pp. 1761, 1822.

48. Dwyer, "Parent's Religion and Children's Welfare," p. 1378.

49. Urie Bronfenbrenner, "Discovering What Families Do," in David Blankenhorn et al, eds., *Rebuilding the Nest: A New Commitment to the American Family* (Milwaukee, WI: Family Service America, 1990), p. 29.

50. Ibid., p. 33.

51. Woodhouse, "Hatching the Egg," pp. 1818-19.

52. Marian L. Faupel, "The 'Baby Jessica Case' and the Claimed Conflict Between Children's and Parents' Rights," *Wayne Law Review* 40 (1994), p. 305.

53. See, James Garbarino, "The Child's Evolving Capacities," in *Children's Rights in America*, p. 19.

54. Mary Ann Glendon, *Abortion and Divorce in Western Law* (Cambridge, MA: Harvard University Press, 1987), quoted in Bruce C. Hafen, "Individualism and Autonomy in Family Law: The Waning of Belonging," *Brigham Young University Law Review* (1991), p. 6.

55. Bartlett, "Re-expressing Parenthood," pp. 301, 295.

56. Ibid., p. 337.

57. Public Law 105-89, 42 USCA Section 675, *et seq.* On November 19, 1997, President Clinton signed into law the Adoption and Safe Families Act of 1997 (ASFA). Each state was required to implement provisions of the federal statute to continue receiving federal funding. The purpose of the legislation is to improve the safety of children, to promote adoption and other permanent homes for children who need them, and to support families.

58. Case Notes.

Chapter 9

The Right to Be Heard:
The Child as a Legal Person[1]

Lewis Pitts

The legal status of children in the United States today is comparable to that of women and African Americans in the past. Children are denied basic rights that, as persons rather than property, they ought to be accorded under the Constitution. The call for children's rights includes a broad spectrum of rights, some of which are more controversial than others. This essay will focus on what I call "first stage" rights. By this I mean the child's right to protection in cases involving abuse, neglect, abandonment, and custody. I shall argue that children, like other persons with interests, have the right to be heard in such cases, which means that they should have due process rights of access to court and representation through independent counsel who present the views and preferences that children themselves express. The right to due process is essential for securing protection rights for children. For, in the words of the United States Supreme Court, the right of access to court is "the right conservative of all other rights."[2] Furthermore, due process rights are not only basic; they are urgent, given that the mistreatment of children in the United States amounts to a "national emergency."[3]

In theory, Supreme Court rulings have established that the child is a person under the Constitution and possesses constitutional rights. In practice, however, children are routinely treated as property in the legal system and denied their protective due process rights.[4] After briefly clarifying the status of children under the Constitution, I shall illustrate the gap between theory and practice with four case studies taken from my first-hand experience as a legal activist and practicing attorney.

These case studies also demonstrate the harm to which children can be exposed if their voices are not heard, which is why they need due process rights. In this connection, I shall explain how, paradoxically, the principle of the best interests of the child can work against the child's best interests. I shall then discuss some of the fears and misconceptions that underlie the resistance to granting children protective due process rights. Finally, I shall conclude by returning to the point with which I began, that the position of children in the United States is analogous to that of other groups whose civil rights historically have been denied. I shall mention two initiatives that can and should be taken to enhance the status of children and improve their lives: passage of a constitutional amendment that provides for due process and protection rights for children, and ratification of the United Nations Convention on the Rights of the Child (UNCRC).

The Constitutional Status of Children

On paper, in court and statutory language, children are persons with constitutional rights. The 1967 Supreme Court decision of *In re Gault* stated that "neither the Fourteenth Amendment nor the Bill of Rights is for adults alone," and that "[u]nder our Constitution, the condition of being a boy does not justify a kangaroo court."[5] Two years later, in the famous arm band case, *Tinker v. Des Moines Community School District*, the Court stated that children are persons and "possessed of fundamental rights which the state must respect."[6] In 1972, in *Wisconsin v. Yoder*, the Court wrote, "These children are 'persons' within the meaning of the Bill of Rights. We have so held over and over again."[7] In 1976, the Court reiterated its position in *Planned Parenthood v. Danforth*: "Constitutional rights do not mature and come into being magically only when one attains the state-defined age of majority. Minors, as well as adults, are protected by the Constitution and possess constitutional rights."[8] Moreover, every state constitution, as well as the United States Constitution itself, contains language declaring that each "person" shall enjoy due process and equal protection of the law.

In 1979, the American Bar Association (ABA) adopted stringent standards for lawyers representing children. These standards, reflecting the constitutional status of children, treat them as legal persons entitled to due process. They state:

Justice requires that all parties (including children as well as parents and other adults) subject to juvenile and family court proceedings are represented. Children and their parents (or guardians) should have independent counsel at all stages of legal proceedings concerning charges of delinquency, status offenses, and cases involving child abuse, neglect, custody and adoption, except in temporary emergencies where immediate participation of counsel cannot be arranged.[9]

However, if "justice requires" legal representation for children when their essential interests are at stake, then justice is not being done. In their 1993 report, the ABA Presidential Working Group on the Unmet Legal Needs of Children and Their Families found as follows: "Our society is failing to protect its children and fails them even more once they are in crisis...Children too frequently find themselves before courts without benefit of counsel, despite their constitutional and statutory rights to counsel in many kinds of cases."[10]

This situation is not new. There has been a long history in the United States of treating children as mere objects of court proceedings, rather than as participants with rights and interests to be weighed and respected alongside competing adult rights and interests. In the following section, I shall illustrate this point with four examples taken from my own experience as a lawyer.

Case Studies

Gregory K

In 1992, Gregory K., who was ten years old, had been left "double-parked" in the Florida foster care system well beyond the statutory time limit. The child protective system (CPS) had custody of Gregory, and the court appointed a guardian *ad litem* to represent his best interests.[11] Gregory was placed with a foster family with whom he wished to continue living. The family was ready to adopt him, but the CPS refused to initiate "termination of parental rights" proceedings against his biological parents.[12] So, Gregory found a lawyer to represent him. His lawyer petitioned for parental rights to be terminated and for an order of adoption to be granted. During that time, Gregory's appointed guardian *ad litem* did not meet with him or speak to him about his needs or desires. Predictably, the lawyer for the CPS moved to dismiss Gregory's petition, claiming he lacked standing and capacity to bring a legal action.

Gregory (who could be called the Rosa Parks of the children's rights movement) aroused national attention by his claim that he had a right to be heard on such matters as his own safety, liberty from state custody, and his desire for a permanent loving family. As Director of the Legal Action Project of the National Committee for the Rights of the Child, I filed and argued an *amicus* brief before the trial judge, opposing the CPS motion to dismiss.[13] The judge, denying the motion to dismiss, accepted the petition for termination of parental rights to be brought on for a hearing. The trial was nationally televised on the fledgling Court TV network, and the judge, based on strong evidence, ordered parental rights terminated. Gregory's adoption was approved, and he became part of a wonderful family.

Following the trial, there was a storm of controversy. Critics described the decision as one in which a child was allowed to "divorce" his parents. CPS appealed, and the Florida Court of Appeals reversed the decision, holding that Gregory did not have the capacity to bring the action. There is, however, a twist to the story. CPS successfully filed their *own* petition for termination of parental rights with the trial court. Consequently, the Court of Appeals was able to allow Gregory's adoption to stand, based upon CPS's petition. In short, the court recognized that Gregory had a meritorious claim, but denied his right to knock at the courthouse door on the grounds that he was a minor.[14]

The Grissom Children

In 1992, the three Grissom teenagers were living with their mother in Missouri. The parents were divorced. Under a divorce and custody order, the children were supposed to visit their father. However, they refused to do so, testifying that he abused them. The father sought to have their mother held in contempt for disobeying the court order. The trial judge, without notice to either parent, and without any legal representation for the children, placed the children under the "custody and control" of the Division of Family Services, leaving physical custody with the mother, but threatening state custody if she did not make the children visit their father. When the children renewed their contentions of abuse and refused to visit their father, a hearing was scheduled with the real possibility that the children would be taken from their mother and ordered into a foster home or institutional placement. Along with local counsel, I moved on behalf of the children to intervene because their fundamental liberty and safety interests were at stake. Not only was the motion denied, but the trial judge sanctioned both counsel for filing a frivolous motion. An appeal was filed, and the

Missouri Court of Appeals affirmed the denial of the motion to intervene (although reversing the sanctions).[15]

Fortunately, following anguished negotiations, the children were kept from being placed in state custody, nor did they have to endure visits with their father. However, the court decision remains, denying children their right to be heard when their fundamental interests are at risk.

Samantha

Samantha was nine years old when the CPS in Delaware petitioned for termination of parental rights. Four years earlier, her biological mother, a long time substance abuser, had abandoned her and moved to another state with a substance-abusing boyfriend. In the intervening years, Samantha went from one foster home to another, in one of which she was the victim of abuse. Eventually, she entered the home of a stable family that wanted to adopt her. At the termination of parental rights hearing, her biological mother was represented by a lawyer. Samantha's own interests were represented by a court-appointed lay advocate with a lawyer.

Samantha wanted to be adopted, but her testimony and desires were never heard by the court. Her advocate urged, against Samantha's wishes, that Samantha be sent to live with her mother who was still in drug rehabilitation. The CPS attorney did not present the case for termination of parental rights vigorously, and the judge ordered her to live with her mother. The CPS attorney allowed the time for appeal to expire.

Recognizing that Samantha's voice had not been heard in court, a handful of Delaware advocates for children's rights took up her cause. I was approached, and drafted a simple four-page *pro se* complaint for a writ of certiorari to the Delaware Supreme Court, asking the court to review her case.[16] The complaint pointed out that Samantha's constitutional right to safety had been denied, and that she had a liberty interest in maintaining her relationship with the new family with whom she had been living. It also asserted that she was the real party in interest and had a fundamental due process right to court access. Samantha read the complaint, corrected certain factual statements, and signed the document *pro se*. With the help of the local advocates for children's rights, she filed the complaint with the Delaware Supreme Court.

The morning after Samantha filed her complaint, details of her unhappy story and her efforts to seek legal redress were front-page news in the statewide newspaper, and were reported in newspapers in other states. Her story was featured that same morning on ABC's Good Morning America with a live interview of Samantha.

The Delaware Supreme Court accepted Samantha's complaint and reviewed the case. Seventeen days later, the court issued an order declaring:

> It would thus appear that as a matter of statutory entitlement, under Delaware law, a child who is the subject of the termination proceedings may not institute an appeal in the child's own name. This is not to say that the child, whose very future as a member of a family unit may be in the balance, is not an interested party...As an interested party in the termination proceedings, the child's right to be heard must be protected...The [court-appointed advocate], like [the CPS], claims that it acted in Samantha's best interest, but that claim is open to significant doubt...A Guardian ad Litem, if true to the role, must assume a role closer to the child's wishes, while affording the minor the benefit of the guardian's counsel and advice.[17]

The court remanded the case for another hearing where Samantha would finally have a chance to be heard. Her story shows that in order to be heard, she had to overcome the representations made on her behalf by her court-appointed advocate — who was, in effect, her adversary.

Chris B.

Chris, a ten-year-old deaf boy, had been severely neglected and sexually abused by his mother and stepfather. For six years, he was a ward of North Carolina, during which time he lived with a wonderful foster family that included other deaf children. The family intended to adopt him. Chris showed clear signs of Reactive Attachment Disorder, and for over ten months his foster mother pleaded with the CPS and the local public mental health center to get appropriate mental health treatment for him. However, the mental health center, operating under stringent managed care techniques, did not evaluate Chris, much less provide treatment. When repeated intra-system advocacy at many levels failed, his foster mother publicized her pleas for mental health and legal services for Chris.

The court had appointed a lay guardian *ad litem* and a staff attorney — known in North Carolina as an "attorney advocate" — for Chris. However, during the six years Chris had been in foster care, his attorney advocate only met with him once — for approximately fifteen minutes — and never visited his foster home. Further, after the foster mother publicly advocated for Chris and consulted with me in my capacity as a lawyer, the attorney advocate filed a motion alleging the foster mother had violated confidentiality rules and harmed the best interest of the child.

I agreed to represent Chris. I met with him out of the foster mother's presence. Communicating through a sign language interpreter, Chris told me that he wanted legal counsel to help him get treatment and to assist him in becoming adopted by his foster family. He signed a retainer agreement for my *pro bono* legal services.[18] I made full oral argument on Chris's behalf, supported by an *amicus* brief written by two experts: a professor of law and a child psychiatrist who specializes in deaf children. Chris had fundamental and protected rights that were being denied, including the right to safety, liberty, and health care under the federal Medicaid law. Nonetheless, he was not given the right to be heard through his retained *pro bono* attorney in the ongoing foster care proceedings.

Soon after, in what appeared to be a retaliatory move against the foster mother for having publicly advocated for Chris to receive treatment and meaningful representation, the CPS decided to remove Chris from his foster family — the only loving family he had ever known. Extraordinary writs to appeal the decision were denied without opinion by both the North Carolina Court of Appeals and the North Carolina Supreme Court. The only opposition to these writs came from Chris's guardian *ad litem*, who hired a private attorney to prepare and file a brief in opposition in the state Supreme Court. The upshot was that Chris was removed from his family of six years and moved to another town. Several weeks later, he was moved once again. At the time of writing, I have no idea where he is, whether he has received appropriate treatment, or how he is doing. Truly, this deaf child was never heard in court.

Two Kinds of Legal
Representation for the Child

These are just some of the many cases of injustice suffered by children in the child welfare system and the court extensions of that system. The crucial issue in such cases is the constitutionally significant difference between two kinds of legal representation for the child: *expressed* interest and *best* interest representation. In the relevant ABA Standards of Practice, the "child's attorney" is defined as "a lawyer who provides legal services for a child and who owes the same duties of undivided loyalty, confidentiality, and competent representation to the child as is due to an adult client."[19] The Commentary to this definition adds, "These standards explicitly recognize that the child is a separate individual with potentially discrete and independent views. To ensure that the child's independent voice is heard, the child's attorney must advocate the child's articulated position." In other words, the "child's attorney" represents the *expressed* interest of the child, as in the traditional attorney-client relationship. In contrast, the role of the lawyer appointed as guardian *ad litem* is "to protect the child's interests without being bound by the child's expressed preferences." (This is also the role of the lawyer appointed to act in conjunction with a lay guardian *ad litem*, as in the cases of Samantha and Chris B.)

The ABA document explains, "The chief distinguishing factor between the two roles is the manner and method to be followed in determining the legal position to be advocated." It is true that the child's attorney "[a]s with any client...may counsel against the pursuit of a particular position sought by the child."[20] It is also true that the lawyer acting as (or with) a guardian *ad litem* should "take the child's point of view into account." But in the latter case, "the child's preferences are not binding, irrespective of the child's age and the ability or willingness of the child to express preferences."[21]

Not only is the difference between these two roles significant constitutionally, but it also has implications for the operation of the judicial system and the well-being of the child. Because Chris B. was denied *pro bono* traditional representation, the factual issues in his case were not fully explored and certain legal arguments were not even presented. His attorney advocate, basing her advocacy on her judgment of what was in Chris's best interest, rather than on Chris's own expressed preferences, ignored or overruled his desire for adoption. Moreover, she did not make the case for additional Medicaid-guaranteed mental health treatment. Without traditional counsel to represent his needs and interests, the fact-finding process in Chris's case was crucially defective. Supreme Court Justice Rehnquist has acknowledged the harm that can be caused to children from a defective fact-finding process:

> The child has an interest in the outcome of the fact-finding hearing independent of that of the parent. To be sure, "the child and his parents share a vital interest in preventing erroneous termination of their natural relationship." But the child's interest in a continuation of the family unit exists only to the extent that such a continuation would not be harmful to

him. An error in the fact-finding hearing that results in a failure to terminate a parent-child relationship that rightfully should be terminated may well detrimentally affect the child.[22]

That Chris was detrimentally affected is an understatement. He suffered re-abuse from his stepfather because of the misguided attempts by the child welfare system to reunify him with his biological parents. He suffered by being "double-parked" in state custody as a foster child for six years and being denied a permanent home. He was traumatized when moved from the foster home in which he had lived for six years to another placement, and again when placed subsequently in yet another home. Had Chris been allowed to have his own attorney, a lawyer who represented his expressed wishes, he might not have suffered the trauma of being removed from the only loving family and home he ever had. As it is, he probably assumes that I abandoned him, since his new placement and location were withheld in the name of confidentiality.

The 1993 ABA report *America's Children at Risk* observes, "Even when children are represented, the representation they receive is sometimes inadequate. Children's cases are often 'processed,' not advocated, and too frequently children's interests are poorly represented."[23] In the light of the case studies presented here, we can conclude that a system that provides for representation of the "best interests" of the child is not necessarily in the child's best interests.

Three Fears and Misconceptions About Children's Protective Due Process Rights

At the heart of this paper is the principle that children, on account of their inherent dignity as human beings, and in view of our society's ethic of care, have rights of protection in cases involving abuse, neglect, abandonment, and custody. I have called these rights "first stage" rights, and I have argued that children have the right to be heard in such cases. Further, I have argued that in order for their voice to be heard, children must have due process rights of access to court and representation through competent, loyal counsel who present the views and preferences that children themselves express.

In theory, children are entitled to such protective due process rights as persons under the Constitution. In practice, however, as illustrated by the four stories I have told, children are routinely treated as mere objects of legal proceedings, with no standing in their own right. This gap between theory and practice is due, in part, to the consternation caused by what appears to be an open-ended call for children's rights. In this section, I shall identify and discuss three such fears and the misconceptions that attend them.

Confusing the Right to Be Heard
with the Right to Decide

When Gregory K., through his lawyer, successfully petitioned for termination of parental rights, there was a widespread fear that the court had granted children the right to "divorce" their parents — as if a child need simply check the "divorce" box on some legal form and leave home as a matter of "right." This fear is based on confusing the child's right to be *heard*, which is an appropriate right in the circumstances, and the child's right to *decide*, which is not at all what Gregory or his lawyer or his supporters maintained. It is the judge, in each case, who must make a decision, having heard from all parties. The claim being advanced in this essay is only that the child's voice, along with the voices of parents and other interested adult parties, should be considered and given the appropriate weight by the judge.

Arguably, in a case like Gregory's, or more generally in cases that affect a child's basic welfare, the child is the person who has most to gain or lose — their security, their safety, their attachment to a loving caretaker, their childhood, even their life. Yet, time and again, courts rule that children do not have standing to bring a legal action to secure their basic needs and interests. A child should be able to knock at the courthouse door seeking protection and have that knock answered.

Confusing the Child's Protection Rights
with Parental Rights

Some people fear that granting children the right to be heard will open the floodgates to lawsuits in which children challenge the basic rights of parents to raise their children as they see fit. However, children's rights are not unbounded. In particular, the call for "first stage" rights does not in any way impugn parental rights to decide when children should go to bed, whether to buy a child an expensive computer game, who should do which household chores, and other matters of family life.

Nor do "first stage" rights imply that a child should be removed from the parental home if they can be placed with someone else who can "do a better job." There are only two circumstances in which the protection rights of the child should limit parental rights of custody. First, where birth parents are abusive, neglectful, or abandon the child, parental rights are balanced by considerations of the child's best interest. Every state has laws that recognize this principle, and these laws are not vulnerable to constitutional challenge by parents. Second, where a child has little or no relationship with the biological parents because the child has been in the long-term custody of third parties and the removal would impose significant trauma to the child, parental rights should be balanced by considerations of the best interest of the child. Several states recognize this principle through statute or case law.[24]

As demonstrated by these exceptions, parents do not have an absolute constitutional right to custody of their children. In fact, probably no right is absolute, and courts routinely balance competing rights. "First stage" rights for children simply mean that in cases of abuse, neglect, abandonment, or long term custody with a third party, children should be recognized by the legal system as persons entitled to have *their* rights weigh in the balance. The corollary of this is that children should have due process rights of access to court and representation through independent counsel.

As regards the child's rights to freedom of association, freedom of expression, and so on, reasonable people differ over the age at which such rights are appropriate and the degree to which such rights exist — if at all. Let the debate continue as expeditiously as possible; but the question of whether children should have the protective due process rights that are the subject of this essay need not and should not wait upon the outcome of that debate.

Confusing Denial of Children's Due Process Rights with Protection of Minors

As minors lacking capacity, children are protected from injuring their own interests and from being exploited by others. This gives rise to the fear that if children are granted due process rights, they will be at risk.

It is true that the ancient legal concept of minors as infants and incompetents is intended as a shield to protect children from their immaturity and vulnerability. Thus, a child cannot enter into a contract to purchase a set of encyclopedias from a door-to-door salesperson; the contract would be deemed void by the court because the child lacked the capacity to enter into it. However, this doctrine is sound as long as it is being used as a shield to protect children. It is obviously illogical to allow the doctrine to become a sword against the child. Yet, that is exactly what happened when the Florida Court of Appeals told Gregory K. that it could not hear his petition because he was only a child and had no capacity to file.

In fact, most, if not all, states have modified the legal concept of capacity when appropriate to protecting children. For example, minors have the capacity to be named as respondents in petitions alleging delinquency, to have legal counsel in such proceedings, and to waive basic constitutional rights to remain silent or to have a trial. Most states recognize a child's capacity to contract for the necessities of life, such as food, clothing, and shelter. Some states recognize the child's right to contract for an education. Given these precedents, it is reasonable to argue that the child should have the capacity to be a party in court and to be represented by an attorney where basic interests are at stake. It is certainly absurd to think that the child is *protected* by being denied the right to be heard.

Existing concepts and principles of law that shield and protect children should not be abandoned. However, they should not be allowed to hurt more than they help. Telling children that they are legally incompetent and must find an adult to act on their behalf simply puts another obstacle in the way of justice — especially when the adult most likely to go to court in their behalf is frequently told that he or she has no standing to bring the matter to court. (Grandparents or adoptive parents are often turned away by the court on this ground.) If the child cannot bring the action, and if the adults who are most involved with the child cannot or will not act either, the child has no recourse; it is like playing a shell game with no pea.

A Civil Rights Approach

The cornerstone of the argument in this essay is that children are persons, not property, and thereby are entitled to the human dignity of due process of law. Over the last thirty years or so, Supreme Court rulings have established the principle that children, under the Constitution, are persons with rights. However, in practice this is not how they are treated in the courts and the child welfare system. Children continue to be treated as mere objects of proceedings or as property, and as incompetents lacking capacity to take legal action in their own behalf.

The position of children today is comparable to the historical treatment of women and African Americans. Both these groups were excluded initially from the founding vision of our nation. In both cases, they were recognized as persons under the Constitution long before society in general, and the legal system in particular, actually treated them as such. The parallel suggests that we should adopt a "civil rights" approach in seeking justice for children. This implies a range of legal and political initiatives. In closing, I shall single out two proposals in particular that embody this approach.

A Constitutional Amendment for Children

The federal Constitution is the document in which we state in general terms the values, protections, and promises of fundamental fairness and equality for which the nation stands. Accordingly, the struggle to extend fair treatment and due process to those groups who were initially excluded has led to the Constitution being amended; for example, the post-Civil War amendments (XIII, XIV, XV) and the Women's Suffrage amendment (XIX). Similarly, the cause of justice for children would be served by an amendment to the Constitution guaranteeing the rights of children to protection and due process.

Unlike the constitutions of many countries, the United States Constitution does not mention children. This leaves their constitutional status uncertain, despite Supreme Court rulings in favor of the principle that children are persons.[25] Noting that "the state of the child in this country...is a disgrace," Chief Justice A. J. Toal of the South Carolina Supreme Court gave the following opinion: "If our state and federal constitutions do not protect our children from abuse and an unstable family life in their formative years, then they should be amended so that they do."[26] Judge Charles D. Gill, former Connecticut Superior Court Judge, has observed, "It is ironic that, although corporations in the United States have long been held to be 'persons,' and thus eligible for constitutional protection, the extent to which children, as individuals, have comparable constitutional rights is still not entirely clear."[27]

In 1988 Judge Gill co-founded the National Task Force for Children's Constitutional Rights. The Task Force seeks to improve the condition of our nation's children through passage of a constitutional amendment. With this end in view, twenty children's advocates from the fields of medicine, education, and law met in Washington, D.C. on October 18, 1997, and drafted the following text:

The rights of persons under the age of eighteen years shall include all the due process and protective rights possessed by those over the age of eighteen years. Such rights may be limited only upon demonstration of a compelling state interest, and any such limitation shall be accomplished by the least intrusive means. Nothing herein shall be construed to diminish any rights of persons under the age of eighteen years, nor to preclude the enhancement of rights of such persons.[28]

The group decided not to include an itemized wish list for children, such as the provision of health care and education. It was agreed that a more general statement of principle regarding due process and protective rights would have the best chance of passage; such rights could be developed and defined subsequently by case law, as with other rights for which the Constitution provides.

The very process of organizing around a constitutional amendment can have a positive effect. Even though the campaign to introduce an Equal Rights amendment for women was not successful, the national dialogue it generated promoted awareness of the unequal treatment of women. Likewise, the campaign for a constitutional amendment for children serves the purpose of educating the public and building broad support for the cause of justice for children.[29]

Ratification of the United Nations Convention on the Rights of the Child (UNCRC)

The UNCRC was adopted by the United Nations General Assembly in 1989. It is a shared global statement of directions and goals for improving the lives of children. Forty-one substantive articles comprehensively define the rights of the child. They include provisions for the protective due process rights that are the subject of this essay; and they go further. Provision is made for education and health care. Certain articles recognize that children, relative to their stage of development, have rights of privacy, as well as freedom of expression, religion, and association. Thus, with the UNCRC we progress from the "first stage" of children's rights to the next.

The United States was active in the ten-year drafting process, and signed the UNCRC in 1995. However, other than Somalia, the United States is the only member of the United Nations that has failed to ratify the Convention. Despite widespread support within the country for ratification, there is also a degree of opposition based, in part, on certain misplaced fears and misconceptions, some of which are similar to the ones discussed in this essay. In particular, contrary to the impression that some people have gained, the UNCRC repeatedly underscores the primary role that parents play in the lives of children and the importance of family life.

Three procedural articles establish a body called the Committee on the Rights of the Child. The role of the Committee is to monitor progress in individual jurisdictions and to foster implementation of the Convention. The Committee has no powers of enforcement, relying on moral and public pressure to promote better policies for children in individual jurisdictions. Despite the lack of enforcement power, ratification would not be an empty gesture. Just as a federal constitutional amendment is an act of commitment on the part of the nation, so ratifying the UNCRC would be an act of commitment by the United States to join the international community in promoting the goals and vision of the Convention.

Ultimately, the two proposals — a constitutional amendment for children and ratification of the UNCRC — go hand in hand. They belong together as pledges to make a better world for children: to accord them the rights that flow from their inherent dignity as human beings, and to rescue them from the "national emergency" that lies in the background of the argument of this essay.[30]

Notes

1. An earlier, more extensive version of this article was published by the American Bar Association Center on Children and the Law as part of the publication *Perspectives on Child Advocacy Law in the Early 21ˢᵗ Century* (June 2000). The development of the article was made possible by a grant to the American Bar Association from the Foundation for Child Development.

2. *Chambers v. Baltimore and Ohio Railroad*, 207 U.S. 142 (1907).

3. The U.S. Advisory Board on *Child Abuse and Neglect, Child Abuse and Neglect: Critical First Steps in Response to a National Emergency* (1990), available from the U.S. Government Printing Office, stock no. 017-092-001045-5. The report said, "The Board bases this conclusion on three findings: 1) each year hundreds of thousands of children are being starved and abandoned, burned and severely beaten, raped and sodomized, berated and belittled; 2) the system the nation has devised to respond to child abuse and neglect is failing; and 3) the United States spends billions of dollars on programs that deal with the results of the nation's failure to treat child abuse and neglect." The report commented, "All Americans should be outraged by child maltreatment." This "national emergency" is part of a larger picture described by the National Commission on Children in their final report in 1991: "As a commission on children, we could not avoid questioning the moral

character of a nation that allows so many children to grow up poor, to live in unsafe dwellings and violent neighborhoods, to lack access to basic health care and a decent education. In our visits to communities across the country, we saw the consistent presence of institutional immorality — often unintended, but present nonetheless. We were shocked by the callous treatment of children in the child welfare system and the public health system" (*Beyond Rhetoric: A New American Agenda for Children and Families*, p. 84). These indictments of our nation's treatment of children provide the social context for this essay.

4. When I refer to "protective due process rights," I mean due process rights to secure rights of protection as indicated above. These are the due process rights for children for which I am specifically arguing in this essay.

5. *In re Gault*, 387 U.S. 1, 13, 26 (1967). The Fourteenth Amendment to the Constitution grants equal protection and due process to all "persons."

6. *Tinker v. Des Moines Community School District*, 393 U.S. 503, 511 (1969).

7. *Wisconsin v. Yoder*, 406 U.S. 205 (1972).

8. *Planned Parenthood v. Danforth*, 428 U.S. 52, 74 (1976).

9. IJA/ABA, *Juvenile Justice Standards: Standards Relating to Counsel for Private Parties* (1980).

10. ABA, *America's Children at Risk: A National Agenda for Legal Action*, Executive Summary, p. ix (1993).

11. The child protective system comprises all those agencies involved when the state intervenes on behalf of a child who is alleged to be the victim of neglect, abuse, or abandonment. A guardian *ad litem* (guardian "for the suit") is a person appointed by the court to protect the best interests of a child during legal proceedings concerning alleged abuse, neglect or abandonment. The guardian *ad litem* may, but need not, be a lawyer.

12. "Termination of parental rights" means parents' loss of rights in their natural child, normally upon a finding (in Family Court) of neglect, abuse or abandonment.

13. An *amicus curiae* ("friend of the court") is a person who submits a brief on a point of law concerning a case to which they are not themselves a party.

14. For a detailed recounting of the case and analysis of the legal issues, see George Russ, "Through the Eyes of a Child, 'Gregory K.': A Child's Right to be Heard," *Family Law Quarterly*, vol. 27, no. 3 (Fall 1993). Mr. Russ and his wife adopted Gregory.

15. *Grissom v. Grissom*, 886 S.W.2d 47 (Mo Ct. App. 1994).

16. A *pro se* ("for self") complaint is one that a person submits directly, rather than through a lawyer. A writ of certiorari ("to be informed about") is an order by a higher court to review a case heard by a lower court.

17. Unpublished Order by Chief Justice Veasey and Justices Walsh and Holland of Supreme Court of Delaware, decided June 19, 1998, Case No. 234, 1998.

18. Compensation was not an issue because Chris qualified for *pro bono* — free — representation by Legal Services of North Carolina, by whom I am employed. "*Pro bono*" is short for "*pro bono publico*" ("for the public good").

19. ABA Standards of Practice for Lawyers Who Represent Children in Abuse and Neglect Cases. These standards were developed by the ABA Family Law Section, 1996.

20. Ibid.

21. Ibid.

22. *Santosky v. Kramer*, 455 U.S. 745, 788 n. 13 (1982). (Rehnquist, J., dissenting, joined by Burger, C.J., and O'Connor, J.)

23. ABA, *America's Children at Risk*, p. 7.

24. New York's highest court dealt with this issue in 1976, saying there had been a "shifting of emphasis" in the case law reflecting "more the modern principle that a child is a person, and not a subperson over which the parent has an absolute possessory interest" (*Bennet v. Jeffreys*, 356 N.W.2d 277, 281).

25. See the section of this essay entitled "The Constitutional Status of Children."

26. *Greenville County DSS v. Bowes, et al*, 437 S.E.2d 107, 114 (1993). Chief Justice Toal's was a dissenting opinion in a case involving reunification of a child with a biological parent who had previously harmed the child.

27. Charles D. Gill, "Essay on the Status of the American Child, 2000 A.D.: Chattel or Constitutionally Protected Child-Citizen?", *Ohio Northern University Law Review*, vol. XVII, no. 3 (1991), p. 548.

28. The meeting was organized by the National Task Force for Children's Constitutional Rights and hosted by the American Academy of Child and Adolescent Psychiatry. The drafting group also included top ranking leadership from the American Academy of Pediatrics and the American Association of School Administrators. All three professional organizations support the amendment as written, though none is attached to this precise wording.

29. While a federal amendment for children is the ideal, local efforts to amend state constitutions are also worth pursuing and might be more feasible.

30. See note 3.

Chapter 10

Child Advocacy in the United States and the Power of International Human Rights Law

Roger J. R. Levesque

Many legal scholars posit that the ratification of international human rights treaties adds little to the protection of rights in the United States. Commentaries about the United Nations Convention on the Rights of the Child (UNCRC) provide no exception. Some legal analyses suggest that the 1989 Convention virtually mimics United States law.[1] Other analyses find some differences but note that the attachment of a small number of "reservations" — statements explaining that a nation does not commit itself to certain treaty provisions — would free the United States from having to make changes in existing laws and policies.[2] Indeed, commentators generally doubt that ratification of the treaty would present much improvement in current approaches to children's issues.[3] Given these sentiments, it is no surprise that the United States has yet to ratify the UNCRC.

It is true that the history of international law reveals that international treaties do not readily impact nations' internal policies and that international human rights law may not readily influence domestic policies. Moreover, history reveals how struggles to secure fundamental human rights ultimately remain local and that progress only emerges through domestic activism. Nonetheless, despite the need to look to a nation's own laws to envision and ensure basic human rights, local activists around the world recognize that the most serious domestic rights problems have an international dimension and that the ability of international human rights law to apply pressure and scrutiny

can ameliorate adverse domestic conditions.[4] Given the potential reach
of international law, and given the UNCRC's approach to children's
rights, it is no surprise to find that the treaty has been hailed by
children's advocacy groups, elicited policy commitments from
international agencies, and prompted numerous conferences dedicated
to implementing the Convention's objectives.[5] Indeed, even the legal
analyses that perceive little benefit from ratification urge ratification.[6]
Although international law historically has focused on concerns
between nations rather than on the internal affairs of individual states,
human rights advocacy suggests that the UNCRC and other significant
human rights documents could make a difference to current legal
approaches to children in the United States and to the nation's
obligations to children.

Existing commentaries dealing with the Convention and the nature
of human rights law leave two points of discussion open for those
interested in understanding the potential role that international human
rights law can play in child advocacy in the United States. First, how
does international law actually impact the laws of the United States?
Second, how different are the provisions of the UNCRC from United
States legislation concerning children? As regards the first question,
there are a variety of views about the potential impact of international
human rights laws on domestic laws. As regards the second question,
there are widely different commentaries relating to the actual nature of
the UNCRC. In light of these differences, this essay seeks to
accomplish two goals: to explore the different ways to implement
international treaties concerning children's rights and to compare and
contrast the international approach to children's rights with the United
States' approach. The two analyses suggest that many commentators
take an unnecessarily narrow approach to international law; that human
rights law actually may have more power than currently envisioned by
those who comment on the UNCRC; and that the UNCRC calls for
change which holds the potential to transform child policy-making in
the United States. This potential is jeopardized when commentators
play down visions of childhood in international human rights law and
when their discussions essentially stifle the process of ratification and
implementation that otherwise would set in motion forces that would
lead to change.

The "Domestication" of International Law

As suggested above, the ratification and implementation of international human rights law allows for very different interpretations of the eventual impact such treaties may have on domestic law. Recent commentaries draw from traditional and modern jurisprudence to suggest that international law actually operates in various ways, and that all of these ways must be considered when evaluating the power of international mandates.[7]

Broadly speaking, there are two different views of international law: the traditional and the modern. The traditional view focuses on two very narrow approaches to the domestication of international law: formal and informal ratification. Formal ratification involves signature of the President upon the advice and consent of the Senate (U.S. Constitution. Art II.s. 2 cl.2). Although that process seems quite straightforward, several limitations may be placed on a treaty and narrow its eventual impact. The first applies to a treaty that is not "self-executing," i.e. one whose provisions do not come into force in U.S. law automatically. In such a case, the treaty binds domestic courts only if Congress has passed legislation for the specific purpose of implementing the treaty provisions domestically. The need for such legislation may narrow the treaty's impact.[8] Second, limitations arise to the extent that the treaty may conflict with existing law. Thus, if the treaty conflicts with state law, then the treaty prevails[9]; if it conflicts with federal law, the most recent provision rules[10]; lastly, if the treaty conflicts with the Constitution, the treaty loses.[11] Third, potential limitations arise when the ratification process results in reservations and other devices that clarify the extent of the obligation the ratifying state views itself as undertaking.[12] In short, formal ratification, which involves specific rules and relatively clear outcomes, can result in narrowing the impact of the ratified treaty.

The traditional view also focuses on a process that could be called "informal ratification." This process is less clear-cut, with less clear outcomes, than formal ratification. The informal ratification of a treaty makes use of customary law, a process that is often ignored but which is rather significant. The legal rule regarding this form of law is simple: If law is customary, it is "part of our law."[13] However, the scope of this use of international law remains rather limited. The Supreme Court urges lower courts to turn to customary law "where there is no treaty, and no controlling executive or legislative act or judicial decision."[14] Yet, even the Court's own use of customary international law remains inconsistent. In important children's rights cases, for example, it turned to customary norms to interpret the Eighth Amendment as prohibiting execution of a minor under the age of sixteen (*Thompson v. Oklahoma*, 1988),[15] only to ignore such standards for a similar issue one year later (*Stanford v. Kentucky*, 1989).[16] Reviews of these and other cases suggest, as several commentators have noted, that courts rest their decisions on some alternative source of values when they seek support from international law.[17] Be that as it may, informal ratification, like formal ratification, represents a narrow approach to the domestication of international law.

In contrast to the traditional view, the modern view of international law recognizes that there is more to the domestication of a treaty than mere ratification, and finds ways around the limits states attempt to impose on their obligations to the international community and their own citizens. Commentators who address the impact of international human rights law on children's rights in the United States often fail to consider and report how these alternative methods may lead to changes in the nation's approach to children's rights. A cursory glance at international law reveals that these commentators miss a critical part of otherwise routine legal analyses. Although the ratification process can limit the impact of a treaty, there are three methods to circumvent this.

The first method has to do with the use of executive and administrative discretion. The rule that deals with self-execution of treaties has been designed for judges. In theory, a non-self-execution declaration is a *non sequitur* as a matter of executive policy.[18] In other words, from the fact that a treaty is declared non-self-executing, nothing follows for the purposes of executive policy and action; it is the judicial branch of government, not the executive branch, that is constrained by the non-self-executing treaty provisions. This leaves open the issue of whether executive and administrative officials whose work is affected by treaties must follow the judiciary's "non-self-executing" rule. Non-judicial use of international standards is significant for four major reasons. First, the executive branch is free to enter into agreements which, as federal law, prevail over inconsistent state law by reason of the Supremacy Clause.[19] Thus, both states and the federal government would be bound by the executive agreement unless the federal legislature or executive branches decided to enact new rules. Second, statutes and regulations inevitably leave considerable discretion to those entrusted with their implementation.[20]

The practical result of this view suggests that thousands of national and local decision-makers who have discretion to enforce, interpret and implement laws could be encouraged to administer laws in a more progressive manner consistent with the UNCRC. This would affect, for example, prosecutors, welfare officials, school principals, doctors, lawyers, psychologists, and those who have direct contact with children. Third, article four of the UNCRC holds that "States Parties shall undertake all appropriate legislative, *administrative*, and other measures, for the implementation of the rights recognized in this Convention" (emphasis added). The UNCRC's own language, then, mandates the use of alternative methods. Lastly, as will be discussed below, the Convention places obligations on private parties. Admittedly, the link between international treaties and private parties is not necessarily direct, but the UNCRC requires states to place obligations on private parties, and modern international law increasingly creates methods to hold private parties accountable.[21] Importantly, in some instances, governments are obliged to recognize children's rights directly and to play down the traditional role caretakers have in controlling children's legal rights.[22]

Even if reservations have been attached, once the treaty has been ratified there is a second method by which attempts to narrow states' treaty obligations can be circumvented. This second method involves monitoring states' compliance with the terms of the treaty. The focus on monitoring is an important development in human rights law. The United States, like all other ratifying parties, would not be able to avoid the obligation to publicize, report on, and monitor the enforcement, and failures of enforcement, of all rights found in the UNCRC (articles 42 and 44-6). In this regard, ratification would necessarily open the U.S. to domestic and international scrutiny based on agreed international norms. The power of the global community derives from a surprisingly broad base. Formal quasi-governmental organizations with a global reach, such as the World Bank, have a tremendous influence on the lives of families and children.[23] Likewise, nongovernmental organizations (NGOs) forcefully mobilize interest in children's human rights.[24] International professional organizations also play important roles in that they help discover, define, and influence public reaction to social issues.[25] Lastly, private citizens increasingly form local social movements that ultimately have global repercussions; the reach and activism of the children's rights movement in the United States, including organizations like the Children's Defense Fund, provides a powerful case in point.[26] Thus, although a cooperative and educational approach to enforcing international law may seem to be a rather weak and unsophisticated method of enforcement, it has become, in practice, a major weapon in the struggle to ensure human rights.[27] Human rights treaties seemingly function best indirectly, through pushing, prodding, and even embarrassing states that fail to take steps to guarantee the proper implementation of rights.

The third method to circumvent limitations set in the ratification process pertains to the status of those limitations with respect to international obligations. Reservations and other limiting additions to treaties apply domestically; they do not affect the treaty in terms of obligations to foreign parties. This is critical for two reasons. First, States Parties to the UNCRC must act in "good faith" and implement its core values and standards, an obligation that arises with any ratification.[28] Second, human rights are *erga omnes*: all states, all "world citizens," have an interest in their recognition and enforcement.[29] This point is of significance in that the interest goes beyond making rights judicially enforceable; rights are to be recognized and enforced in other arenas of lawmaking.[30] Thus, although the black letter obligations set forth in the UNCRC may not impose direct obligations on the United States or subject it to foreign jurisdictions,[31] the rights enumerated in the Convention are, nonetheless, universal in the eyes of States Parties: every individual is seen to have an interest in such rights being recognized and enforced. It would be unwise to discount the power of such rights, as reflected by calls to enact treaties that would have universal jurisdiction and reach rights violators essentially anywhere in the world.[32]

As the preceding discussion suggests, it is important to understand the various methods that may be used to domesticate international law. Those methods can be subsumed under two headings: the more traditional approach to international treaties, which focuses on obligations to other states, and a more modern approach which recognizes that a nation's international obligations to other states must include fulfilling the obligations it has toward its own citizens. When we examine the potential impact of international law on United States law and policy regarding children, families, and the broader society, we shall reach fundamentally different conclusions according to which approach guides our analysis.

As numerous commentators have said, if the narrow, traditional view of international law is taken, then the UNCRC's direct impact is likely to be negligible. Two reasons support this claim. First, the Convention is not self-executing,[33] and therefore will not automatically come into force in United States law. Second, even if individual articles were self-executing, the United States has already ratified other treaties that cover several of the points that commentators have identified as potentially problematic. Ratification of international human rights treaties as such does not necessarily have a significant effect on domestic law.[34] Taking the most technical, narrow view then, the UNCRC's impact could well be quite negligible.

The modern, broader approach to the domestication of international law, however, suggests that children's international human rights may make a difference to the way the United States approaches children's lives and social environments. This approach suggests a need to do two things: to focus on different avenues of implementation that find ways around efforts to limit the impact of international treaties and to foster discourse about alternative approaches to children's rights. Ultimately, however, the practical difference that the alternative approach can make rests on the extent to which the international mandates differ from current U.S. policy and laws regulating the place of children in families and society. We now turn to those differences.

The Convention's Radical Departures

In terms of laws that affect family policy and child development, four areas of fundamental difference exist between the UNCRC and United States law. The divergence suggests that, if taken seriously, the UNCRC should dramatically transform U.S. family policy. First, the UNCRC diverges significantly from current U.S. jurisprudence and policy that generally bestow rights on adults who care for children, rather than the children themselves. For example, in the case of children's rights to relationships, the UNCRC places these rights in the child, rather than the parent or state. Parties have the obligation to "respect the right of the child to preserve his or her...family relations" (article 8). States further must respect the "right of the child...to maintain personal relations and direct contact" with parents from whom the child has been separated (article 9). The Supreme Court's recent analysis of this issue adopts a different posture. In *Michael H. v Gerald D.* (1989) the Court did not uphold a child's right to retain her relationship with her natural father. In fact, the Court concluded that neither natural parents nor their children have a constitutionally cognizable right to maintain relationships with each other.[35] But in general, courts take an adult-centered approach when determining the weight given to a child's right to maintain relationships with parent-like individuals.[36] This approach has serious implications for other aspects of children's rights, such as those that involve the juvenile justice system, the child protection systems, and the educational rights of youths.[37]

Second, the UNCRC's vision of family life differs sharply from the family ideology the Supreme Court espouses in its interpretation of the Constitution. For example, in *Hodgson v. Minnesota* (1990) the Court refused to intervene in family life and protect what would otherwise have been a child's right to obtain an abortion.[38] Although children may have rights to privacy under U.S. law, this case suggests that they have limited authority to exercise that right. The Constitution permits states to have children assert their claims only vicariously through parents.[39] The issue may have been resolved differently under the UNCRC because, although it does not deal with the issue of abortion, it entitles children to rights even when the rights are tied to family relationships, particularly to parents. For example, it clearly aims to give children privacy rights (article 16) and decision-making authority to exercise those rights, commensurate with the child's development and evolving capacities (article 12). The potential impact of these two articles is likely to be revolutionary: it allows for the creation of an "adolescent jurisprudence" currently absent from United States law, policymaking, and even academic discourse.[40]

Third, even more radical than entitling children with rights, the UNCRC contains a vision of society in which the state is involved in actively supporting children and families (e.g. articles 19, 23, 24, 26 and 27). The UNCRC identifies specific areas for state involvement, such as child abuse and maltreatment cases (article 19), enforcement of child support payments, as well as state assistance for the poorest children (article 27). In addition to affirming the rights of mentally and physically disabled children to appropriate care and support, the UNCRC calls for states to provide assistance to parents of such children who lack resources (article 23). In contrast, the ideology of family life envisioned by the Constitution is one which protects family integrity by a principle of state noninterference, barring caretaker criminal abuse or failure to realize basic responsibilities.[41]

Fourth, the UNCRC adopts an approach to rights that moves beyond the United States' minimalist approach. Indeed, it aims for higher standards than the rights the Constitution presently protects. Taking the UNCRC's mandates seriously would mean revisiting the vast majority of children's rights cases developed haphazardly during the last century. Among the most obvious constitutional children's issues addressed by the Supreme Court which would need to be reconsidered in a more systematic manner would be those involving: freedom of expression (compare article 13 with *Hazelwood School*

District v. Kuhlmeier, 1988); freedom to seek, receive and impart information (compare article 13 with *Ginsberg v. New York*, 1968); freedom to practice one's own religion (compare article 30 with *Prince v. Massachusetts*, 1944); special treatment in juvenile penal codes (compare article 37(a) with *Stanford v. Kentucky*, 1989), including detention of juveniles (compare article 37(b) with *Schall v. Martin*, 1984 and *Flores v. Reno*, 1993); the right to education (compare article 29 with *San Antonio Independent School District v. Rodriguez*, 1973); protection from corporal punishment (compare article 28 with *Ingraham v. Wright*, 1977); the right to be heard in proceedings (compare article 12 with *Parham v. J. R.*, 1979); protection from child abuse and neglect (compare article 19 with *DeShaney v. Winnebago County Dept. of Social Services*, 1989; *Suter v. Artist*, 1992); the right to housing (compare article 27 with *Lindsey v. Normet*, 1972); and freedom of association and the right to social development (compare article 15 with *Dallas v. Stanglin*, 1989).[42] As the Supreme Court and other branches of government would revisit these issues, their potential transformation would be quite great given that the UNCRC imposes duties of a positive nature as it moves away from simply imposing duties that can be substantially fulfilled by government inaction.

As aptly noted by many who aim to assuage fears that the UNCRC would radically transform U.S. jurisprudence and legislation affecting children and families, the UNCRC does emphasize that the positive rights, those that require states to act in a supportive manner (e.g., providing welfare services) are to be achieved more progressively through programmatic implementation (article 4). Taken as a whole, however, the UNCRC envisions compliance as meaning more than a matter of establishing programs. Compliance would mean taking steps to implement programs that are effective; otherwise there would not be much use for the UNCRC. Importantly, even though some states in the United States arguably have moved toward ensuring children's rights in a manner consistent with the Convention's aspirations,[43] it would be difficult and disingenuous to conclude that current state constitutional and legislative provisions actually meet those aspirations. They fall short, most notably, in relation to the right to an adequate standard of living (articles 26 and 27) and health care (article 24), as well as the right to protection from child labor and exploitation (article 32), and abuse and neglect (articles 19, 34, 35 and 36). These shortcomings are all part of societal failures culminating in the current "national emergency" in child protection announced a decade ago.[44] Again, the UNCRC requires States Parties to respect and ensure *all* of the children's rights it enumerates.

Conclusion

The UNCRC was meant to be, and undoubtedly is, a milestone in a global strategy that aims to change our attitudes toward children and families. The Convention urges us to rethink current policies marked by contradictory visions about the proper role of children's voices, parents' authority and obligations, and the state's responsibilities in matters concerning children. That fundamental mandate is the most critical contribution the UNCRC offers those interested in changing the place children occupy in our society.

As mentioned at the beginning of this essay, the current discourse about the UNCRC plays down its impact on United States law and policy. Several simple reasons suggest the need to rethink this discourse. First, the UNCRC is a "living document." It would be a mistake to shut out arguments about its aspirations. The need to consider possibilities is a well-established proposition in human rights law; human rights consist largely of norms *de lege ferenda*, the law that ought to be made, as opposed to *lex lata*, the law that is already made. Second, since the UNCRC is about law that is about to be made, it makes sense to think about the transformative power of human rights law. Human rights law deals with cultural change, with the ways in which cultures address competing interests, groups, and needs. Discourse about the UNCRC should generate discussion of the future of children's rights, not only a debate about ratification and the potentially narrow impact that the Convention will have on the United States. Such a limited debate will fail to realize the transformative power of human rights law. This is borne out by the history of ratified treaties in the United States, which shows that they have had little impact; typically, treaty obligations have been watered down to the point that they comport with American law, and discussion has focused on how the treaties would not change the nation's obligations. Third, this very fact — the fact that previous treaties have failed to foster change within the United States — offers the critical insight that current discourse about a treaty truly matters. A fundamental rule of legal interpretation is to rely on legislative history when there is ambiguity in legal texts. If our discourse about the UNCRC fails to provide history with a broader vision of what may be found in that document, this will ensure that those who see no fundamental difference between children's rights in the United States and international children's rights will prevail. Lastly, legal documents play a critical role in cultural change. That is why human rights law focuses first and foremost on the process of deliberating about human rights, and on protecting that process. For example, the United Nations High Commissioner for Human Rights is not a prosecutor but an official who works through diplomatic channels;[45] in other words, the UNCRC itself works through the use of reports and efforts to publicize the Convention, rather than by trying to forcibly impose external values on particular societies. If we do not engage in the process of deliberation, there will be no meaningful cultural change; trying to assure others that the UNCRC would not impact polices affecting their lives seems to be the surest way to ensure that the Convention will do just that.

Child advocates who wish to benefit from international human rights law must aim not only to change United States law as it is, but also to change the context of law and ensure that the Convention's principles infiltrate cultural and individual consciousness. The point is of utmost significance. Human rights gain their legitimacy from being rooted in people, in humanity. Faith in public discourse reflects what developments in international law, both historical and modern, are all about. A vision of humanity that champions equality, inclusion, and respect for human dignity, and the basic faith in human interactions that goes along with that vision, forms the very foundation of human rights law. These democratic principles apply not only to what governments should strive for, but also what individuals should aspire to in their everyday interactions. That is why the UNCRC should be used to rethink United States law, and why it seems to be mistaken to propose and defend the view that the Convention merely replicates existing conceptions of rights.

Notes

1. Cynthia Price Cohen and Howard A. Davidson, eds., *Children's Rights in America: U.N. Convention on the Rights of the Child Compared with United States Law* (Washington, DC: American Bar Association, 1990).

2. American Bar Association, *Report of the Working Group on the United Nations Convention on the Rights of the Child* (Washington, DC: American Bar Association, 1993).

3. Homer H. Clark, Jr., "Children and the Constitution," *University of Illinois Law Review* (Spring 1992), pp. 1-4.

4. Charlotte Bunch and Niamh Reilly, *Demanding Accountability: The Global Campaign and Vienna Tribunal for Women's Human Rights* (New York: United Nations Development Fund for Women, 1994).

5. Sharon Stephens, ed., *Children and the Politics of Culture* (Princeton: Princeton University Press, 1995); Gary B. Melton, "The Right to a Family

Environment for 'children living in exceptionally difficult conditions'," *Law and Policy* 17 (1995), pp. 345-351.

6. Cohen and Davidson, eds., *Children's Rights*.

7. Roger J. R. Levesque, "International Children's Rights: Can They Make a Difference in American Family Policy?" *American Psychologist* 51 (1996), pp. 1251-1256; "Educating American Youth: Lessons from Children's Human Rights Law," *Journal of Law and Education* 27 (1998), pp. 173-209.

8. *Foster v. Nelson*, 27 U.S. (2 Pet.) 253 (1829), p. 314.

9. *Whitney v. Robertson*, 124 U.S. 190 (1888), p. 194; *Reid v. Covert*, 354 U.S. 1 (1957), p. 18.

10. *Missouri v. Holland*, 252 U.S. 416 (1920), pp. 433-35; *Zschernig v. Miller*, 389 U.S. 429 (1968), pp. 440-41.

11. *Reid v. Covert*, p. 16.

12. These mechanisms, however phrased or named, simply clarify the specific obligations ratifying states actually view themselves as either adopting or rejecting. Although such reservations may narrow the effect of the treaty, they nonetheless must be accepted by other parties to the treaty. Louis Henkin, *Constitutionalism, Democracy and Foreign Affairs* (New York: Columbia University Press, 1990); Roger J. R. Levesque, "International Children's Rights Grow Up: Implications for American Jurisprudence and Domestic Policy," *California Western International Law Journal* 24 (1994), pp. 193-240.

13. *The Paquete Habana*, 175 U.S. 677, 700 (1900), p. 700.

14. Ibid., pp. 710-11.

15. *Thompson v. Oklahoma*, 487 U.S. 815 (1988), p. 831.

16. *Stanford v Kentucky*, 492 U.S. 361, 369 (1989), p. 369.

17. See for example, Anne Bayefsky and Joan. Fitzpatrick, "International Human Rights Law in United States Courts: A Comparative Perspective," *Michigan Journal of International Law* 14 (1992), pp. 1-89.

18. Jordan J. Paust, "Avoidant 'Fraudulent' Executive Policy: Analysis of Non-Self-execution of the Covenant on Civil and Political Rights," *DePaul Law Review* 42 (1993), pp. 1257-85.

19. *U.S. v. Belmont*, 301 U.S. 324 (1937), pp. 331-32.

20. Richard H. Gaskins, "Default Presumptions in Legislation: Implementing Children's Services," *Harvard Journal of Law & Public Policy* 17:3 (1994), pp. 779-800.

21. Roger J. R. Levesque, "Piercing the Family's Private Veil: Family Violence, International Human Rights, and the Cross-Cultural Record," *Law and Policy* 21 (1999), pp. 161-87.

22. Roger J. R. Levesque, *Sexual Abuse of Children: A Human Rights Perspective* (Bloomington: Indiana University Press, 1999).

23. See George Kent, *Children in the International Political Economy* (New York: St. Martin's Press, 1995).

24. Michael Longford, "NGOs and the Rights of the Child," in Peter Willetts, ed., *'The Conscience of the World:' The Influence of Non-*

Governmental Organizations in the UN System (Washington, DC: Brookings Institute, 1996), pp. 214-40.

25. Joel Best, ed., *Troubling Children: Studies of Children and Social Problems* (New York: Aldine de Gruyter, 1994).

26. Chadwick F. Alger "Citizens and the United Nations System in a Changing World," in Yoshikazu Sakamoto, ed., *Global Transformation: Challenges to the State System* (New York: United Nations University Press, 1994); on the Children's Defense Fund see Marian Wright Edelman, *Families in Peril: An Agenda for Social Change* (Cambridge, MA: Harvard University Press, 1987).

27. Ann Fagan Ginger, "The Energizing Effect of Enforcing a Human Rights Treaty," *DePaul Law Review* 42 (1993), pp. 1341-1404; Kevin T. Jackson, *Charting Global Responsibilities: Legal Philosophy* (Lanham, MD: University Press of America, 1994).

28. Ian Brownlie, *Principles of Public International Law*, 4th ed., (New York: Oxford University Press, 1990).

29. Maurizio Ragazzi, *The Concept of International Obligations Erga Omnes* (New York: Oxford University Press, 1997).

30. Levesque, "International Children's Rights: Can They Make A Difference?"

31. American Bar Association, *Report of the Working Group*.

32. Levesque, *Sexual Abuse*.

33. See Gary B. Melton, "Is There a Place for Children in the New World Order?" *Notre Dame Journal of Law, Ethics, and Public Policy* 7 (1993), pp. 491-529.

34. Examples are the Convention on the Prevention and Punishment of the Crime of Genocide (1948), International Covenant on Civil and Political Rights (1966), Convention against Torture and Other Cruel, Inhuman or Degrading Treatment or Punishment (1985), and the Convention on the Elimination of All Forms of Racial Discrimination (1966), which respectively entered into force for U.S. law in 1989, 1992, 1994 and 1994; Levesque, *Sexual Abuse*.

35. *Michael H. v. Gerald D.*, 109 S. Ct. 2333 (1989).

36. For reviews of these cases, see Gilbert A. Holmes, "The Tie That Binds: The Constitutional Right of Children to Maintain Relationships with Parent-like Individuals," *Maryland Law Review* 53 (1994), pp. 358-411; for a review of statutes, see Levesque, "Maintaining Children's Familial Relationships with Mentally Disabled Parents: Recognizing Difference and the Difference that it Makes," *Children's Legal Rights Journal* 16 (1996), pp. 14-22.

37. Levesque, "Future Visions of Juvenile Justice: Lessons from International and Comparative Law," *Creighton Law Review* 29 (1996), pp. 1563-1585; Levesque, "Combating Child Sexual Maltreatment: Advances and Obstacles in International Progress," *Law and Policy* 17 (1995), pp. 441-69; Levesque, "Educating America's Youth."

38. *Hodgson v. Minnesota*, 110 S. Ct. 2926 (1990).

39. Levesque, "International Children's Rights Grow Up."

40. Levesque, *Adolescents, Society, and the Law: Interpretive Essays and Bibliographic Guide* (Chicago: American Bar Association, 1997).

41. *Baltimore City Dept. Social Services v. Bouknight*, 110 S. Ct. 900 (1990); Levesque, "International Children's Rights Grow Up," and "The Failures of Foster Care Reform: Revolutionizing the Most Radical Blueprint," *Maryland Journal of Contemporary Legal Issues* 9 (1994), pp. 1-39.

42. *Hazelwood School District v. Kuhlmeier*, 484 U.S. 260 (1988); *Ginsberg v. New York*, 390 U.S. 629 (1968); *Prince v. Massachusetts*, 321 U.S. 158 (1944); *Stanford v. Kentucky*, 492 U.S. 361, 369 (1989); *Schall v. Martin*, 467 U.S. 253 (1984); *Flores v. Reno*, 113 S. Ct. 1439 (1993); *San Antonio Independent School District v. Rodriguez*, 411 U.S. 1 (1973); *Ingraham v. Wright*, 430 U.S. 651 (1977); *Parham v. J. R.*, 442 U.S. 584 (1979); *DeShaney v. Winnebago County Dept of Social Services*, 489 U.S. 189 (1989); *Suter v. Artist*, 112 S. Ct. 1360 (1992); *Lindsey v. Normet*, 405 U.S. 56 (1972); *Dallas v. Stanglin*, 109 S. Ct. 1591 (1989).

43. Levesque, "International Children's Rights: Can They Make a Difference?"

44. U.S. Advisory Board on Child Abuse and Neglect, Department of Health and Human Services, *Neighbors Helping Neighbors: A New National Strategy for the Protection of Children* (Washington, DC: United States Government Printing Office, 1993).

45. Levesque, *Sexual Abuse*.

Chapter 11

Children's Rights in the Curriculum

Sara Ellen Kitchen

A recent American Association of Colleges and Universities monograph entitled *Liberal Learning and the Arts of Connection for the New Academy* states that "an old era is coming to a close: a new vision of the intimate connections between higher learning and the quality of human community is coming clearly into focus."[1] One might see in this vision a response to the late Ernest Boyer, who questioned nearly a decade ago why the most deeply felt issues, the most haunting questions and the most creative moments are so often relegated to the margins of university life.[2] Children's rights are a case in point. Establishing children's rights as a focus of study in the curriculum is an example of making the connection between higher education and the conditions of human life in our world.

This essay describes several ways in which children's rights have been introduced into the curriculum at Chestnut Hill College. It focuses on a multidisciplinary course in children's rights that has been successfully taught for over a decade, and argues that such curricular innovation is essential if colleges and universities are to meet the challenge of preparing students to be future citizens of the world.

For the past decade children's rights have been incorporated into the social science curriculum of Chestnut Hill College, a small liberal arts college in Philadelphia, PA. With the assistance of a Pew grant to internationalize the curriculum, and the support of a Dean who believed in the mission of the College to educate students for their role in the global community, I developed a course entitled "World Justice and Care for Children." I was also influenced by my experiences as a Watson Fellow studying the rights of children in Europe, a Fulbright-

Hayes study tour with a focus on children in Costa Rica and Nicaragua, and practice in juvenile court as a public defender.

The Chestnut Hill College Catalogue offers the following course description for the Sociology course SOC 200, World Justice and Care for Children:

> A global study of human rights for children including an examination of historical and contemporary conditions, legal developments, child welfare programs, and current social and moral issues.

This three-credit course, which is interdisciplinary in content, is offered by the Sociology Department as an elective. Students interested in the topic and the issues it raises may select this course to supplement any major or concentrated course of study. The course has been taught seven times with different texts, assigned readings, videos, and guest speakers. When it was first developed in the late 1980s, resources were difficult to find. Today ample materials make it possible to vary the readings from semester to semester. Consequently, each time the course is taught students have a different educational experience. Nonetheless, student evaluations of the course have been uniformly positive and enthusiastic.

One of the educational aims of this ambitious course is to acquaint the student with ideas and issues not often included in a college curriculum but essential for global citizenship. It has been my experience that few students or faculty are familiar with the United Nations Convention on the Rights of the Child (UNCRC) or any other international human rights convention. Robert Muller, the Chancellor emeritus of the University of Peace in Costa Rica has written, "Even if progress at the level of the child may still be distant, owing to the idiosyncrasies of national education, at least at the university level the time has come to make progress and to establish entirely new global curricula aimed at the needs of the new emerging world society."[3] In other words, the university curriculum should have a global dimension. The course, World Justice and Care for Children, not only brings children's rights into the curriculum but also draws attention to the UNCRC, thereby introducing an international human rights convention into the college curriculum.

Topics for the course include the definition of a child, the history of childhood, socialization of children across cultures, the development of human rights for children, education, health, child labor, children and war, refugee children, child abuse, juvenile justice and national policies. The UNCRC provides an ideal framework for the course design, especially under the broad headings of three kinds of rights of the child: the right to survival, the right to protection, and the right to develop.

When the course was first offered in 1987, the UNCRC was still in the draft stage, and so the Declaration of the Rights of the Child, adopted by the General Assembly of the United Nations in 1959, served as a focus. As part of the initial course development, the United Nations Children's Fund (UNICEF) and Defense for Children International-USA were generous with resources and suggestions. Maryknoll House in Philadelphia provided valuable resources, including printed materials, videos and guest speakers.[4] *The State of the World's Children*, a UNICEF annual publication, has been a consistent required text and an excellent source of current information and statistics.[5] Upon the recommendation of the first group of students, who desired more information and connection with children in the United States, I sometimes require *The State of America's Children*, a yearbook published by the Children's Defense Fund.[6] Other texts have varied in the past decade due to the contemporary context of the course and the fact that some texts went out of print. For the spring of 2001, I assigned *Abandoned Children*, a book emphasizing recent cross-cultural scholarship on children in historical and current circumstances.[7] A world map and a copy of the UNCRC are also essential.

In addition to assigned readings, there are video presentations and guest speakers, which have added a more human dimension to the course content. Videos put a face on statistics. However, they must be used with caution. Students in the class critique videos in terms of content and the portrayal of children's circumstances. Students consider several questions in this process. Are the children speaking for themselves or are they scripted? Is the video producer manipulating the emotions of the viewer? Are children's rights being violated in the making of the video? Many excellent videos are available through UNICEF, Maryknoll World Productions, and educational video catalogues. However, an instructor must be conscious of "compassion fatigue" that results from only depicting the situation of children in desperate circumstances. Guest speakers are other credible resources. Returned Maryknoll lay missioners have shared their experiences in refugee camps in Somalia and the Sudan, balancing the "social pornography" images of starving children with accounts of children's lives that reveal a broader range of experiences. Other speakers have related their firsthand knowledge of children in South Africa, El Salvador, Honduras, Nicaragua, Russia, and Korea. Videoconferencing through Global Education Motivators can bring a speaker or group of students to a class for interactive education.[8] By this means, Olara Otunnu, the Special Representative for the

Secretary-General for Children and Armed Conflict, together with other representatives from his office at the United Nations (U.N.), have interacted with students in their classroom. Students in my class have also participated in a field trip to the U.N. and participated in briefings by representatives of UNICEF.

Pedagogically, this course incorporates a number of Freirean and feminist ideas. According to Paulo Freire, the primary purpose of education is to sensitize students to the human condition and to empower them to respond to social justice.[9] To help meet this challenge, students are required to write a Letter to the Editor about a children's rights issue of their own choice. This exercise compels students to formulate and articulate their opinions. Students generally write to their local paper, such as the *Philadelphia Inquirer*, or to *Time* and *Newsweek* magazines, regarding the failure of the United States to ratify the UNCRC, or child labor, or the death penalty for juveniles. It has been a rewarding experience for students to see their thoughts published in newspapers and magazines and it offers a lesson in citizenship. Feminist pedagogy attempts to create a classroom atmosphere of collaboration and concern.[10] Two assignments are designed with this objective in mind. First, students are required to keep a reading and reflection journal, where they can react to the readings, videos, guest speakers, or class discussions. I advise them to use the journal to ask questions, challenge assumptions, and imagine areas of social change. Second, students extend the course topics through individual research; by presenting their research to the class, they engage in a mutual learning experience. The range of topics that students have chosen for research has contributed to the global reach of the course. A student from Japan researched the children's peace movement in Japan. A pre-med major wrote a paper on the forensic and DNA analysis that helped to reunite some of the *abuelas* of the Plaza de Mayo in Argentina with their grandchildren. A student from Kenya studied children in armed conflict on American streets. Other research topics have included child prostitution, international adoptions, children and AIDS, and street children.

In addition to a research project, students are sometimes required to write a report based on an observational visit and/or interview with a child or children or a local agency or facility. The purpose of this assignment is to make clear the connection between children in the United States and the mandates of the UNCRC (even though the U.S. has not ratified the Convention). It also offers students the chance to compare and contrast the lives of American children with children globally. Students have visited classes for the developmentally disabled, daycare centers, juvenile detention facilities, homeless shelters, and toy stores. The supermarket toy store provides an opportunity for social analysis as students are confronted with the military toy arsenals and doll role models. A final examination essay calls for the student to integrate course content with appropriate articles of the UNCRC.

The following excerpts from student evaluations indicate the impact of this course:

> My most genuine personal response to this course is summed up in the word gratitude. It has not only been a rewarding academic experience, but a very moving and significant experience in terms of my personal life...I feel a much greater personal responsibility to engage in dialogue and action around these issues.

> Because of this course, I read the newspapers more carefully. I watch the international news...with more interest...I will teach my children, my future students, anyone who will listen...

> I have never taken a college course before this one that has had such an emotional impact on me...I aspire to be a writer of children's books, which is one of the main reasons I took this course. Perhaps through the knowledge I have gained from this course I can better relate to the children I want to reach through my writing.

> Before taking this course, I had always pushed such problems as poverty and child abuse from my mind — they were not directly affecting my life, and they were unpleasant to think about, so I chose not to think about them unless I had to. But I realize now that such an attitude will do nothing to help...children and that such an attitude on a large-scale basis is what keeps solutions to these problems from being found. At the moment, I feel that I can take the knowledge that I have gained in this course and the understanding that goes along with it and educate myself further...

Comments such as these show that students respond warmly and deeply when children's rights are moved from "the margins of university life" to the center of their education. Furthermore, this course has influenced the career choices of several students. Many have opted for human service positions in juvenile court or related agencies, while others have volunteered a postgraduate year of service. Two students are studying medicine to be public health physicians. Several are studying international development. Those who have become teachers are bringing the world into their classrooms. In my view, these career choices demonstrate that this course has met the educational objective of helping students to become informed and responsible global citizens.[11]

The success of this course and the enthusiastic response of the students were instrumental in the development of another interdisciplinary course, "Psychology and the Law: The Rights of Children." This two-semester seminar course was offered as part of the Interdisciplinary Scholars Program at Chestnut Hill College. It was team-taught by myself, a law professor, and my colleague, Dr. Judith Gay, a professor of psychology. To facilitate discussion and analysis of course topics, students read extensively from a law school casebook on children's rights, in addition to psychology journal articles and the UNCRC. Child custody, competence of children to make decisions and to act as witnesses, student rights, multicultural education, child labor, mental health commitments, the death penalty for juveniles, and juvenile justice were among the areas covered in the seminar.[12]

So far I have focused on the development of new courses devoted to the study of children's rights. This represents one approach to the challenge of connecting learning with social change. Another approach is to modify the content of existing courses by including material on children's rights as a course component. For example, an art history professor and myself team-teach another interdisciplinary honors course at Chestnut Hill College, "Cities and Peoples of the World." The course, offered for the past three years, explores city architecture and urban culture in major world cities. To make the connection between children's rights and urban life, readings for this seminar include studies on street children in Brazil and New York City.[13] Other courses in the Sociology Department have come under the influence of children's rights as an area of academic study. SOC 101 Introduction to Sociology provides opportunities to illustrate sociological concepts with examples from children's rights issues. SOC 103 Social Problems and SOC 104 Major Global Problems now include children in their social analysis. SOC 220 Juvenile Justice and Child Welfare refers to the UNCRC in comparing the juvenile justice and child welfare systems of the United States with those other nations.

Secondary schools as well as colleges and universities offer many courses where the study of children's rights can be incorporated as a component or as the basis for examples and case studies. The following list contains some brief suggestions for integrating children's issues, including their rights, across the curriculum:

- Political Science: study the history of the UNCRC as part of the focus on human rights theory, and explore the case for and against United States ratification as part of international affairs and world politics.
- History: assign research projects related to the history of childhood and children in a particular time period or as part of a national history.
- Philosophy: explore the work of Gareth Matthews and others in the field of the philosophy of childhood.
- Religious Studies: examine the many moral and ethical issues raised by children's rights in the context of world religions.
- Children's Literature: include the writings of children that reflect childhood experiences.
- Art History: take up the work of Philippe Ariès on the depiction of children in early modern European art and explore the portrayal of children in art around the world and throughout history.
- Foreign Languages: use videos in the language studied that focus on children's issues. (Many United Nations videos are produced in Spanish or French. The UNCRC is also available in several translations.)
- Natural Science: use illustrations such as ORT (Oral Rehydration Therapy) to explain how millions of children's lives have been saved.
- Environmental Science: focus on identifying environmental issues affecting children and include children's participation in action plans.
- Psychology: include children's rights in developmental studies, and incorporate research on children traumatized by war and refugee life.
- Education: include children's rights in the curriculum, particularly the UNCRC and the provisioning of education to the children of the world.
- Economics: study the effect of national debt on children via its effect on the nation's economy.
- Business: include the issue of national and international child labor.
- Communications: utilize child advocacy assignments.
- Information Technology: include communications with children worldwide.

Children's rights do not belong on the margins of university life. Consequently, it is encouraging to see that *The Chronicle of Higher Education* has recognized the pioneering work of Gertrud Lenzer, founder of the Children's Studies program at Brooklyn College.[14] Just as women's studies and peace studies have had an impact on educational curricula, the era of children's studies has arrived. This is signaled by the fact that the United Nations, upon the "Appeal" of the living Nobel Peace Prize Laureates, has declared the decade 2001 to 2010 "The International Decade for a Culture of Peace and Non-Violence for the Children of the

World."[15] The Appeal calls upon educational institutions to support the Decade for the benefit of every child in the world. Since the UNCRC is viewed as an integral part of achieving the objectives of the Decade, children's rights should be integrated into the curriculum, not least in the United States, with a view to reducing the suffering of children. Here is an extract from the appeal:

> Today, in every single country throughout the world, there are many children silently suffering the effects and consequences of violence. This violence takes many different forms: between children on streets, at school, in family life and in the community. There is physical violence, psychological violence, socio-economic violence, environmental violence and political violence. We wish to contribute to reduce their suffering. We believe that each child can discover, by himself, that violence is not inevitable. We can offer hope, not only to the children of the world, but to all of humanity, by beginning to create, and to build, a new culture of non-violence.[16]

Grace Abbott, director of the United States Children's Bureau from 1921 to 1934, and author of the classic work, *The Child and the State*, believed that the progress of a state might be measured by the extent to which it safeguards the rights of children.[17] If education is the institutionalization of what a society deems important, may a curriculum be measured by the extent to which it teaches the rights of children?

Notes

1. Elizabeth K. Minnich, *Liberal Learning and the Arts of Connection for the New Academy* (Washington, DC: Association of American Colleges and Universities, 1995).
2. Ernest Boyer, *College: The Undergraduate Experience in America* (New York: Harper & Row, 1988).
3. Robert Muller, *New Genesis: Shaping a Global Spirituality* (New York: Image Books, 1982), p. 23.
4. Maryknoll House is a United States-based Roman Catholic mission movement of priests, sisters, brothers, and laity committed to working with and for the poor and oppressed of the world in pursuit of peace and social justice.
5. United Nation's Children's Fund, *The State of the World's Children* (Oxford: Oxford University Press, 1988-2001).
6. Children's Defense Fund, *The State of America's Children* (Boston: Beacon Press, 2000).

7. Catherine Panter-Brick and Malcolm T. Smith, eds., *Abandoned Children* (Cambridge: Cambridge University Press, 2000).

8. Global Education Motivators (GEM), headquartered at Chestnut Hill College, a non-profit educational corporation and a nongovernmental organization in association with the United Nations Department of Public Information provides global education programs including interactive videoconferencing for all educational levels. Website: www.gem-ngo.org.

9. Paulo Freire, *The Pedagogy of the Oppressed* (New York: Continuum, 1970).

10. Carol Gilligan, *In A Different Voice: Psychological Theory and Women's Development* (Cambridge, MA: Harvard University Press, 1982).

11. Elise Boulding, *Building a Global Civic Culture: Education for an Interdependent World* (Syracuse, NY: Syracuse University Press, 1990).   '

12. Benn, Sara Kitchen and Judith Gay, "A Course on the Rights of Children," *Teaching of Psychology* 19 (1992), pp. 226-228.

13. Tobias Hecht, "In Search of Brazil's Street Children," in Panter-Brick and Smith, eds., *Abandoned Children*, pp. 146-160.

14. Gertrud Lenzer, "Children's Studies: Beginnings and Purposes," *The Lion and The Unicorn* 25 (2001), pp. 181-186.

15. *International Decade for a Culture of Peace and Non-Violence for the Children of the World (2001-2010),* Implementation of the Resolution A/RES/53/25/ (19/11/98, 53rd session).

16. Ibid.

17. Grace Abbott, *The Child and the State: Select Documents, with Introductory Notes* [1938] (New York: Greenwood Press, 1968).

Chapter 12

Children's Studies and the Human Rights of Children: Toward a Unified Approach

Gertrud Lenzer

This essay attempts to demonstrate the intimate connections that exist between, on the one hand, the agenda of the rights of children within the international human rights movement since the middle of the twentieth century and, on the other hand, the interdisciplinary field of Children's Studies, founded in 1991. The principal arguments presented here concern the following:

- Academic and policy research on infants, children, and youth is segmented into a multitude of disciplines and subdisciplines. By contrast, the new interdisciplinary field of Children's Studies aims at viewing children and youth in a holistic, comprehensive manner in order to bring about an integration of the different perspectives of the many child-related disciplines and bodies of knowledge.

- The human rights agenda has splintered exponentially into manifold special and narrow fields, of which children's rights and the United Nations Convention on the Rights of the Child (UNCRC) represents one example. Moreover, the field of children's rights itself is further subdivided into many different topics that focus upon the lives of children and youth. By contrast, the arguments presented here promote a comprehensive perspective on children's rights. As this perspective develops, it should lead in turn to a reintegration of the isolated segments of the children's rights agenda within the framework of human rights.

• Finally, the temper and methods of Children's Studies and the rights of children complement and reinforce one another. The widely ranging academic fields in Children's Studies — the history of childhood, child development, children's health, children's imagination and the arts, the ethnic diversity of children, the sociology of children, and so on — individually relate to one another. The articles of the UNCRC are similarly interrelated and encompass many of the same developmental, social, economic, educational, and cultural themes and problems, expressed in terms of the propensities and needs of the child. In other words, the interdisciplinary perspectives of Children's Studies supply the scholarly information and knowledge that are indispensable to the implementation of the UNCRC. Reciprocally, the focus on the human rights of children gives new directions to the fields included in Children's Studies and provides another general framework for scholars in these fields.

Children's Rights and Children's Studies

Children's Rights and Their History

What do we mean when we speak of the "rights of the child" or "the rights of children"? To be sure, the UNCRC, as a comprehensive human rights covenant and generational compact, represents a historical watershed. However, since its adoption in 1989, it has become customary to date the "true" history of children's rights from that year. Moreover, in certain quarters there has been a perceptible tendency to dismiss virtually all previous preoccupation with children's well-being and rights as the work of those who were *merely* concerned with the *protection* of children. From this perspective, the approach taken by the so-called child protection movement was qualitatively different from the approach found in the UNCRC, which considers children to be full participants in society with human rights and the legal competence to exercise these rights. Although the Geneva Declaration (1924) and the United Nations Declaration of the Rights of the Child (1959) are commonly recognized as important milestones on the way toward the UNCRC, this new perspective has for the moment

— at least in the United States — all but eclipsed any interest in the long history of what has been called the "children's rights movement" in this country.

This is not the place to examine that history, but it is worth recalling the Progressive Era with its policies for children and children's rights (1890s-1920s), the National Child Labor Committee and the campaigns for child labor legislation during the first four decades of the twentieth century, and the establishment of the Children's Bureau and of government programs and social services for children from the 1930s onward. The 1960s and 1970s produced an energetic discussion of children's rights, needs, and entitlements, as illustrated by the U.S. Supreme Court decision *In re Gault* (which extended procedural rights to young people), the creation of the Head Start Program, and the landmark publication of *Beyond the Best Interests of the Child* (1973) — to mention only a few major developments. [1] Also during the early 1970s in the United States, prominent members of the Society of Jesus, such as Bernard J. Coughlin and Robert F. Drinan, were already actively involved in children's rights issues and wrote such papers as "The Rights of Children" and "The Rights of Children in Modern American Family Law." [2] In other words, it is important to recall that the Year of the Child in 1979 and the Polish Draft Convention on the Rights of the Child in 1978 — an initiative that eventually led to the UNCRC in 1989 — were preceded by a historical period with an all-consuming interest in children and youth: their needs, their problems, their rights. In my view, it is altogether essential to connect — or reconnect — this history to the ongoing efforts on behalf of the UNCRC.

Children's Studies and the Academic Disciplines

The new and interdisciplinary field of Children's Studies was founded in the autumn semester of 1991 at Brooklyn College of The City University of New York. Two central observations led to its establishment.

First, with the notable exceptions of children's literature, child psychology, and pediatrics, most disciplines — including disciplines in the arts and humanities, the social and medical sciences, and law — had failed to provide a special focus on children. In brief, most disciplines did not regard children as both a separate social class and a human transhistorical condition. Childhood was conceived of as a transitory stage on the way toward future adulthood. To the extent that children received any specialized attention, they were subsumed under such different categories as education, the family, generational and life course studies, socialization, juvenile delinquency, deviant behavior, and peer group analysis. This general neglect of children and childhood as a distinct focus of analysis in the academic disciplines was even more remarkable when we consider that the corporate sector had been well ahead of the academic disciplines. During recent decades, this sector discovered, singled out, and "developed" children and young people as a separate new market, a new "continent" for capital expansion. Moreover, political parties have used children extensively, especially during periods of elections, to demonstrate their socially responsible intentions and for purposes of legitimation. (Such child-oriented rhetoric, however, usually disappears after the election.) In other words, the increasing visibility of and concentration on children as a social class in the economic and political realms antedates, as it were, the "discovery" of children by the scholarly community.

The last two decades have witnessed an increasing number of disciplines in the arts and sciences manifesting an interest in children and youth. In the humanities, these growing subfields include children's literature, history of childhood, and the philosophy of children. Among the social sciences, there is the newly emerging area of the sociology of children in the United States. Other disciplines, such as anthropology, political science, and economics, have also produced, in rapidly increasing numbers, studies on child-related topics without, however, establishing a primary focus on children as a special branch of scholarship and analysis within their disciplines and professional organizations. In addition, with the adoption of the UNCRC, the field of children's rights has been growing rapidly since 1989.

Second, while the recent sharpening focus on children and youth in the humanities, social sciences, and international law represents a welcome development, the intellectual division of labor in child-related scholarship across the disciplines has largely added new subspecialties within those disciplines, and produced studies that are disconnected from one another. This had become evident even as I first founded and established the Sociology of Children as a new field and section within the American Sociological Association in 1991. Those of us involved in this initiative felt that it was incumbent on us to develop a holistic conceptualization of children, both as individuals and as a class, in order to overcome the disciplinary fragmentation that creates an incoherent manifold of specialized perspectives on children; we also felt we must develop a commensurate perspective on and analysis of children, one that is genuinely comprehensive.

Along with this realization came the recognition that the disparate disciplinary undertakings in question — the findings, theories, and codes of assumption — needed to be complemented by a reconstruction or synthesis at another level of integration; for children are not fully characterized by psychological developmental processes, nor indeed by processes seen from any single perspective. In our view, children are not only individuals, they are also a social and cultural class and a historical generation.

Hence, we cannot arrive at a comprehensive understanding of children by simply accumulating or aggregating segmented findings from a far-flung variety of inquiries in various disciplines. In response to the increasing fragmentation in child research, Children's Studies was conceived as a new, genuinely interdisciplinary and multidisciplinary field of study. Children's Studies represents an attempt to bring knowledge from the different sectors of the arts and sciences to bear on the conception of children as a class and to integrate this knowledge at an appropriate level of understanding and articulation. Children's Studies does not aim simply to gather a sum of findings from diverse perspectives. Rather, by bringing carefully chosen knowledge from different studies to bear on the class or category of children, and by introducing this knowledge to liberal arts students, a more holistic understanding of children and childhood should emerge, which in the end will represent more than merely the sum of its parts. In this conception, a child — or children, for that matter — does not consist of a multitude of disconnected propensities, interests, or realities as they appear refracted in a congeries of disconnected disciplinary pursuits. Instead, children and youth, both individually and as a class, are foregrounded as human beings.

This is the aim of Children's Studies, which makes the ontological claim that children must be viewed in their fullness as human beings. The various child-focused disciplinary endeavors must contribute to such a holistic understanding of children rather than reducing them to specialized abstract fragments that then in turn are hypostatized as representing "the child," "children," or "childhood." Such were among the ideas and methodological reflections that led to the conception of the interdisciplinary field of Children's Studies.

The Children's Studies Program at Brooklyn College includes courses on children's literature, the history of childhood, child development, speech and language development, sociology of children, children and the media, children in education, child health, the African American child, the Puerto Rican child, children and the law, and the rights of children. Other courses in preparation are: children and the arts, children and the mass media, new technologies and the internet, children and the environment, and children of the world, emphasizing cross-cultural and global perspectives on children. In this way, a range of disciplines — including the visual and performing arts, music, film, literature, philosophy, history, the social sciences, medical sciences, and law — are brought together to provide a combined focus on children and to bring about new understanding in the form of a series of new conceptualizations of children. From this perspective, the emerging subject of the rights of children is not conceived as a separate formal inquiry that confronts other studies dealing with children and youth. On the contrary, the human rights of children are regarded as an intrinsic component of all the disciplinary studies concerned with children.

It should be stressed that in including a Children's Studies Program in a liberal arts curriculum, our overarching goal is to educate students to more adequate, knowledge-based representations of children and youth in society, utilizing a new pedagogy and research methodology. At Brooklyn College, we conceive of Children's Studies as a part of a student's general education. We have found that our students have interests in children and childhood that are widespread and cut across the fields in which they are majoring.

We also hope that these new perspectives on children will have wider social benefits. We envision that the Children's Studies Program will enable the educated public and society at large to gain an improved, knowledge-based understanding of children's capacities, capabilities, needs, and desires, as well as of their civil, political, economic, and cultural human rights; and thus contribute to the well-being of children. Our approach is to concentrate our efforts on creating an infrastructure of students with enlightened knowledge. We thus envision a future in which the multidisciplinary field of Children's Studies will play a significant role in promoting an enhanced understanding of children, not only by reaching across the disciplines, but also by exposing students to knowledge that will deepen their understanding of children, and prepare them for their future roles in all walks of life: as professionals, as citizens, and as parents. For the time has passed when the specialized knowledge we derive from child research, scholarship, and practice is available only to the experts. The time has also passed when individual citizens are simply left to depend on unquestioned and unexamined conceptions about child development, child rearing, and indeed the very experiences of children. It is time that the privileged knowledge of the expert is shared with the so-called non-expert. We hope that Children's Studies will contribute to changing public awareness, so that children are viewed as human subjects, not merely as objects of specialized scholarly research or of social policies and social action. It is for this reason also that we hope other academic institutions will introduce Children's Studies into their curricula.

George Orwell observes:

> The real question is whether it is still normal for a schoolchild to live for years amid irrational terrors and lunatic misunderstandings. And here one is up against the very great difficulty of knowing what a child really feels and thinks. A child which appears reasonably happy may actually be suffering horrors which it cannot or will not reveal. It lives in a sort of alien under-water world which we can only penetrate by memory or divination. Our chief clue is the fact that we were once children ourselves, and many people appear to forget the atmosphere of their own childhood almost entirely.[3]

He goes on to say, "Treacherous though memory is, it seems to me the chief means we have of discovering how a child's mind works...The child and the adult live in different worlds." His essay powerfully dramatizes our general condition: We know very little about the inner life of children, about their desires, aspirations, or fears and sorrows, the imaginative creation of their own world and how the world of adults appears to the child. Children are indeed confronted with the considerable power the adult world has over them. Children cannot represent themselves, unlike other powerless groups that have made their claims heard. For most of what we know about children has been created by adults, as Orwell suggests — adults who in most instances have forgotten what it was like to be a child. Much of our most intimate knowledge of children and childhood has traditionally come from writers, poets, and artists, and not from scholars, educators, and policymakers. Perhaps Children's Studies can contribute to providing children and childhood with a voice that is commensurate with their reality, and which is not exclusively an adult construction.

The Children's Rights Perspective in Children's Studies

We therefore envision the multidisciplinary subject of Children's Studies as playing a significant role in the understanding and lives of children in the future. In addition to the human rights laid down in the UNCRC and other children's rights instruments, children can, so to speak, claim that they deserve to be understood and analyzed in the whole of their existence by the research, academic and policy community. We do not find this implicit claim and comprehensive vision articulated in most discussions of our human rights conventions relating to children.

In fact, such discussions reflect the fragmentation of concerns about different social areas and problems that intimately involve and affect children, a situation of incoherence that characterizes social and historical reality as well as policies in different societies. Children's rights documents themselves mirror this fragmentation. There are, to be sure, articles in the UNCRC that address children's general and universal needs, interests and rights. But since most articles attend to particular and separately specifiable historical problems, many scholars and advocates concerned with the well-being and rights of children divide the labor among themselves. There are, of course, the generalists in the new field of children's rights, people who address such important questions as the history, basic principles, and goals of the UNCRC and similar instruments, their place in the arena of human rights, and the tasks of monitoring and implementing the Convention on a global scale. Yet, in addition to the generalists, a large number of child rights experts deal exclusively with separate articles of the Convention and concentrate on specific areas, such as education, health care, child labor, street children, child abuse, and child soldiers.

In short, alongside other compartmentalized child-focused fields of study in the arts and sciences, the field of child rights has emerged in the 1990s as a separate field of study with a wide variety of subspecialties and experts. However, given the comprehensive nature of children's rights on a global scale, the time has come to forge intimate relations with the relevant fields of child research in the arts and sciences. It is, after all, these fields that examine and cover most areas of the individual, political, social, economic, and cultural realities of childhood. In order to overcome the disciplinary fragmentation, both in the established arts and sciences and in the new field of children's rights, and in order to achieve a synthesis, we need to aim at a unified representation of children in research and policy, in society and the polity of nations, and in the evolving jurisprudence of the rights of the child. In the vision of the new and interdisciplinary field of Children's Studies, children are human beings with all their capacities, competencies, interests, and needs, and — last but not least — all the rights that attach to them as members of the human community. On this view, Children's Studies, together with the goal of synthesizing the representation of children, can become an important, if not essential, ally in the global movement for children's rights.[4]

Human Rights and the
Rights of Children[5]

The Human Rights of Children: the Quest for Legitimacy

A new era in the history of children's rights began with the adoption of the UNCRC in 1989. Now, after more than a decade, all nations of the world — with the exception of the United States and Somalia — have ratified or acceded to the Convention. Hence, according to the standards of international law, the UNCRC has acquired the status of international *legality*. But, to use Max Weber's useful distinction, the historical task of achieving *legitimacy* for the Convention as a whole and for its specific articles and provisions still lies ahead. This means that it is not sufficient that the provisions of the Convention are legally binding on those countries that have ratified it. For, unless the citizens of a country uphold those provisions as valid, the articles of the Convention will not effectively guide the social and political action taken by that country on behalf of children and youth. This means that the "validity of the claims to legitimacy" for the articles of the Convention must be based, at a minimum, "on a belief in the legality of enacted rules."[6] In other words, it is not sufficient for governments to become States Parties to the Convention. The next and more difficult steps entail incorporating the Convention into the legal and administrative structures of each nation, and applying newly adapted laws and procedures in the everyday affairs of governments and society. They entail, as well, the establishment of foundations of legitimacy for these new legal realities in the public at large.

When the term "implementation" is used in the Convention itself, it means such attempts at transforming international agreements and standards into the laws, practices, and belief systems of each participating nation. Once we disaggregate the meaning of "implementation of the Convention," the difficulties that confront such attempts become immediately apparent. At stake are not only the good intentions of legislators, government officials, and administrators to honor the terms of these international agreements, but also the values, belief systems, customs, and traditional practices that have heretofore governed society's attitudes and behavior toward children and youth. When it is considered in its entirety, the Convention both presupposes and requires formidable changes in the political, economic, social, and cultural realities of children. These changes will often run against the grain of popular beliefs and practices of elected officials, administrators, and the generality of citizens. The task of implementing the Convention goes far beyond the legal realms of the international community and nations. The problem is to achieve legitimate authority for the Convention.[7]

This problem is further exacerbated by the fact that much criticism has been directed against those Western hegemonic intentions that are widely supposed to inform the human rights movement in general and the UNCRC in particular. Such criticism emanates not only from representatives of the developing world but also from certain intellectual quarters in Western industrialized societies.[8] To be sure, the history of human rights after the Second World War and the articulation of two categories of 1) civil and political rights and 2) economic, social, and cultural rights largely took place in the context of the Cold War. In the words of Lawrence LeBlanc, during this period "these categories were fixtures of international ideological dispute between East and West, with some Western states, especially the United States, emphasizing civil and political rights and with some socialist and Third World states emphasizing economic, social, and cultural rights."[9]

There can be no doubt that the history of East-West conflict and North-South relations is refracted in the contemporary human rights movement and in the UNCRC as well. (After all, it was the Polish delegation that began the process that led to the eventual drafting of the UNCRC.) Equally, there can be no doubt that Western conceptions of the child, of what constitutes the best interests of the child, and of what enhances child development, preponderate in the articles of the Convention. This underscores the problems that will have to be faced by both Western and non-Western States Parties in the future when it comes to implementing the Convention.

Universality, Complementarity, and Indivisibility of Human Rights

It is important to discuss the UNCRC within the larger framework of human rights. Even though human rights have been held to be universal, interdependent and indivisible, the writings of many scholars and activists in the arena of international law and human rights demonstrate that there has been an ever-increasing specialization of topics and interests. This is the result of an increasingly dense context of international conventions, treaties, and declarations, as well as administrative bodies to enact them. Among the milestones in the history of human rights since the Second World War are such important treaties and instruments as: the United Nations Charter (1945), the Universal Declaration of Human Rights (1948), the European Social Charter (1961), the International Covenant on Civil and Political Rights (1966), the International Covenant on Economic, Social and Cultural Rights (1966), the American Convention on Human Rights (1969), the Convention on the Elimination of all Forms of Discrimination Against Women (1979), the African Charter on Human Rights and Peoples' Rights (1981), the UNCRC (1989), and the Rio Declaration on Environment and Development (1992).[10] Such agreements and instruments have resulted in new and ever-growing fields of expertise, scholarship, and advocacy concerning groups and issues ranging from children and women to indigenous people, the environment, labor, health, education, and so on.

As a related development, however, groups of experts in any particular human rights field are often only dimly aware of the nature of the conventions, treaties, and agreements in other human rights fields. Moreover, within a given field, and with respect to any convention or treaty, there is a tendency to more and more specialization and subspecialization. The need for unified perspectives has become increasingly acute in view of such pervasive division and fragmentation in international human rights law in general, together with the proclaimed rights of special groups or classes in particular.

Unless we attempt to unify our perspectives, particularized concerns and scholarly competencies will continue to proliferate. This in turn will generate still more specialized subdivisions in each human rights field. Given the tendency among individual scholars, activists, and consultants to specialize, and given the manifold institutions that fund their special interests, the time has come to initiate a counter-movement that stresses the communality and interdependence of such separate pursuits within the larger framework of human rights. It amounts to a truism to say that when experts and publics divide their attention and concentrate their energies on so many different sub-problems and subjects in isolation from one another, the overall effectiveness of their efforts is weakened.

It does not require much reflection to see that although international human rights declarations and treaties cover different groups or issues, most of the social, economic, political, and cultural problems that have given rise to them are closely connected. If we isolate single areas of highly specialized circumstances, we run the risk of establishing nothing more than a symptomatology. This is manifest if we take the larger view and consider the historical forces that have been changing individual nations and the world community, forces that continue to operate in the new millennium. The transformations of sovereignty; the expansions of trade, finance and capital markets; the free and often instantaneous transfer of capital across national borders — to invoke merely a few global developments — have ushered in historical changes with major repercussions on national social and political infrastructures. Their implications for the social well-being of children, women, and families, or for the relations between racial and ethnic groups, or for the environment, must be comprehended in their totality and inform the particular strategies devoted to the realization and implementation of children's human rights. Obviously, an exclusively specialized approach to each separately perceived human rights problem, without comprehending the wider forces that give rise to these problems, is doomed to failure.

On this basis, I would argue that the rights of children should be promoted within the context of a unified approach to human rights. In calling for a general framework of human rights, I do not mean to imply that it is wrong to focus on the rights of one particular group, or that efforts to bring about the implementation of the UNCRC are unworthy. But on the view for which I am arguing, all such efforts must be regarded as having both a narrower significance for children and a broader significance for human rights in general. Even in terms of practical politics, promoting the children's rights agenda within the framework of the wider human rights movement might prove to be a more efficacious way of reaching the public at large, at least in Western industrialized nations. Events in the Balkans during the 1990s and the response of American and European publics to the intervention in Yugoslavia strongly indicate that popular support for human rights is based not merely on international law, but on grounds of legitimacy; that is, human rights are held to be morally valid.[11]

In the case of the UNCRC, the unified approach for which I am arguing might usefully lead to reflection on more general human rights positions. These would include not only the rights proclaimed in the Universal Declaration of Human Rights, but also first, second, and third generation rights as they are articulated in international covenants of civil and political rights; international covenants on economic, social and cultural rights; and solidarity rights. In light of such declarations and instruments, the UNCRC, despite its unique and innovative character, appears as a particular embodiment and application of these earlier, broad articulations of the human rights agenda — an agenda that has been developing since the Second World War.

Civil Society and Human Rights

Almost all discussions of the history of the UNCRC stress the importance and significance of the contributions made by nongovernmental organizations (NGOs). The same claims about NGOs are made in many other human rights fields as well. There can be no doubt that NGOs have played, and are still playing, a salient role in the human rights arena generally, and on behalf of children in particular. Indeed, there continues to be an extraordinary proliferation of NGOs worldwide. In the 1990s, major funding agencies and international bodies — such as the World Bank, the International Monetary Fund (IMF), the United Nations Development Program, and the United Nations Educational, Scientific and Cultural Organization — changed their official attitudes and policies toward NGOs. This change in attitude, as a matter of international policy, has led to a significant re-channeling of funds to NGOs. This change in funding policies is of considerable historical importance. If we examine this change, we can find some of the deeper-lying roots of the increasing fragmentation of, and specialization in, human rights projects in our era, as I shall now explain.

Especially since 1989, the virtues and benefits of "civil society" have been extolled in such quarters as the World Bank, the IMF, and the United Nations Children's Fund. The term "civil society" has a long and venerable history. However, in most recent human rights discussions, "civil society" has become synonymous with the aggregate of NGOs and their role vis-à-vis the state and sovereign governments. In this recent usage, proponents of "civil society" use the phrase as shorthand for initiatives that they wish to promote in *all* societies, not just in the developing societies of the South. However, scholars and activists who frequently use the term are hard-pressed to explain its wider significance. More importantly, they do not seem to appreciate the implications it has for the human rights causes to which their energies are dedicated.

In order to understand these implications, it is necessary to trace certain historical developments in the second half of the twentieth century. (For reasons of limited space, this historical analysis must remain condensed and simplified.) Ever since the Bretton Woods Conference in 1944,[12] but especially since the demise of communism, there has been an ever-accelerating growth of economic and financial institutions that serve as the most powerful integrative forces of a global system. By the same token, the competitive economic and financial pressures on governments to open their borders to free trade in goods and services (especially to the free flow of short-term capital) have been mounting. During this same period, developing countries have pursued a quest for higher living standards, while developed and industrialized nations have sought a more equitable distribution of resources and opportunities. With these developments, the role and capacity of the modern state, to which citizens have turned for redress, has become a central focus of debate and discussion. Demands have been made on developing countries to curtail their infrastructural expenditures (education, health, etc.) in order to satisfy the requirements of international loan repayment — a development that has become known as "structural adjustment." These demands have now reached back into the developed world. One example of this is the federal welfare reform carried out in 1996, designed to reduce the number of people receiving welfare assistance checks.[13] In a similar vein, European countries have been under pressure to cut down on their infrastructural spending, which has contributed to the dismantling of the highly developed "welfare states" of these nations. These examples illustrate how structural adjustment has been brought home, as it were, in the service of the generation of wealth and the growth of international capital.

Hand in hand with these developments, demands for "less government" (or for getting "big government" out of people's lives) have been insistent, both on the international level, as advanced by the World Bank, and on the national level, as in the United States. Proponents of such neo-liberal views aim at scaling down the state to the bare functions of military defense, the maintenance of social order, and minimal infrastructural provisions. In this conception of society, the intermediary groups — voluntary organizations, "secondary groups" or NGOs, and charitable organizations — are expected to attend to society's affairs and to remedy many of the social problems that need public attention. On this view, the state as such and society as a whole are only minimally responsible for assuring human well-being. This responsibility devolves largely onto all those groups that serve an intermediary function among the state, the economy, and the individual.

In short, there are close connections between, first, recent policies aimed at paring down the welfare states in the North; second, the assertion that it is not economically feasible to implement welfare states in the Third World; third, the promotion of "civil society" by leading international policy institutions, such as the World Bank. Only if we consider the larger context of prevailing international policies will we be able to understand why it is that voluntary organizations and NGOs have been broadly promoted and generously funded in recent years.

It is here that the argument comes full circle. No matter how well intentioned and effective such NGOs are at times, they nonetheless represent a multitude of competing causes and interests that, in the neo-liberal model, are not the responsibility of the modern state. Human rights are a case in point. We need to understand the intimate connections between the structures of our societies and the problems that give rise to human rights advocacy — whether on behalf of women, ethnic minorities, or any other group, including children. If we fail to emphasize these connections, and if we fall back on "civil society" to supply the remedies to social ills, our good intentions, as well as our efforts at amelioration, are liable to result in mere band-aid measures that hold little promise of leading to meaningful social change.

A Strategy for the New Millennium

In light of the forces of international finance, capital and trade — forces that continue to shape and transform our societies in the new millennium — the neo-liberal model of "civil society" must be revised, if not abandoned. In this model, the task of assuring human well-being has been delegated to an exponentially increasing multitude of social action groups, social interest groups, NGOs, charitable and voluntary organizations. These intermediary groups and organizations are in uninterrupted competition with one another for scarce resources. Anyone familiar with this situation at the national or international level comes to realize that these groups and organizations are no match for the economic and financial conglomerates in their global advance.

Accordingly, the children's rights movement cannot afford to continue its activities without regard to the larger social and economic developments that are shaping the world for future generations. Nor can it afford to proceed in isolation from the general human rights agenda. The cause of advancing the human rights of children will stand a genuine chance only when securely situated within the general framework of the Universal Declaration of Human Rights, the Covenant on Civil and Political Rights, and the Covenant on Economic, Social and Cultural Rights. In short, in order to advance its cause, the children's rights movement needs to adopt a strategy in which it attempts to do the following:

- connect the rights of children with the human rights movement of the post-Second World War era;

- work toward a unified and integrated approach to human rights in general and the UNCRC in particular;
- base its advocacy on a more thoroughgoing understanding of those forces and policies that are maintaining — rather than transforming for the better — those structural realities that give rise to the very problems it is attempting to solve;
- devise ways of reaching the public and instructing it about the relevance of human rights in general, and of children's human rights in particular, bearing in mind that governments and elected officials tend, as a rule, to listen only to those constituencies that are conversant with, and affirmative of, the legitimacy of human rights claims.

Children's Studies and Human Rights: Toward a Unified Agenda

All signs point to the conclusion that the prevalent fragmentation in the fields of human rights, the rights of children, and child-focused academic disciplines, hinders rather than promotes the understanding of children and youth and the promotion of their well-being. In place of this fragmentation, we need to substitute a comprehensive approach to the academic study of children and to their human rights, an approach that views children as whole human individuals and as a distinct order of social beings endowed with human needs, capacities, and rights. Only thus will it be possible to provide children with the intellectual and political representation they need and deserve. Since children cannot organize and represent themselves like other social groups or minorities, scholars and advocates alike must become conscious of the fact that they perform these representative functions on behalf of children. Both Children's Studies, as a subject that seeks to integrate our knowledge of children, and a comprehensive human rights approach to children, carry the promise of promoting their general well-being. Moreover, collaboration and cross-fertilization between, on the one hand, Children's Studies, and on the other hand, human rights of children perspectives, appear to hold out the only promise for enhancing the lives and opportunities of children everywhere.

Notes

1. *In re Gault*, 387 U.S. 1, 13, 26 (1967); Joseph Goldstein, Anna Freud, and Albert J. Solnit, *Beyond the Best Interests of the Child* (New York: Free Press, 1973).

2. In Albert E. Wilkerson, ed., *The Rights of Children: Emergent Concepts in Law and Society* (Philadelphia: Temple University Press, 1974).

3. George Orwell, "Such, Such Were the Joys" in Sonia Orwell and Ian Angus, eds., *In Front of Your Nose, 1945-1950: The Collected Essays, Journalism and Letters of George Orwell*, vol. 4 (New York: Harcourt, Brace & World, 1968), pp. 366-68.

4. To give just one of many examples: The fragmentation and lack of a unifying and coherent conception could be seen in the program for the Second World Congress on Family Law and the Rights of Children and Youth (June 2-7, 1997), in San Francisco. The program represented a potpourri of topics including violence, female genital mutilation, sexual exploitation, child soldiers, divorce, foster care, and so forth and so on. This comprises a catalogue of abuses and problems — that is, a veritable victimology of childhood. What is lacking is a unifying vision derived from the UNCRC itself, which in its totality is a comprehensive human rights treaty with an underlying holistic vision of the child. Moreover, we must not forget that the abject conditions of children are the symptoms of deeper social and structural problems on a global scale, which none of the sessions of this World Congress appeared ready to address. In all fairness, however, it must be observed that only a major shift in the social and economic priorities of nations will lead to conditions that ultimately will allow the realization of the provisions of the Convention for the benefit of all children.

5. The ideas in this section of the essay were developed during a resident fellowship at the Rockefeller Foundation Study and Conference Center in Bellagio, Italy, in Spring 1998. I would like, in particular, to acknowledge with gratitude discussions with Alan E. Boyle and Dan Connell at the Bellagio Center.

6. Max Weber, *Economy and Society: An Outline of Interpretive Sociology*, vol. 1, Guenther Roth and Claus Wittich, eds. (New York: Bedminster Press, 1968), p. 215.

7. The role of states needs to be clarified in relation to international and transnational nonstate actors. According to Lawrence J. LeBlanc, "A great deal has been said in recent years about the emergence of various international and transnational nonstate actors in international politics, but it is generally agreed that states remain the primary actors in the international system...This is certainly the case for human rights treaties. States — and only states — can ratify such treaties, so they can be expected to play the most important role in drafting them." In LeBlanc, *The Convention on the Rights of the Child: United Nations Lawmaking on Human Rights* (Lincoln: University of Nebraska Press, 1995), p. 26.

8. For example, Jens Quortrup, a scholarly activist on behalf of children, says: "The UN-convention is a political document of Western provenance, it is a very abstract document, which glosses over enormous differences of conditions between childhoods, as these are found in many parts of the world." But Quortrup concedes that it "is nevertheless a useful document of highly symbolic value with far-reaching signaling effects." In "Sociological Perspectives on Childhood," in Eugeen Verhellen, ed., *Collected Papers Presented at the First International Interdisciplinary Course on Children's Rights* (Ghent: Children's Rights Centre, University of Ghent, 1996), p. 109. In response to a presentation I gave on the UNCRC at the Rockefeller Foundation Study and Conference Center in Bellagio, a number of colleagues (social scientists and others) indicated to me in private conversations their problems with such conceptions as "autonomy" or "the child as an individual" in the field of human rights and in the Convention. According to their arguments, these ideas are not applicable in a non-Western context such as in the case of Japan or most developing countries.

9. LeBlanc, *The Convention on the Rights of the Child*, p. xvii.

10. With the exception of the Rio Declaration, the text of all of these documents, in whole or in part, can be found in P. R. Ghandhi, ed., *Blackstone's International Human Rights Documents* (London: Blackstone Press, 2000).

11. Certain experts in international law and human rights have made similar observations when commenting on fragmentation in the human rights arena. These observers have also advocated, either directly or by implication, what I am calling a "unified approach." For example, here is how G.J. Merrill describes the current situation: "Proponents of new human rights, of those seeking to further existing rights, sometimes present their arguments in terms which appear to overlook the existence of other rights, or the need to relate the right under consideration to them. This is understandable, given that those concerned with certain rights often come to these matters from a background of special expertise or interest. Nevertheless, the tendency for rights to be discussed, as it were, in separate compartments, which is encouraged by the practice just mentioned of formulating certain rights in rather vague terms, is not acceptable. A coherent concept of rights calls for a given right, whether actual or proposed, to be considered alongside other rights, for only thus is it possible to appreciate what any existent right really means, or to understand the possible impact of a new right on a moral or legal system." He adds, "The need to avoid thinking in absolutist terms, which is a major risk if rights are treated in isolation, can be seen if we consider first of all the ways in which nearly all rights have to be qualified to take account of other interests." In "Environmental Protection and Human Rights: Conceptual Aspects," in Alan E. Boyle and Michael R. Anderson, eds., *Human Rights Approaches to Environmental Protection* (Oxford: Clarendon Press, 1996), pp. 36-7.

12. This refers to the United Nations Monetary and Financial Conference held at Bretton Woods, New Hampshire, July 1-22, 1944, which led, among other things, to the creation of the IMF.

13. "Welfare reform" refers to the changes in the federal welfare system in the United States introduced by the Personal Responsibility and Work Opportunity Reconciliation Act, 1996.

Appendix

United Nations Convention on the Rights of the Child

Adopted and opened for signature, ratification and accession by General Assembly resolution 44/25 of 20 November 1989

Entry into force 2 September 1990, in accordance with article 49

Preamble

The States Parties to the present Convention,

Considering that, in accordance with the principles proclaimed in the Charter of the United Nations, recognition of the inherent dignity and of the equal and inalienable rights of all members of the human family is the foundation of freedom, justice and peace in the world,

Bearing in mind that the peoples of the United Nations have, in the Charter, reaffirmed their faith in fundamental human rights and in the dignity and worth of the human person, and have determined to promote social progress and better standards of life in larger freedom,

Recognizing that the United Nations has, in the Universal Declaration of Human Rights and in the International Covenants on Human Rights, proclaimed and agreed that everyone is entitled to all the rights and freedoms set forth therein, without distinction of any kind, such as race,

colour, sex, language, religion, political or other opinion, national or
social origin, property, birth or other status,

Recalling that, in the Universal Declaration of Human Rights, the
United Nations has proclaimed that childhood is entitled to special care
and assistance,

Convinced that the family, as the fundamental group of society and the
natural environment for the growth and well-being of all its members
and particularly children, should be afforded the necessary protection
and assistance so that it can fully assume its responsibilities within the
community,

Recognizing that the child, for the full and harmonious development of
his or her personality, should grow up in a family environment, in an
atmosphere of happiness, love and understanding,

Considering that the child should be fully prepared to live an individual
life in society, and brought up in the spirit of the ideals proclaimed in
the Charter of the United Nations, and in particular in the spirit of
peace, dignity, tolerance, freedom, equality and solidarity,

Bearing in mind that the need to extend particular care to the child has
been stated in the Geneva Declaration of the Rights of the Child of
1924 and in the Declaration of the Rights of the Child adopted by the
General Assembly on 20 November 1959 and recognized in the
Universal Declaration of Human Rights, in the International Covenant
on Civil and Political Rights (in particular in articles 23 and 24), in the
International Covenant on Economic, Social and Cultural Rights (in
particular in article 10) and in the statutes and relevant instruments of
specialized agencies and international organizations concerned with the
welfare of children,

Bearing in mind that, as indicated in the Declaration of the Rights of
the Child, "the child, by reason of his physical and mental immaturity,
needs special safeguards and care, including appropriate legal
protection, before as well as after birth",

Recalling the provisions of the Declaration on Social and Legal
Principles relating to the Protection and Welfare of Children, with
Special Reference to Foster Placement and Adoption Nationally and
Internationally; the United Nations Standard Minimum Rules for the

Administration of Juvenile Justice (The Beijing Rules); and the Declaration on the Protection of Women and Children in Emergency and Armed Conflict,

Recognizing that, in all countries in the world, there are children living in exceptionally difficult conditions, and that such children need special consideration,

Taking due account of the importance of the traditions and cultural values of each people for the protection and harmonious development of the child,

Recognizing the importance of international co-operation for improving the living conditions of children in every country, in particular in the developing countries,

Have agreed as follows:

PART I

Article 1

For the purposes of the present Convention, a child means every human being below the age of eighteen years unless under the law applicable to the child, majority is attained earlier.

Article 2

1. States Parties shall respect and ensure the rights set forth in the present Convention to each child within their jurisdiction without discrimination of any kind, irrespective of the child's or his or her parent's or legal guardian's race, colour, sex, language, religion, political or other opinion, national, ethnic or social origin, property, disability, birth or other status.

2. States Parties shall take all appropriate measures to ensure that the child is protected against all forms of discrimination or punishment on the basis of the status, activities, expressed opinions, or beliefs of the child's parents, legal guardians, or family members.

Article 3

1. In all actions concerning children, whether undertaken by public or private social welfare institutions, courts of law, administrative authorities or legislative bodies, the best interests of the child shall be a primary consideration.

2. States Parties undertake to ensure the child such protection and care as is necessary for his or her well-being, taking into account the rights and duties of his or her parents, legal guardians, or other individuals legally responsible for him or her, and, to this end, shall take all appropriate legislative and administrative measures.

3. States Parties shall ensure that the institutions, services and facilities responsible for the care or protection of children shall conform with the standards established by competent authorities, particularly in the areas of safety, health, in the number and suitability of their staff, as well as competent supervision.

Article 4

States Parties shall undertake all appropriate legislative, administrative, and other measures for the implementation of the rights recognized in the present Convention. With regard to economic, social and cultural rights, States Parties shall undertake such measures to the maximum extent of their available resources and, where needed, within the framework of international co-operation.

Article 5

States Parties shall respect the responsibilities, rights and duties of parents or, where applicable, the members of the extended family or community as provided for by local custom, legal guardians or other persons legally responsible for the child, to provide, in a manner consistent with the evolving capacities of the child, appropriate direction and guidance in the exercise by the child of the rights recognized in the present Convention.

Article 6

1. States Parties recognize that every child has the inherent right to life.

2. States Parties shall ensure to the maximum extent possible the survival and development of the child.

Article 7

1. The child shall be registered immediately after birth and shall have the right from birth to a name, the right to acquire a nationality and. as far as possible, the right to know and be cared for by his or her parents.

2. States Parties shall ensure the implementation of these rights in accordance with their national law and their obligations under the relevant international instruments in this field, in particular where the child would otherwise be stateless.

Article 8

1. States Parties undertake to respect the right of the child to preserve his or her identity, including nationality, name and family relations as recognized by law without unlawful interference.

2. Where a child is illegally deprived of some or all of the elements of his or her identity, States Parties shall provide appropriate assistance and protection, with a view to re-establishing speedily his or her identity.

Article 9

1. States Parties shall ensure that a child shall not be separated from his or her parents against their will, except when competent authorities subject to judicial review determine, in accordance with applicable law and procedures, that such separation is necessary for the best interests of the child. Such determination may be necessary in a particular case such as one involving abuse or neglect of the child by the parents, or one where the parents are living separately and a decision must be made as to the child's place of residence.

2. In any proceedings pursuant to paragraph 1 of the present article, all interested parties shall be given an opportunity to participate in the proceedings and make their views known.

3. States Parties shall respect the right of the child who is separated from one or both parents to maintain personal relations and direct contact with both parents on a regular basis, except if it is contrary to the child's best interests.

4. Where such separation results from any action initiated by a State Party, such as the detention, imprisonment, exile, deportation or death (including death arising from any cause while the person is in the custody of the State) of one or both parents or of the child, that State Party shall, upon request, provide the parents, the child or, if appropriate, another member of the family with the essential information concerning the whereabouts of the absent member(s) of the family unless the provision of the information would be detrimental to the well-being of the child. States Parties shall further ensure that the submission of such a request shall of itself entail no adverse consequences for the person(s) concerned.

Article 10

1. In accordance with the obligation of States Parties under article 9, paragraph 1, applications by a child or his or her parents to enter or leave a State Party for the purpose of family reunification shall be dealt with by States Parties in a positive, humane and expeditious manner. States Parties shall further ensure that the submission of such a request shall entail no adverse consequences for the applicants and for the members of their family.

2. A child whose parents reside in different States shall have the right to maintain on a regular basis, save in exceptional circumstances personal relations and direct contacts with both parents. Towards that end and in accordance with the obligation of States Parties under article 9, paragraph 1, States Parties shall respect the right of the child and his or her parents to leave any country, including their own, and to enter their own country. The right to leave any country shall be subject only to such restrictions as are prescribed by law and which are necessary to

protect the national security, public order (ordre public), public health or morals or the rights and freedoms of others and are consistent with the other rights recognized in the present Convention.

Article 11

1. States Parties shall take measures to combat the illicit transfer and non-return of children abroad.

2. To this end, States Parties shall promote the conclusion of bilateral or multilateral agreements or accession to existing agreements.

Article 12

1. States Parties shall assure to the child who is capable of forming his or her own views the right to express those views freely in all matters affecting the child, the views of the child being given due weight in accordance with the age and maturity of the child.

2. For this purpose, the child shall in particular be provided the opportunity to be heard in any judicial and administrative proceedings affecting the child, either directly, or through a representative or an appropriate body, in a manner consistent with the procedural rules of national law.

Article 13

1. The child shall have the right to freedom of expression; this right shall include freedom to seek, receive and impart information and ideas of all kinds, regardless of frontiers, either orally, in writing or in print, in the form of art, or through any other media of the child's choice.

2. The exercise of this right may be subject to certain restrictions, but these shall only be such as are provided by law and are necessary: (a) For respect of the rights or reputations of others; or (b) For the protection of national security or of public order (ordre public), or of public health or morals.

Article 14

1. States Parties shall respect the right of the child to freedom of thought, conscience and religion.

2. States Parties shall respect the rights and duties of the parents and, when applicable, legal guardians, to provide direction to the child in the exercise of his or her right in a manner consistent with the evolving capacities of the child.

3. Freedom to manifest one's religion or beliefs may be subject only to such limitations as are prescribed by law and are necessary to protect public safety, order, health or morals, or the fundamental rights and freedoms of others.

Article 15

1. States Parties recognize the rights of the child to freedom of association and to freedom of peaceful assembly.

2. No restrictions may be placed on the exercise of these rights other than those imposed in conformity with the law and which are necessary in a democratic society in the interests of national security or public safety, public order (ordre public), the protection of public health or morals or the protection of the rights and freedoms of others.

Article 16

1. No child shall be subjected to arbitrary or unlawful interference with his or her privacy, family, home or correspondence, nor to unlawful attacks on his or her honour and reputation.

2. The child has the right to the protection of the law against such interference or attacks.

Article 17

States Parties recognize the important function performed by the mass media and shall ensure that the child has access to information and material from a diversity of national and international sources, especially those aimed at the promotion of his or her social, spiritual and moral well-being and physical and mental health. To this end, States Parties shall:

(a) Encourage the mass media to disseminate information and material of social and cultural benefit to the child and in accordance with the spirit of article 29;

(b) Encourage international co-operation in the production, exchange and dissemination of such information and material from a diversity of cultural, national and international sources;

(c) Encourage the production and dissemination of children's books;

(d) Encourage the mass media to have particular regard to the linguistic needs of the child who belongs to a minority group or who is indigenous;

(e) Encourage the development of appropriate guidelines for the protection of the child from information and material injurious to his or her well-being, bearing in mind the provisions of articles 13 and 18.

Article 18

1. States Parties shall use their best efforts to ensure recognition of the principle that both parents have common responsibilities for the upbringing and development of the child. Parents or, as the case may be, legal guardians, have the primary responsibility for the upbringing and development of the child. The best interests of the child will be their basic concern.

2. For the purpose of guaranteeing and promoting the rights set forth in the present Convention, States Parties shall render appropriate

assistance to parents and legal guardians in the performance of their child-rearing responsibilities and shall ensure the development of institutions, facilities and services for the care of children.

3. States Parties shall take all appropriate measures to ensure that children of working parents have the right to benefit from child-care services and facilities for which they are eligible.

Article 19

1. States Parties shall take all appropriate legislative, administrative, social and educational measures to protect the child from all forms of physical or mental violence, injury or abuse, neglect or negligent treatment, maltreatment or exploitation, including sexual abuse, while in the care of parent(s), legal guardian(s) or any other person who has the care of the child.

2. Such protective measures should, as appropriate, include effective procedures for the establishment of social programmes to provide necessary support for the child and for those who have the care of the child, as well as for other forms of prevention and for identification, reporting, referral, investigation, treatment and follow-up of instances of child maltreatment described heretofore, and, as appropriate, for judicial involvement.

Article 20

1. A child temporarily or permanently deprived of his or her family environment, or in whose own best interests cannot be allowed to remain in that environment, shall be entitled to special protection and assistance provided by the State.

2. States Parties shall in accordance with their national laws ensure alternative care for such a child.

3. Such care could include, inter alia, foster placement, kafalah of Islamic law, adoption or if necessary placement in suitable institutions for the care of children. When considering solutions, due regard shall

be paid to the desirability of continuity in a child's upbringing and to the child's ethnic, religious, cultural and linguistic background.

Article 21

States Parties that recognize and/or permit the system of adoption shall ensure that the best interests of the child shall be the paramount consideration and they shall:

(a) Ensure that the adoption of a child is authorized only by competent authorities who determine, in accordance with applicable law and procedures and on the basis of all pertinent and reliable information, that the adoption is permissible in view of the child's status concerning parents, relatives and legal guardians and that, if required, the persons concerned have given their informed consent to the adoption on the basis of such counselling as may be necessary;

(b) Recognize that inter-country adoption may be considered as an alternative means of child's care, if the child cannot be placed in a foster or an adoptive family or cannot in any suitable manner be cared for in the child's country of origin; (c) Ensure that the child concerned by inter-country adoption enjoys safeguards and standards equivalent to those existing in the case of national adoption;

(d) Take all appropriate measures to ensure that, in inter-country adoption, the placement does not result in improper financial gain for those involved in it;

(e) Promote, where appropriate, the objectives of the present article by concluding bilateral or multilateral arrangements or agreements, and endeavour, within this framework, to ensure that the placement of the child in another country is carried out by competent authorities or organs.

Article 22

1. States Parties shall take appropriate measures to ensure that a child who is seeking refugee status or who is considered a refugee in accordance with applicable international or domestic law and procedures shall, whether unaccompanied or accompanied by his or her

parents or by any other person, receive appropriate protection and humanitarian assistance in the enjoyment of applicable rights set forth in the present Convention and in other international human rights or humanitarian instruments to which the said States are Parties.

2. For this purpose, States Parties shall provide, as they consider appropriate, co-operation in any efforts by the United Nations and other competent intergovernmental organizations or non-governmental organizations co-operating with the United Nations to protect and assist such a child and to trace the parents or other members of the family of any refugee child in order to obtain information necessary for reunification with his or her family. In cases where no parents or other members of the family can be found, the child shall be accorded the same protection as any other child permanently or temporarily deprived of his or her family environment for any reason , as set forth in the present Convention.

Article 23

1. States Parties recognize that a mentally or physically disabled child should enjoy a full and decent life, in conditions which ensure dignity, promote self-reliance and facilitate the child's active participation in the community.

2. States Parties recognize the right of the disabled child to special care and shall encourage and ensure the extension, subject to available resources, to the eligible child and those responsible for his or her care, of assistance for which application is made and which is appropriate to the child's condition and to the circumstances of the parents or others caring for the child.

3. Recognizing the special needs of a disabled child, assistance extended in accordance with paragraph 2 of the present article shall be provided free of charge, whenever possible, taking into account the financial resources of the parents or others caring for the child, and shall be designed to ensure that the disabled child has effective access to and receives education, training, health care services, rehabilitation services, preparation for employment and recreation opportunities in a manner conducive to the child's achieving the fullest possible social

integration and individual development, including his or her cultural and spiritual development

4. States Parties shall promote, in the spirit of international cooperation, the exchange of appropriate information in the field of preventive health care and of medical, psychological and functional treatment of disabled children, including dissemination of and access to information concerning methods of rehabilitation, education and vocational services, with the aim of enabling States Parties to improve their capabilities and skills and to widen their experience in these areas. In this regard, particular account shall be taken of the needs of developing countries.

Article 24

1. States Parties recognize the right of the child to the enjoyment of the highest attainable standard of health and to facilities for the treatment of illness and rehabilitation of health. States Parties shall strive to ensure that no child is deprived of his or her right of access to such health care services.

2. States Parties shall pursue full implementation of this right and, in particular, shall take appropriate measures:

(a) To diminish infant and child mortality;

(b) To ensure the provision of necessary medical assistance and health care to all children with emphasis on the development of primary health care;

(c) To combat disease and malnutrition, including within the framework of primary health care, through, inter alia, the application of readily available technology and through the provision of adequate nutritious foods and clean drinking-water, taking into consideration the dangers and risks of environmental pollution;

(d) To ensure appropriate pre-natal and post-natal health care for mothers;

(e) To ensure that all segments of society, in particular parents and children, are informed, have access to education and are supported in the use of basic knowledge of child health and nutrition, the advantages of breastfeeding, hygiene and environmental sanitation and the prevention of accidents;

(f) To develop preventive health care, guidance for parents and family planning education and services.

3. States Parties shall take all effective and appropriate measures with a view to abolishing traditional practices prejudicial to the health of children.

4. States Parties undertake to promote and encourage international co-operation with a view to achieving progressively the full realization of the right recognized in the present article. In this regard, particular account shall be taken of the needs of developing countries.

Article 25

States Parties recognize the right of a child who has been placed by the competent authorities for the purposes of care, protection or treatment of his or her physical or mental health, to a periodic review of the treatment provided to the child and all other circumstances relevant to his or her placement.

Article 26

1. States Parties shall recognize for every child the right to benefit from social security, including social insurance, and shall take the necessary measures to achieve the full realization of this right in accordance with their national law.

2. The benefits should, where appropriate, be granted, taking into account the resources and the circumstances of the child and persons having responsibility for the maintenance of the child, as well as any other consideration relevant to an application for benefits made by or on behalf of the child.

Article 27

1. States Parties recognize the right of every child to a standard of living adequate for the child's physical, mental, spiritual, moral and social development.

2. The parent(s) or others responsible for the child have the primary responsibility to secure, within their abilities and financial capacities, the conditions of living necessary for the child's development.

3. States Parties, in accordance with national conditions and within their means, shall take appropriate measures to assist parents and others responsible for the child to implement this right and shall in case of need provide material assistance and support programmes, particularly with regard to nutrition, clothing and housing.

4. States Parties shall take all appropriate measures to secure the recovery of maintenance for the child from the parents or other persons having financial responsibility for the child, both within the State Party and from abroad. In particular, where the person having financial responsibility for the child lives in a State different from that of the child, States Parties shall promote the accession to international agreements or the conclusion of such agreements, as well as the making of other appropriate arrangements.

Article 28

1. States Parties recognize the right of the child to education, and with a view to achieving this right progressively and on the basis of equal opportunity, they shall, in particular:

(a) Make primary education compulsory and available free to all;

(b) Encourage the development of different forms of secondary education, including general and vocational education, make them available and accessible to every child, and take appropriate measures such as the introduction of free education and offering financial assistance in case of need;

(c) Make higher education accessible to all on the basis of capacity by every appropriate means;

(d) Make educational and vocational information and guidance available and accessible to all children;

(e) Take measures to encourage regular attendance at schools and the reduction of drop-out rates.

2. States Parties shall take all appropriate measures to ensure that school discipline is administered in a manner consistent with the child's human dignity and in conformity with the present Convention.

3. States Parties shall promote and encourage international cooperation in matters relating to education, in particular with a view to contributing to the elimination of ignorance and illiteracy throughout the world and facilitating access to scientific and technical knowledge and modern teaching methods. In this regard, particular account shall be taken of the needs of developing countries.

Article 29

General comment on its implementation

1. States Parties agree that the education of the child shall be directed to:

(a) The development of the child's personality, talents and mental and physical abilities to their fullest potential;

(b) The development of respect for human rights and fundamental freedoms, and for the principles enshrined in the Charter of the United Nations;

(c) The development of respect for the child's parents, his or her own cultural identity, language and values, for the national values of the country in which the child is living, the country from which he or she may originate, and for civilizations different from his or her own;

(d) The preparation of the child for responsible life in a free society, in the spirit of understanding, peace, tolerance, equality of sexes, and friendship among all peoples, ethnic, national and religious groups and persons of indigenous origin;

(e) The development of respect for the natural environment.

2. No part of the present article or article 28 shall be construed so as to interfere with the liberty of individuals and bodies to establish and direct educational institutions, subject always to the observance of the principle set forth in paragraph 1 of the present article and to the requirements that the education given in such institutions shall conform to such minimum standards as may be laid down by the State.

Article 30

In those States in which ethnic, religious or linguistic minorities or persons of indigenous origin exist, a child belonging to such a minority or who is indigenous shall not be denied the right, in community with other members of his or her group, to enjoy his or her own culture, to profess and practise his or her own religion, or to use his or her own language.

Article 31

1. States Parties recognize the right of the child to rest and leisure, to engage in play and recreational activities appropriate to the age of the child and to participate freely in cultural life and the arts.

2. States Parties shall respect and promote the right of the child to participate fully in cultural and artistic life and shall encourage the provision of appropriate and equal opportunities for cultural, artistic, recreational and leisure activity.

Article 32

1. States Parties recognize the right of the child to be protected from economic exploitation and from performing any work that is likely to

be hazardous or to interfere with the child's education, or to be harmful to the child's health or physical, mental, spiritual, moral or social development.

2. States Parties shall take legislative, administrative, social and educational measures to ensure the implementation of the present article. To this end, and having regard to the relevant provisions of other international instruments, States Parties shall in particular:

(a) Provide for a minimum age or minimum ages for admission to employment;

(b) Provide for appropriate regulation of the hours and conditions of employment;

(c) Provide for appropriate penalties or other sanctions to ensure the effective enforcement of the present article.

Article 33

States Parties shall take all appropriate measures, including legislative, administrative, social and educational measures, to protect children from the illicit use of narcotic drugs and psychotropic substances as defined in the relevant international treaties, and to prevent the use of children in the illicit production and trafficking of such substances.

Article 34

States Parties undertake to protect the child from all forms of sexual exploitation and sexual abuse. For these purposes, States Parties shall in particular take all appropriate national, bilateral and multilateral measures to prevent:

(a) The inducement or coercion of a child to engage in any unlawful sexual activity;

(b) The exploitative use of children in prostitution or other unlawful sexual practices;

(c) The exploitative use of children in pornographic performances and materials.

Article 35

States Parties shall take all appropriate national, bilateral and multilateral measures to prevent the abduction of, the sale of or traffic in children for any purpose or in any form.

Article 36

States Parties shall protect the child against all other forms of exploitation prejudicial to any aspects of the child's welfare.

Article 37

States Parties shall ensure that:

(a) No child shall be subjected to torture or other cruel, inhuman or degrading treatment or punishment. Neither capital punishment nor life imprisonment without possibility of release shall be imposed for offences committed by persons below eighteen years of age;

(b) No child shall be deprived of his or her liberty unlawfully or arbitrarily. The arrest, detention or imprisonment of a child shall be in conformity with the law and shall be used only as a measure of last resort and for the shortest appropriate period of time;

(c) Every child deprived of liberty shall be treated with humanity and respect for the inherent dignity of the human person, and in a manner which takes into account the needs of persons of his or her age. In particular, every child deprived of liberty shall be separated from adults unless it is considered in the child's best interest not to do so and shall have the right to maintain contact with his or her family through correspondence and visits, save in exceptional circumstances;

(d) Every child deprived of his or her liberty shall have the right to prompt access to legal and other appropriate assistance, as well as the right to challenge the legality of the deprivation of his or her liberty before a court or other competent, independent and impartial authority, and to a prompt decision on any such action.

Article 38

1. States Parties undertake to respect and to ensure respect for rules of international humanitarian law applicable to them in armed conflicts which are relevant to the child.

2. States Parties shall take all feasible measures to ensure that persons who have not attained the age of fifteen years do not take a direct part in hostilities.

3. States Parties shall refrain from recruiting any person who has not attained the age of fifteen years into their armed forces. In recruiting among those persons who have attained the age of fifteen years but who have not attained the age of eighteen years, States Parties shall endeavour to give priority to those who are oldest.

4. In accordance with their obligations under international humanitarian law to protect the civilian population in armed conflicts, States Parties shall take all feasible measures to ensure protection and care of children who are affected by an armed conflict.

Article 39

States Parties shall take all appropriate measures to promote physical and psychological recovery and social reintegration of a child victim of: any form of neglect, exploitation, or abuse; torture or any other form of cruel, inhuman or degrading treatment or punishment; or armed conflicts. Such recovery and reintegration shall take place in an environment which fosters the health, self-respect and dignity of the child.

Article 40

1. States Parties recognize the right of every child alleged as, accused of, or recognized as having infringed the penal law to be treated in a

manner consistent with the promotion of the child's sense of dignity and worth, which reinforces the child's respect for the human rights and fundamental freedoms of others and which takes into account the child's age and the desirability of promoting the child's reintegration and the child's assuming a constructive role in society.

2. To this end, and having regard to the relevant provisions of international instruments, States Parties shall, in particular, ensure that:

(a) No child shall be alleged as, be accused of, or recognized as having infringed the penal law by reason of acts or omissions that were not prohibited by national or international law at the time they were committed;

(b) Every child alleged as or accused of having infringed the penal law has at least the following guarantees:

(i) To be presumed innocent until proven guilty according to law;

(ii) To be informed promptly and directly of the charges against him or her, and, if appropriate, through his or her parents or legal guardians, and to have legal or other appropriate assistance in the preparation and presentation of his or her defence;

(iii) To have the matter determined without delay by a competent, independent and impartial authority or judicial body in a fair hearing according to law, in the presence of legal or other appropriate assistance and, unless it is considered not to be in the best interest of the child, in particular, taking into account his or her age or situation, his or her parents or legal guardians;

(iv) Not to be compelled to give testimony or to confess guilt; to examine or have examined adverse witnesses and to obtain the participation and examination of witnesses on his or her behalf under conditions of equality;

(v) If considered to have infringed the penal law, to have this decision and any measures imposed in consequence thereof reviewed by a higher competent, independent and impartial authority or judicial body according to law;

(vi) To have the free assistance of an interpreter if the child cannot understand or speak the language used;

(vii) To have his or her privacy fully respected at all stages of the proceedings. 3. States Parties shall seek to promote the establishment of laws, procedures, authorities and institutions specifically applicable to children alleged as, accused of, or recognized as having infringed the penal law, and, in particular:

(a) The establishment of a minimum age below which children shall be presumed not to have the capacity to infringe the penal law;

(b) Whenever appropriate and desirable, measures for dealing with such children without resorting to judicial proceedings, providing that human rights and legal safeguards are fully respected.

4. A variety of dispositions, such as care, guidance and supervision orders; counselling; probation; foster care; education and vocational training programmes and other alternatives to institutional care shall be available to ensure that children are dealt with in a manner appropriate to their well-being and proportionate both to their circumstances and the offence.

Article 41

Nothing in the present Convention shall affect any provisions which are more conducive to the realization of the rights of the child and which may be contained in:

(a) The law of a State party; or

(b) International law in force for that State.

PART II

Article 42

States Parties undertake to make the principles and provisions of the Convention widely known, by appropriate and active means, to adults and children alike.

Article 43

1. For the purpose of examining the progress made by States Parties in achieving the realization of the obligations undertaken in the present Convention, there shall be established a Committee on the Rights of the Child, which shall carry out the functions hereinafter provided.

2. The Committee shall consist of ten experts of high moral standing and recognized competence in the field covered by this Convention. The members of the Committee shall be elected by States Parties from among their nationals and shall serve in their personal capacity, consideration being given to equitable geographical distribution, as well as to the principal legal systems. (amendment)

3. The members of the Committee shall be elected by secret ballot from a list of persons nominated by States Parties. Each State Party may nominate one person from among its own nationals.

4. The initial election to the Committee shall be held no later than six months after the date of the entry into force of the present Convention and thereafter every second year. At least four months before the date of each election, the Secretary-General of the United Nations shall address a letter to States Parties inviting them to submit their nominations within two months. The Secretary-General shall subsequently prepare a list in alphabetical order of all persons thus nominated, indicating States Parties which have nominated them, and shall submit it to the States Parties to the present Convention.

5. The elections shall be held at meetings of States Parties convened by the Secretary-General at United Nations Headquarters. At those

meetings, for which two thirds of States Parties shall constitute a quorum, the persons elected to the Committee shall be those who obtain the largest number of votes and an absolute majority of the votes of the representatives of States Parties present and voting.

6. The members of the Committee shall be elected for a term of four years. They shall be eligible for re-election if renominated. The term of five of the members elected at the first election shall expire at the end of two years; immediately after the first election, the names of these five members shall be chosen by lot by the Chairman of the meeting.

7. If a member of the Committee dies or resigns or declares that for any other cause he or she can no longer perform the duties of the Committee, the State Party which nominated the member shall appoint another expert from among its nationals to serve for the remainder of the term, subject to the approval of the Committee.

8. The Committee shall establish its own rules of procedure.

9. The Committee shall elect its officers for a period of two years.

10. The meetings of the Committee shall normally be held at United Nations Headquarters or at any other convenient place as determined by the Committee. The Committee shall normally meet annually. The duration of the meetings of the Committee shall be determined, and reviewed, if necessary, by a meeting of the States Parties to the present Convention, subject to the approval of the General Assembly.

11. The Secretary-General of the United Nations shall provide the necessary staff and facilities for the effective performance of the functions of the Committee under the present Convention.

12. With the approval of the General Assembly, the members of the Committee established under the present Convention shall receive emoluments from United Nations resources on such terms and conditions as the Assembly may decide.

Article 44

1. States Parties undertake to submit to the Committee, through the Secretary-General of the United Nations, reports on the measures they have adopted which give effect to the rights recognized herein and on the progress made on the enjoyment of those rights:

(a) Within two years of the entry into force of the Convention for the State Party concerned;

(b) Thereafter every five years.

2. Reports made under the present article shall indicate factors and difficulties, if any, affecting the degree of fulfilment of the obligations under the present Convention. Reports shall also contain sufficient information to provide the Committee with a comprehensive understanding of the implementation of the Convention in the country concerned.

3. A State Party which has submitted a comprehensive initial report to the Committee need not, in its subsequent reports submitted in accordance with paragraph 1 (b) of the present article, repeat basic information previously provided.

4. The Committee may request from States Parties further information relevant to the implementation of the Convention.

5. The Committee shall submit to the General Assembly, through the Economic and Social Council, every two years, reports on its activities.

6. States Parties shall make their reports widely available to the public in their own countries.

Article 45

In order to foster the effective implementation of the Convention and to encourage international co-operation in the field covered by the Convention:

(a) The specialized agencies, the United Nations Children's Fund, and other United Nations organs shall be entitled to be represented at the consideration of the implementation of such provisions of the present Convention as fall within the scope of their mandate. The Committee may invite the specialized agencies, the United Nations Children's Fund and other competent bodies as it may consider appropriate to provide expert advice on the implementation of the Convention in areas falling within the scope of their respective mandates. The Committee may invite the specialized agencies, the United Nations Children's Fund, and other United Nations organs to submit reports on the implementation of the Convention in areas falling within the scope of their activities;

(b) The Committee shall transmit, as it may consider appropriate, to the specialized agencies, the United Nations Children's Fund and other competent bodies, any reports from States Parties that contain a request, or indicate a need, for technical advice or assistance, along with the Committee's observations and suggestions, if any, on these requests or indications;

(c) The Committee may recommend to the General Assembly to request the Secretary-General to undertake on its behalf studies on specific issues relating to the rights of the child;

(d) The Committee may make suggestions and general recommendations based on information received pursuant to articles 44 and 45 of the present Convention. Such suggestions and general recommendations shall be transmitted to any State Party concerned and reported to the General Assembly, together with comments, if any, from States Parties.

PART III

Article 46

The present Convention shall be open for signature by all States.

Article 47

The present Convention is subject to ratification. Instruments of ratification shall be deposited with the Secretary-General of the United Nations.

Article 48

The present Convention shall remain open for accession by any State. The instruments of accession shall be deposited with the Secretary-General of the United Nations.

Article 49

1. The present Convention shall enter into force on the thirtieth day following the date of deposit with the Secretary-General of the United Nations of the twentieth instrument of ratification or accession.

2. For each State ratifying or acceding to the Convention after the deposit of the twentieth instrument of ratification or accession, the Convention shall enter into force on the thirtieth day after the deposit by such State of its instrument of ratification or accession.

Article 50

1. Any State Party may propose an amendment and file it with the Secretary-General of the United Nations. The Secretary-General shall thereupon communicate the proposed amendment to States Parties, with a request that they indicate whether they favour a conference of States Parties for the purpose of considering and voting upon the proposals. In the event that, within four months from the date of such communication, at least one third of the States Parties favour such a conference, the Secretary-General shall convene the conference under the auspices of the United Nations. Any amendment adopted by a majority of States Parties present and voting at the conference shall be submitted to the General Assembly for approval.

2. An amendment adopted in accordance with paragraph 1 of the present article shall enter into force when it has been approved by the General Assembly of the United Nations and accepted by a two-thirds majority of States Parties.

3. When an amendment enters into force, it shall be binding on those States Parties which have accepted it, other States Parties still being bound by the provisions of the present Convention and any earlier amendments which they have accepted.

Article 51

1. The Secretary-General of the United Nations shall receive and circulate to all States the text of reservations made by States at the time of ratification or accession.

2. A reservation incompatible with the object and purpose of the present Convention shall not be permitted.

3. Reservations may be withdrawn at any time by notification to that effect addressed to the Secretary-General of the United Nations, who shall then inform all States. Such notification shall take effect on the date on which it is received by the Secretary-General.

Article 52

A State Party may denounce the present Convention by written notification to the Secretary-General of the United Nations. Denunciation becomes effective one year after the date of receipt of the notification by the Secretary-General.

Article 53

The Secretary-General of the United Nations is designated as the depositary of the present Convention.

Article 54

The original of the present Convention, of which the Arabic, Chinese, English, French, Russian and Spanish texts are equally authentic, shall be deposited with the Secretary-General of the United Nations.

IN WITNESS THEREOF the undersigned plenipotentiaries, being duly authorized thereto by their respective governments, have signed the present Convention.

Suggestions for Further Reading

In addition to the books and articles listed in the endnotes to each of the chapters in this book, we suggest the following titles for those who wish to further explore the issue of children's rights. These suggestions, limited to English language publications, are illustrative of the growing body of work on the topic and are not intended to be comprehensive. Interested readers should also consult UNICEF's website <www.unicef.org> as well as the publications of their International Child Development Centre/Innocenti Centre, Florence, Italy.

Angel, William D., ed. *The International Law of Youth Rights: Source Documents and Commentary.* Dordrecht: Martinus Nijhoff Publishers, 1995.

Alston, Philip, Stephen Parker, and John Seymour, eds. *Children, Rights and the Law.* Oxford: Clarendon Press, 1992.

Andrews, Arlene Bowers and Natalie Hevener Kaufman, eds. *Implementing the U.N. Convention on the Rights of the Child: A Standard of Living Adequate for Development.* Westport, CT: Praeger Publishers, 1999.

Boulding, Elise. *Children's Rights and the Wheel of Life.* New Brunswick, NJ: Transaction Books, 1979.

Clinton, Hillary Rodham. *It Takes a Village and Other Lessons Children Teach Us.* New York: Simon and Schuster, 1996.

Douglas, Gillian and Leslie Sebba, eds. *Children's Rights and Traditional Values.* Aldershot, UK: Ashgate/Dartmouth Publishing, 1998.

Fagan, Jeffrey and Franklin E. Zimring, eds. *The Changing Borders of Juvenile Justice: Transfer of Adolescents to the Criminal Court.* Chicago: The University of Chicago Press, 2000.

Fletcher, Anthony and Stephen Hussey, eds. *Childhood in Question: Children, Parents and the State.* Manchester, UK: Manchester University Press, 1999.

Fortin, Jane. *Children's Rights and the Developing Law.* London: Butterworths, 1998.

Fottrell, Deidre, ed. *Revisiting Children's Rights: Ten Years of the UN Convention on the Rights of the Child.* The Hague: Kluwer Law International, 2000.

Freeman, Michael, ed. *Children's Rights: A Comparative Perspective.* Aldershot, UK: Dartmouth Publishing Company, 1996

Freeman, Michael, and Philip Veerman, eds. *The Ideologies of Children's Rights.* Dordrecht: Martinus Nijhoff Publishers, 1992.

Gross, Beatrice and Ronald Gross, eds. *The Children's Rights Movement: Overcoming the Oppression of Young People.* Garden City, NY: Anchor Books, 1977.

Hart, Roger A., et el. *Children's Participation: The Theory and Practice of Involving Young Citizens in Community Development and Environmental Care.* New York: UNICEF; London: Earthscan, 1997.

Henning, James S., ed. *The Rights of Children: Legal and Psychological Perspectives.* Springfield, IL: Charles C. Thomas Publishers, 1982.

Irvine, William B. *Doing Right by Children: Reflections on the Nature of Childhood and The Obligations of Parenthood.* St. Paul, MN: Paragon House, 2001.

Korczak, Janusz. *When I Am Little Again and The Child's Right to Respect.* Trans. E. P. Kulawiec. Lanham, MD: University Press of America, 1992.

Melton, Gary B. ed., *Reforming the Law: Impact of Child Development Research*. New York: Guilford Press, 1987.

Minow, Martha, ed. *Family Matters: Readings on Family Lives and the Law*. New York: New Press, 1993.

Mnookin, Robert H., et. al. *In the Interest of Children: Advocacy, Law Reform and Public Policy*. New York: W. H. Freeman and Co., 1985.

Newell, Peter. *Children Are People Too: The Case Against Physical Punishment*. London: Bedford Square, 1989.

Van Bueren, Geraldine. *The International Law on the Rights of the Child*. The Hague, Netherlands: Martinus Nijhoff, 1995.

Vardin, Patricia A., and Ilene N. Brody, eds. *Children's Rights: Contemporary Perspectives*. New York: Teachers College Press, 1979.

Vittachi, Anuradha. *Stolen Childhood: In Search of the Rights of the Child*. Cambridge, UK: Polity Press, 1989.

Westman, Jack. *Licensing Parents: Can We Prevent Child Abuse and Neglect*. New York: Insight Books, 1994.

Index

Note: The index does not refer to the Foreword, Appendix, or endnotes.

About the Contributors

Kathleen Alaimo is Associate Professor of History at Saint Xavier University. She holds a Ph.D. in History from the University of Wisconsin-Madison and an M.A. in History from the University of Chicago. She has published articles on the history of adolescence in France and the history of juvenile delinquency in Europe. She is a former member of the Editorial Board of the *History of Education Quarterly*.

Christina M. Bellon is Assistant Professor of Philosophy at Ripon College. She holds a Ph.D. in Philosophy from the University of Colorado, Boulder, and an M.A. in Political Theory from Dalhousie University, Canada. She has published articles on Palestinian-Israeli peace prospects and on the theoretical and practical aspects of rights with particular emphasis on the rights of children. She is currently working on a book concerning the ethics of child labor.

Cynthia Price Cohen is Executive Director of ChildRights International Research Institute, New York. She holds a J.D. from New York Law School, an M.A. from City College of New York, and a doctorate in juridical science from the Polish Academy of Sciences in Warsaw. Cohen participated in drafting the United Nations Convention on the Rights of the Child. She has published extensively on child rights and the UNCRC. She is the recipient of a 2001 Lewis Hine Award presented by the National Child Labor Committee and of the Victoria Award presented by the Kapitula Nagrod Humanitarnych and Stowarzyszenie Klub Ludzi Zyczliwych (Poland).

Målfrid Grude Flekkøy is Acting Professional Director and former Chief Psychologist of the Nic Waals Institute for Child and Adolescent Psychiatry, Oslo, Norway. She holds a doctorate in child psychology from the University of Ghent, Belgium. She was a Senior Fellow at UNICEF's International Child Development Centre and is the author of numerous articles and books on child rights and child advocacy.

Flekkøy served as Norway's Ombudsman for Children from 1981 to 1989, the first appointment of its kind in the world.

Sara Ellen Kitchen is Associate Professor of Sociology at Chestnut Hill College. She holds a J.D. from Villanova Law School. As a former Watson Fellow, she studied juvenile justice and child welfare systems in several European countries. In 1993 she examined the status of children in Costa Rica and Nicaragua on a Fulbright-Hays Study Tour. Kitchen is an NGO Representative to the United Nations for Global Education Motivators and a former public defender.

Brian Klug is Associate Professor of Philosophy at Saint Xavier University and Senior Research Fellow in Philosophy, St. Benet's Hall, Oxford. He holds a Ph.D. in Social Thought from the University of Chicago and an M.A. in Philosophy from Bedford College, University of London. He has published in the fields of higher education, ethics, race and racism, and animal rights. He is a Consulting Editor of *Patterns of Prejudice.*

Rosalind Ekman Ladd is Professor of Philosophy, Emerita at Wheaton College, Massachusetts; Lecturer in Pediatrics at Brown University Medical School; and Visiting Professor of Bioethics at Brown University. She holds a Ph.D. and an M.A. in Philosophy from Brown University. She is the author and editor of numerous articles and books concerning children's rights, adolescent values, pediatric ethics, and medical ethics.

Gertrud Lenzer is Professor of Sociology and Director of the Children's Studies Program and Center at Brooklyn College and Professor of Sociology at the Graduate Center of the City University of New York. She is Founding Chair of the Sociology of Children Section of the American Sociological Association and founder of Children's Studies. Lenzer has published on the UNCRC, children's rights and children's studies. She received the 1997 Lewis Hine Award for Service to Children and Youth, held a fellowship at the Rockefeller Foundation Center in Bellagio, Italy in 1998 and is a member of the board of directors of the National Child Labor Committee.

Roger J. R. Levesque is Associate Professor of Psychology and Law at the University of Arizona, Tucson. He holds a J.D. from Columbia University School of Law and a Ph.D. in Cultural Psychology from the University of Chicago. He has published numerous articles and books concerning youth policy and jurisprudence, adolescent sexuality, child protection policies, family life, and human rights law.

Lewis Pitts is Program Director of Advocates for Children's Services, Legal Services of North Carolina, Inc. in Raleigh. He holds a J.D. from the University of South Carolina Law School. He is the former Executive Director of the National Committee for the Rights of the Child (1992-94). His legal work centers on environmental justice, racial justice, and children's rights and includes advocacy on the Gregory Kingsley case. He is the 1994 recipient of the Foundation for Improvement of Justice Award for advancing justice for children.

Joan M. Smith has a family law practice in Melrose Park, Pennsylvania. She holds a J.D. from Temple University School of Law and an M.S. from Millersville University. She is the former chair of the Children's Rights Committee of the Pennsylvania Bar Association and a member of the Board of Directors for the Support Center for Child Advocates, where she also does *pro bono* work. She has written on the connections between NAFTA and child labor.

David S. Tanenhaus is Assistant Professor of History and Law at the University of Nevada, Las Vegas. He holds a Ph.D. in American History from the University of Chicago. He is a coeditor of a book concerning the first one hundred years of the juvenile justice system in Illinois. He served on the Steering Committee of the Children's Court (Illinois) Centennial Committee. His research focuses on legal history and the relationship of the child to the state.